Dummies 101:™ Visual Basic® 5 Programming

CHEAT SHEET

Object Naming Conventions

Object	Prefix	Example
Check box	chk	chkYourMail
Combo box	cbo	cboNation
Command button	cmd	cmdExitOrDie
Directory list box	dir	dirChoice
Drive list box	drv	drvMeHome
File list box	fil	filUpTheGasTank
Form	frm	frmAStraightLine
Frame	fra	fraTheButler
Horizontal scroll bar	hsb	hsbVolumeControl
Image	img	imgMirage
Label	lbl	lblWarning
Line	lin	linEdges
List box	lst	lstGroceries
Menu	mnu	mnuGreenEggsAndHam
Radio button	opt	optRockOrCountry
Picture box	pic	picXRated
Shape	shp	shpStrangeObject
Text box	txt	txtRansomMessage
Vertical scroll bar	vsb	vsbRadiationLevel

Visual Basic Filename Extensions

Extension	Description	Contents
FRM	Form file	Forms and event procedures
BAS	Module file	General procedures
VBP	Project file	List of all files (FRM, BAS, and so on) that make up a single Visual Basic program
VBW	Window file	You won't ever interact with this file directly, but it contains a list of windows in your program and their position on-screen

S0-CCJ-641

Dummies 101:™ Visual Basic® 5 Programming

CHEAT SHEET

Opening Windows

Which Window	Keystroke	Window Is Used To
Code	F7	Edit and examine BASIC code
Debug	Ctrl+Break	Examine the values of variables and expressions; test procedure and function calls
Menu Editor	Ctrl+E	Create and edit pull-down menus
Object Browser	F2	List all the procedures stored in each file of an entire Visual Basic program
Project	Ctrl+R	List all the files that make up your entire Visual Basic program
Properties	F4	Examine and change the value of an object's properties

Starting Visual Basic

1. Click on the Start button in the lower-left corner of the screen

2. Click on Programs

3. Click on the Visual Basic folder

4. Click on Visual Basic in the folder that pops up

Loading a Visual Basic Program

1. With Visual Basic running, click on the Open Project button in the Toolbar

2. Find and double-click on the name of the file you want to open

You may have to click in the Look in list box to find the file, depending on how your files are arranged. See Appendix B for information about the lesson files on the companion CD.

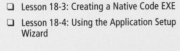

IDG BOOKS WORLDWIDE

Copyright © 1997 IDG Books Worldwide, Inc.
All rights reserved.
Cheat Sheet $2.95 value. Item 0120-8
For more information on IDG Books,
call 1-800-762-2974.

DUMMIES 101:® VISUAL BASIC® 5 PROGRAMMING

by Wallace Wang and John Mueller

IDG BOOKS WORLDWIDE

IDG Books Worldwide, Inc.
An International Data Group Company

Foster City, CA ✦ Chicago, IL ✦ Indianapolis, IN ✦ Southlake, TX

Dummies 101®: Visual Basic® 5 Programming

Published by
IDG Books Worldwide, Inc.
An International Data Group Company
919 E. Hillsdale Blvd.
Suite 400
Foster City, CA 94404
http://www.idgbooks.com (IDG Books Worldwide Web site)
http://www.dummies.com (Dummies Press Web site)

Library of Congress Catalog Card No.: 96-80295

ISBN: 0-7645-0120-8

Printed in the United States of America

10 9 8 7 6 5 4 3 2 1

1M/QS/QU/ZX/IN

Distributed in the United States by IDG Books Worldwide, Inc.

Distributed by Macmillan Canada for Canada; by Transworld Publishers Limited in the United Kingdom and Europe; by WoodsLane Pty. Ltd. for Australia; by WoodsLane Enterprises Ltd. for New Zealand; by Longman Singapore Publishers Ltd. for Singapore, Malaysia, Thailand, and Indonesia; by Simron Pty. Ltd. for South Africa; by Toppan Company Ltd. for Japan; by Distribuidora Cuspide for Argentina; by Livraria Cultura for Brazil; by Ediciencia S.A. for Ecuador; by Addison-Wesley Publishing Company for Korea; by Ediciones ZETA S.C.R. Ltda. for Peru; by WS Computer Publishing Company, Inc., for the Philippines; by Unalis Corporation for Taiwan; by Contemporanea de Ediciones for Venezuela. Authorized Sales Agent: Anthony Rudkin Associates for the Middle East and North Africa.

For general information on IDG Books Worldwide's books in the U.S., please call our Consumer Customer Service department at 800-762-2974. For reseller information, including discounts and premium sales, please call our Reseller Customer Service department at 800-434-3422.

For information on where to purchase IDG Books Worldwide's books outside the U.S., please contact our International Sales department at 415-655-3023 or fax 415-655-3299.

For information on foreign language translations, please contact our Foreign & Subsidiary Rights department at 415-655-3021 or fax 415-655-3281.

For sales inquiries and special prices for bulk quantities, please contact our Sales department at 415-655-3200 or write to the address above.

For information on using IDG Books Worldwide's books in the classroom or for ordering examination copies, please contact our Educational Sales department at 800-434-2086 or fax 817-251-8174.

For press review copies, author interviews, or other publicity information, please contact our Public Relations department at 415-655-3000 or fax 415-655-3299.

For authorization to photocopy items for corporate, personal, or educational use, please contact Copyright Clearance Center, 222 Rosewood Drive, Danvers, MA 01923, or fax 508-750-4470.

is a trademark under exclusive license to IDG Books Worldwide, Inc., from International Data Group, Inc.

About the Authors

John Mueller

John Mueller is a freelance author and technical editor. He has written 31 books and almost 200 articles to date, on topics ranging from networking to artificial intelligence to database management. Some of his current book projects include a Visual C++ programmer's guide and a Windows 95 advanced-user tutorial. In addition to book projects, John has provided technical editing to both *Data Based Advisor* and *Coast Compute* magazines.

When John isn't working at the computer, you can find him in his workshop. He's an avid woodworker and candlemaker. On any given afternoon, you can find him working at a lathe or putting the finishing touches on a bookcase. One of his favorite projects is making candlesticks and the candles to go with them. You can reach John on CompuServe at 71570,641 or on the Internet at JMueller@pacbell.net.

Wallace Wang

Wallace Wang has written over a dozen computer books, including IDG Books' *Visual Basic 5 For Dummies, MORE Visual Basic 5 For Dummies, CompuServe For Dummies,* and *Microsoft Office 97 For Dummies*. When not writing books, he writes a monthly column for *Boardwatch Magazine* and performs stand-up comedy in the San Diego area.

When Wallace isn't working at the computer, he avoids stepping foot in any workshop that involves power tools, flammable items, or sharp objects. He can be reached on CompuServe at 70334,3672.

ABOUT IDG BOOKS WORLDWIDE

Welcome to the world of IDG Books Worldwide.

IDG Books Worldwide, Inc., is a subsidiary of International Data Group, the world's largest publisher of computer-related information and the leading global provider of information services on information technology. IDG was founded more than 25 years ago and now employs more than 8,500 people worldwide. IDG publishes more than 275 computer publications in over 75 countries (see listing below). More than 60 million people read one or more IDG publications each month.

Launched in 1990, IDG Books Worldwide is today the #1 publisher of best-selling computer books in the United States. We are proud to have received eight awards from the Computer Press Association in recognition of editorial excellence and three from *Computer Currents'* First Annual Readers' Choice Awards. Our best-selling *...For Dummies®* series has more than 30 million copies in print with translations in 30 languages. IDG Books Worldwide, through a joint venture with IDG's Hi-Tech Beijing, became the first U.S. publisher to publish a computer book in the People's Republic of China. In record time, IDG Books Worldwide has become the first choice for millions of readers around the world who want to learn how to better manage their businesses.

Our mission is simple: Every one of our books is designed to bring extra value and skill-building instructions to the reader. Our books are written by experts who understand and care about our readers. The knowledge base of our editorial staff comes from years of experience in publishing, education, and journalism — experience we use to produce books for the '90s. In short, we care about books, so we attract the best people. We devote special attention to details such as audience, interior design, use of icons, and illustrations. And because we use an efficient process of authoring, editing, and desktop publishing our books electronically, we can spend more time ensuring superior content and spend less time on the technicalities of making books.

You can count on our commitment to deliver high-quality books at competitive prices on topics you want to read about. At IDG Books Worldwide, we continue in the IDG tradition of delivering quality for more than 25 years. You'll find no better book on a subject than one from IDG Books Worldwide.

John J. Kilcullen

John Kilcullen
CEO
IDG Books Worldwide, Inc.

*Eighth Annual
Computer Press
Awards ≥1992*

*Ninth Annual
Computer Press
Awards ≥1993*

*Tenth Annual
Computer Press
Awards≥1994*

*Eleventh Annual
Computer Press
Awards ≥1995*

IDG Books Worldwide, Inc., is a subsidiary of International Data Group, the world's largest publisher of computer-related information and the leading global provider of information services on information technology. International Data Group publishes over 275 computer publications in over 75 countries. Sixty million people read one or more International Data Group publications each month. International Data Group's publications include: **ARGENTINA:** Buyer's Guide, Computerworld Argentina, PC World Argentina; **AUSTRALIA:** Australian Macworld, Australian PC World, Australian Reseller News, Computerworld, IT Casebook, Network World, Publish, Webmaster; **AUSTRIA:** Computerwelt Osterreich, Networks Austria, PC Tip Austria; **BANGLADESH:** PC World Bangladesh; **BELARUS:** PC World Belarus; **BELGIUM:** Data News; **BRAZIL:** Annuário de Informática, Computerworld, Connections, Macworld, PC Player, PC World, Publish, Reseller News, Supergamepower; **BULGARIA:** Computerworld Bulgaria, Network World Bulgaria, PC & MacWorld Bulgaria; **CANADA:** CIO Canada, Client/Server World, ComputerWorld Canada, InfoWorld Canada, NetworkWorld Canada, WebWorld; **CHILE:** Computerworld Chile, PC World Chile; **COLOMBIA:** Computerworld Colombia, PC World Colombia; **COSTA RICA:** PC World Centro America; **THE CZECH AND SLOVAK REPUBLICS:** Computerworld Czechoslovakia, Macworld Czech Republic, PC World Czechoslovakia; **DENMARK:** Communications World Danmark, Computerworld Danmark, Macworld Danmark, PC World Danmark, Techworld Denmark; **DOMINICAN REPUBLIC:** PC World Republica Dominicana; **ECUADOR:** PC World Ecuador; **EGYPT:** Computerworld Middle East, PC World Middle East; **EL SALVADOR:** PC World Centro America; **FINLAND:** MikroPC, Tietoverkko, Tietoviikko; **FRANCE:** Distributique, Hebdo, Info PC, Le Monde Informatique, Macworld, Reseaux & Telecoms, WebMaster France; **GERMANY:** Computer Partner, Computerwoche, Computerwoche Extra, Computerwoche FOCUS, Global Online, Macwelt, PC Welt; **GREECE:** Amiga Computing, GamePro Greece, Multimedia World; **GUATEMALA:** PC World Centro America; **HONDURAS:** PC World Centro America; **HONG KONG:** Computerworld Hong Kong, PC World Hong Kong, Publish in Asia; **HUNGARY:** ABCD CD-ROM, Computerworld Szamitastechnika, Internetto online Magazine, PC World Hungary, PC-X Magazin Hungary; **ICELAND:** Tolvuheimur PC World Island; **INDIA:** Information Communications World, Information Systems Computerworld, PC World India, Publish in Asia; **INDONESIA:** InfoKomputer PC World, Komputek Computerworld, Publish in Asia; **IRELAND:** ComputerScope, PC Live!; **ISRAEL:** Macworld Israel, People & Computers/Computerworld; **ITALY:** Computerworld Italia, Macworld Italia, Networking Italia, PC World Italia; **JAPAN:** DTP World, Macworld Japan, Nikkei Personal Computing, OS/2 World Japan, SunWorld Japan, Windows NT World, Windows World Japan; **KENYA:** PC World East African; **KOREA:** Hi-Tech Information, Macworld Korea, PC World Korea, Publish in Asia; **MACEDONIA:** PC World Macedonia; **MALAYSIA:** Computerworld Malaysia, PC World Malaysia, Publish in Asia; **MALTA:** PC World Malta; **MEXICO:** Computerworld Mexico, PC World Mexico; **MYANMAR:** PC World Myanmar; **NETHERLANDS:** Computer! Totaal, LAN Internetworking Magazine, LAN World Buyers Guide, Macworld Netherlands, Net, WebWereld; **NEW ZEALAND:** Absolute Beginners Guide and Plain & Simple Series, Computer Buyer, Computer Industry Directory, Computerworld New Zealand, MTB, Network World, PC World New Zealand; **NICARAGUA:** PC World Centro America; **NORWAY:** Computerworld Norge, CW Rapport, Datamagasinet, Financial Rapport, Kursguide Norge, Macworld Norge, Multimediaworld Norge, PC World Ekspress Norge, PC World Nettverk, PC World Norge, PC World ProduktGuide Norge; **PAKISTAN:** Computerworld Pakistan; **PANAMA:** PC World Panama; **PEOPLE'S REPUBLIC OF CHINA:** China Computer Users, China Computerworld, China InfoWorld, China Telecom World Weekly, Computer & Communication, Electronic Design China, Electronics Today, Electronics Weekly, Game Software, PC World China, Popular Computer Week, Software Weekly, Software World, Telecom World; **PERU:** Computerworld Peru, PC World Profesional Peru, PC World Peru, PC World SoHo Peru; **PHILIPPINES:** Click!, Computerworld Philippines, PC World Philippines, Publish in Asia; **POLAND:** Computerworld Poland, Computerworld Special Report Poland, Cyber, Macworld Poland, Networld Poland, PC World Komputer; **PORTUGAL:** Cerebro/PC World, Computerworld/Correio Informático, Dealer World Portugal, Mac*In/PC*In Portugal, Multimedia World; **PUERTO RICO:** PC World Puerto Rico; **ROMANIA:** Computerworld Romania, PC World Romania, Telecom Romania; **RUSSIA:** Computerworld Russia, Mir PK, Publish, Seti; **SINGAPORE:** Computerworld Singapore, PC World Singapore, Publish in Asia; **SLOVENIA:** Monitor; **SOUTH AFRICA:** Computing SA, Network World SA, Software World SA; **SPAIN:** Communicaciones World España, Computerworld España, Dealer World España, Macworld España, PC World España; **SRI LANKA:** Infolink PC World; **SWEDEN:** CAP&Design, Computer Sweden, Corporate Computing Sweden, Internetworld Sweden, it.branschen, Macworld Sweden, MaxiData Sweden, MikroDatorn, Nätverk & Kommunikation, PC World Sweden, PCaktiv, Windows World Sweden; **SWITZERLAND:** Computerworld Schweiz, Macworld Schweiz, PCtip; **TAIWAN:** Computerworld Taiwan, Macworld Taiwan, NEW ViSiON/Publish, PC World Taiwan, Windows World Taiwan; **THAILAND:** Publish in Asia, Thai Computerworld; **TURKEY:** Computerworld Turkiye, Macworld Turkiye, Network World Turkiye, PC World Turkiye; **UKRAINE:** Computerworld Kiev, Multimedia World Ukraine, PC World Ukraine; **UNITED KINGDOM:** Acorn User UK, Amiga Action UK, Amiga Computing UK, Apple Talk UK, Computing, Macworld, Parents and Computers UK, PC Advisor, PC Home, PSX Pro, The WEB; **UNITED STATES:** Cable in the Classroom, CIO Magazine, Computerworld, DOS World, Federal Computer Week, GamePro Magazine, InfoWorld, I-Way, Macworld, Network World, PC Games, PC World, Publish, Video Event, THE WEB Magazine, and WebMaster; online webzines: JavaWorld, NetscapeWorld, and SunWorld Online; **URUGUAY:** InfoWorld Uruguay; **VENEZUELA:** Computerworld Venezuela, PC World Venezuela; and **VIETNAM:** PC World Vietnam.
2/14/97

Dedication

This book is dedicated to all those programmers who want to learn Visual Basic as quickly and painlessly as possible.

Authors' Acknowledgments

Our book agent at Waterside Productions, Matt Wagner, deserves credit for helping us get the contract for this book and taking care of business details that most authors don't really think about. (We have to acknowledge him or else we may not get another book contract through him again.)

A special thank you goes to Rebecca Mueller for her tireless efforts in making the text readable.

We would also like to thank the entire IDG staff, especially Mary Goodwin, for her efforts in producing this final text.

Finally, we wish to extend our thanks to all of our cats. They had absolutely nothing to do with the publication or creation of this book, but without their existence, our lives would be filled with much less mirth, joy, and general happiness (along with cat hair, furballs, and cat box litter).

Publisher's Acknowledgments

We're proud of this book; please send us your comments about it by using the IDG Books Worldwide Registration Card at the back of the book or by e-mailing us at feedback/dummies@idgbooks.com. Some of the people who helped bring this book to market include the following:

Acquisitions, Development, and Editorial

Project Editor: Mary Goodwin

Acquisitions Editor: Mike Kelly

Product Development Director: Mary Bednarek

Copy Editor: Tamara S. Castleman

Technical Reviewer: Garrett Pease

Editorial Manager: Mary C. Corder

Editorial Assistants: Chris H. Collins, Steven H. Hayes, Darren Meiss, and Michael D. Sullivan

Production

Project Coordinator: Regina Snyder

Layout and Graphics: Cameron Booker, Linda M. Boyer, J. Tyler Connor, Dominique DeFelice, Maridee V. Ennis, Angela F. Hunckler, Drew R. Moore, Anna Rohrer, Brent Savage

Proofreaders: Steven Jong, Melissa D. Buddendeck, Joel K. Draper, Dwight Ramsey, Robert Springer

Indexer: Richard T. Evans, Infodex Indexing Services, Inc.

General and Administrative

IDG Books Worldwide, Inc.: John Kilcullen, CEO; Steven Berkowitz, President and Publisher

Dummies, Inc.: Brenda McLaughlin, Senior Vice President & Group Publisher

Dummies Technology Press & Dummies Editorial: Diane Graves Steele, Vice President and Associate Publisher; Judith A. Taylor, Brand Manager; Kristin A. Cocks, Editorial Director

Dummies Trade Press: Kathleen A. Welton, Vice President & Publisher; Stacy S. Collins, Brand Manager

IDG Books Production for Dummies Press: Beth Jenkins, Production Director; Cindy L. Phipps, Supervisor of Project Coordination, Production Proofreading, and Indexing; Kathie S. Schutte, Supervisor of Page Layout; Shelley Lea, Supervisor of Graphics and Design; Debbie J. Gates, Production Systems Specialist; Tony Augsburger, Supervisor of Reprints and Bluelines; Leslie Popplewell, Media Archive Coordinator

Dummies Packaging & Book Design: Patti Sandez, Packaging Specialist; Lance Kayser, Packaging Assistant; Kavish + Kavish, Cover Design

♦

The publisher would like to give special thanks to Patrick J. McGovern, without whom this book would not have been possible.

♦

Files at a Glance

The lesson files on the CD have been arranged so that the Visual Basic Project files (differentiated by the VBP extension in the filename) allow you to access related lesson files. Here's a listing of all the Project files that you install from the CD and where in the book the Project files are first mentioned. Also listed is a database file (Mydata.MDB) that you use for the unit on database files. See Appendix B for installation instructions.

Part I

Part II

Part III

Part IV

Bonus Stuff (Other Items on the CD)

Bonus units

Unit CD1: Pictures, Rectangles, and Lines

Unit CD2: Making Noise

Unit CD3: Playing Animation and Video

Unit CD4: Drawing Business Charts

Unit CD5: Printing a Visual Basic Program

Lesson files (for bonus units)

Contents at a Glance

Table of Contents

Introduction

Welcome to *Dummies 101: Visual Basic 5 Programming*, a book that explains how to write programs in Visual Basic without a lot of the grief, frustration, and confusion normally associated with doing anything on a computer. The book also shows you how to use all those productivity enhancing tools that Visual Basic thoughtfully buries where no one can find them.

Computers may be unnecessarily complicated, but that doesn't mean that books about them have to be. In fact, this book assumes that you're a bright, intelligent, creative person — your computer is the one that doesn't work the way it really should.

This book gently guides you by the hand to learning, using, and programming your computer using Visual Basic 5.0. Take your time. Work through this book at your own pace and feel free to jot notes anywhere in these pages. In no time you will learn enough to write your own Visual Basic programs, and maybe even sell a few in the process.

Why You're Reading This Book

People love learning — they just can't stand school. With that in mind, you may be reading this book for many different reasons:

- The idea of going back to school to learn anything turns your stomach, so you're looking at this book to teach yourself everything you need to get started programming your computer in Visual Basic.

- You're taking a Visual Basic programming class, your textbook is too dull or boring, and you want something easier to read. (Ask your teacher to use this book instead.)

- You want to improve your career opportunities and learn about Visual Basic because so many Help Wanted classified ads keep offering big bucks to anyone with Visual Basic programming knowledge.

- You already know how to program in another language, like C++, and you want to learn Visual Basic quickly so you can write programs even faster than before.

- You want to write a Visual Basic program that works better than the antiquated programs the people in your office are stuck using.

- You have a computer at home and you want to write your own programs just for the fun of it.

Naturally, this book won't make you a Visual Basic programming guru overnight, but it will teach you how to get started using Visual Basic so you can do something useful right away. And maybe what you put into practice will impress your boss enough to buy you a better computer at work.

How This Book Is Organized

Notes:

This book is organized using the time-tested method of gluing pages together along one edge with an adhesive that promises not to fall apart too rapidly when continually flexed and bent. Beyond the physical organization of this book, the actual printed information is organized as follows:

Part I: Introducing Visual Basic

This part of the book introduces you to the mechanics of using Visual Basic, such as loading Visual Basic, saving a Visual Basic program, drawing objects that users will interact with, and manipulating the various parts of Visual Basic. We'll also look at how you can tell Visual Basic to write part of the program for you.

Part II: Designing Your User Interface

Part II explains the fun part about designing what your program will look like to the user. This is where you get to create pull-down menus, dialog boxes, and command buttons, just like professional programs that cost hundreds of dollars, come packaged in fancy boxes, and still don't seem to work right no matter how many times you call technical support.

Part III: Writing BASIC Code

Part III focuses on writing actual commands that make your program do something, such as saving information to a file, calculating a mathematical result, or responding to a user's frantic clicking on a command button or check box. You'll even learn about new technologies on the market, such as ActiveX.

Part IV: Polishing Your Program

Part IV winds up this book by showing you how to write bug-free programs that actually work. You'll also learn how to create your own EXE files so that you can give your program to someone else.

Part V: Appendixes

In Appendix A of Part V, you are rewarded for your diligent reading with the answers to the tests in the part summary sections. Appendix B offers you instructions on how to install the companion CD's lesson files on your computer.

On the CD Bonus Stuff

Even the best program can seem dull if you don't have sound, a little color, or graphics to spice the program up a little. These bonus units explain how to add sound, video, and graphs to your Visual Basic programs to make them fancier than ever before, and to print the programs out.

Recesses, Quizes, Reviews, and Tests

Each of the units includes two features that make learning Visual Basic much easier. First, you'll get to relax a bit in the Recess section. Some of the longer units contain two recesses so that you can double your opportunities for doing absolutely nothing. We usually provide some things for you to think about while you just sit there and do nothing.

After you're fully rested, you can take on the really tough Quiz that appears at the end of each unit. The Quiz will test your knowledge of Visual Basic by using the remarkably accurate testing techniques that we've developed over the years. If you pass, you can rank yourself as a Visual Basic genius in that area and go on to a life of complete fulfillment writing Visual Basic code.

At the end of each part of the book, you'll get another chance to think about all of the new knowledge you've accumulated using the Review section. If you didn't forget everything you learned during Recess, you can move from the Review to the Test section. We'll test your knowledge of Visual Basic again using the same time-honored testing techniques that you found in the Quiz section. Don't try to use the same answers though — the Quizzes and Tests all have different questions.

Icons Used in This Book

Periodically throughout the book, we use icons to point out different kinds of information. Keep your eye peeled for the following icons:

on the CD

This icon lets you know when you need to use a file stored on the enclosed CD-ROM in the back of this book.

on the test

This icon flags important information that you really should know so you don't have to keep looking it up in this book every time you run into trouble. Any information highlighted by this icon will likely show up on the quiz that appears at the end of each unit, so be prepared.

extra credit

This icon highlights advanced information that isn't necessary to know, but can come in handy when you're using Visual Basic.

heads up

Don't overlook any paragraphs marked by this icon. Anything highlighted by the Heads Up icon alerts you to crucial information that can make programming easier or warn you of possible problems that can ruin your day while you're using Visual Basic.

Using the CD-ROM

As long as someone hasn't taken a razor blade to the back of this book and stolen the enclosed CD-ROM, you should find one CD. This CD contains Visual Basic files for you to examine and play with so you don't have to do a lot of unnecessary typing yourself. The CD also contains some bonus units that explain how to use some more advanced features of Visual Basic to brighten up your program. In order to read these bonus units, we also put some software on the CD you need to install.

heads up

Just in case you're wondering, the enclosed CD does not contain the actual Visual Basic program. If you don't already have a copy of Visual Basic, you need to rush right out and buy it before you can even think about using the enclosed CD.

To use this book and the enclosed CD, you need the following:

- Microsoft Windows 95 installed on your computer

- A 486 or faster processor with at least 16MB of RAM

- At least 2.29MB of free hard-disk space available to install all the software from this CD (you'll need less space if you don't install every program)

- A CD-ROM drive — double speed (2x) or faster

- A sound card with speakers

- A display adapter capable of displaying at least 256 colors or grayscale (a 1,024 x 768 minimum resolution is highly recommended)

- A modem with a speed of at least 14,400 bps

If you meet the preceding criteria, you'll be able to use the enclosed CD and all its files.

The exercise files are sample code and documents that you use while following along with the lessons in the book. You need to put these files on your hard drive. After you're done with the book, you can remove the files with a simple uninstall process. To install the files (and the software) on the enclosed CD, follow these instructions:

1 Insert the Dummies 101 CD-ROM (label side up) into your computer's CD-ROM drive.

Be careful to touch only the edges of the CD-ROM. The CD-ROM drive is the one that pops out with a circular drawer.

Wait about a minute before you do anything else; the installation program should begin automatically if your computer has the AutoPlay feature. If the program does not start after a minute, go to step 2. If it does, go to step 4.

2 Double-click on the My Computer icon on the Windows 95 desktop.

3 Double-click on the CD-ROM icon on the desktop.

4 Click on OK.

The installation program will ask if you want to use the CD now.

5 Click on Yes.

You'll see an End User License Agreement dialog box.

6 Click on Accept.

You'll see the main installation dialog box.

7 Choose whether you want to install the exercise files or software by clicking on either Install Exercise Files or Choose Software. . . .

8 Follow the remaining prompts to install your exercise files or software.

After you install the Visual Basic files on the CD, don't mess with the files prematurely. The book explains how to access the files and what to do with them as you progress through the lessons.

heads up

If you have trouble using or installing the files on the enclosed CD, call the IDG Books Worldwide Technical Support Department at 1-800-762-2974. Be nice to the IDG Books representatives. They have problems with their computers too, so they can sympathize with your plight.

Stuff You Should Know

In case you haven't noticed by now, computers require you to do some pretty odd things, like pressing multiple keys at the same time to give a command. So throughout this book, you may see something mathematically impossible that looks like this:

Ctrl+X

Whenever you see something like this, that means you should hold down the Ctrl key with one finger, tap the X key with a second finger, and then let go of both keys.

Notes:

Computers also have funny names for files. Visual Basic is no exception. When you install the files from the CD and look at their names, a typical filename is Obvious.VBP. Basically, Obvious is the name of the file, and VBP is the *extension* — a technical description of the file's contents. You'll learn more about extensions later; for now, know that the important files are the ones with the VBP extension. The VBP stands for Visual Basic Project. While there may be other files that begin with Obvious (or whatever), when this book asks you to call up a project file at the beginning of a lesson, look for the one with the VBP extension.

Depending on what version of Windows you have, filenames may appear all uppercased (OBVIOUS.VBP) or mostly lowercased (Obvious.vbp). This book will refer to filenames in a combination (Obvious.VBP), capitalizing the extension so you can read it more easily.

Visual Basic involves some computer code. When code is included in the lesson steps in this book, you may see some of the code in boldface. That is the part you are being instructed to enter; it does not mean that you have to boldface the code.

All of the illustrations in this book show Visual Basic 5.0 running under Windows 95. If you're using any other 32-bit version of Windows, your screen may look slightly different, so don't panic.

Introducing Visual Basic

Part I

In this part . . .

A computer is only as good as the program that runs on it. To see how this simple truth hits home, look around your computer and count how many programs you never use, rarely use, or wish you didn't have to use. Chances are these programs are either too complicated, too clumsy, or just plain useless when it comes to addressing your particular needs.

Almost everyone has felt the disappointment associated with buying yet another new program that doesn't work as expected. Instead of facing this disappointment time and again, consider another solution: Why not write your own program? That way, you can custom design your program to look and work exactly like you want.

When Microsoft introduced Windows, learning to write your own programs meant studying some cryptic programming language, such as C++, and devoting months out of your life, even to construct the simplest program. Fortunately, Visual Basic makes writing Windows programs a lot easier; those horrid old days of programming have become as obsolete as slide rules.

With Visual Basic, you can draw the way your program looks and then write short and simple BASIC commands to make your program perform a variety of tasks. Millions of people have purchased Visual Basic to write programs ranging from games and utilities to real estate appraisal programs and television network scheduling programs. Whatever problem you need to solve with your computer, Visual Basic can help you write a program that works for you.

The latest version of Visual Basic, Visual Basic 5, makes things even easier. You can now use the Visual Basic Application Wizard to create a program shell that contains all of the basic features of a full-fledged application (such as standard menus and dialog boxes) without doing any programming. The Application Wizard also allows you to add basic Internet and database access to your program without writing one line of code!

Of course, the only drawback to using Visual Basic is that you have to learn how to use it first. To provide a gentle introduction to the way Visual Basic works, this part of the book guides you through the main parts to Visual Basic programming.

Don't worry. You won't find anything complicated in these pages. So relax, load up Visual Basic, and follow along at your own pace. Visual Basic programming is easy and fun.

An Introduction to Visual Basic

Prerequisites
- Turning on your computer (see owner's manual)
- Having Visual Basic installed on your computer (see owner's manual)
- Having CD-ROM files installed or handy (see Appendix B)

- Marquee.VBP

Objectives for This Unit

- ✓ Starting Visual Basic
- ✓ Loading a Visual Basic program
- ✓ Understanding the Visual Basic interface
- ✓ Running and exiting a Visual Basic program

This unit gives you a quick introduction to Visual Basic, helping you feel comfortable with the program even if you don't have the slightest idea how to use Visual Basic yet. Don't worry too much about memorizing anything in this unit for now. Take your time working through this unit and get acquainted with Visual Basic.

Even though everything in this unit is important, you'll want to pay special attention to the two steps required to create a Visual Basic program:

- First you draw the way you want your program to look.
- Then you write BASIC commands to make your program actually do something.

Of course, before you can begin writing a Visual Basic program of your very own, you first must know how to start and load Visual Basic. Just to get things off to a flying start, that's exactly what we teach you in Lesson 1-1, the very first lesson in the book.

<table>
<tr><td>Lesson 1-1</td><td>

Starting Visual Basic and Using the New Project Dialog Box

</td></tr>
</table>

Before you can start Visual Basic, you have to turn your computer on and make sure that Visual Basic is already installed on your computer. (If you haven't installed Visual Basic on your computer, stop right now and install it. Otherwise, you won't be able to relate to the rest of the book.)

Starting Visual Basic

on the test

You'll normally start Visual Basic before you can create a new program or load an existing one. Start Visual Basic by following these steps:

1 Click on the Start button in the lower-left corner of the screen.

A menu pops up on the screen.

2 Click on Programs.

Another menu pops up to the right. If you don't see Visual Basic listed in the offerings, the program isn't installed. Refer to your Visual Basic manual for installation instructions.

3 Click on the Microsoft Visual Basic 5.0 folder.

Another menu pops up to the right.

4 Click on Microsoft Visual Basic 5.0 again.

Visual Basic pops up, as shown in Figure 1-1. Notice that Visual Basic automatically displays a New Project dialog box that asks which New, Existing, or Recent project you want to open.

A project contains all of the files you need for a program; you can think of a project as a container for holding the pieces of your program. Every program you create will contain one or more project files of various types. The most common project file type that you'll create is a form. We'll look more closely at projects in Unit 2. All you need to remember right now is that a project is like a container, and one of the things that it can hold is a form.

heads up

After you have Visual Basic running, get into the habit of exiting Visual Basic (by choosing File⇨Exit) before turning off your computer. If you turn off the computer without exiting Visual Basic, you may lose some of your work.

Loading an existing Visual Basic program

After you have Visual Basic running on your computer, you basically have two choices: You can start writing a new program from scratch, or you can load an existing program. Because writing large Visual Basic programs can take days, months, or even years, most likely you'll create a program and then modify it a little bit over time. Therefore, one of the first skills you need to master is loading an existing Visual Basic program so that you can modify it.

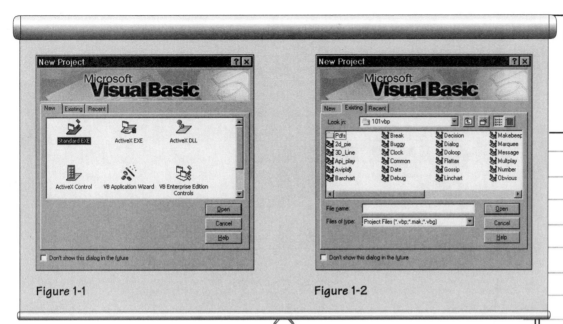

Figure 1-1

Figure 1-2

Figure 1-1: Visual Basic waiting for you to do something.

Figure 1-2: The Existing tab of the New Project dialog box.

on the CD

In this unit, you get a chance to play around with a real-live Visual Basic program called Marquee.VBP, which you can find on your CD, if you haven't misplaced the CD already. (See Appendix B to find out how to install the practice programs to your hard drive.) Make sure that you start Visual Basic and that you can see the New Project dialog box shown in Figure 1-1 before you start this procedure.

1 Click on the Existing tab of the New Project dialog box.

Visual Basic displays a list of the folders and files in the current directory as shown in Figure 1-2. You use the buttons in this dialog box the same way that you use the buttons in Windows Explorer to locate the file you want to open, which in this case is the Marquee file.

You may have to click in the Look in list box and change the drive and directory where the Marquee.VBP file can be found, depending on how you installed the CD files. See Appendix B for the details on the CD.

2 Click on the Marquee file and click on <u>Open</u>.

The Visual Basic Marquee Project window changes as shown in Figure 1-3. Now the Project window contains a Forms folder and a list of files in this project (the Marquee.FRM file). Notice that the Properties and Form Layout windows change appearance as well.

After loading a program, you can either modify the program or run it. You modify an existing program if you want to add new features or correct problems that prevent the program from working correctly. After you test to make sure that your program works right, you can run it.

Figure 1-3: Visual Basic changes the Project window to show what files the Marquee project contains.

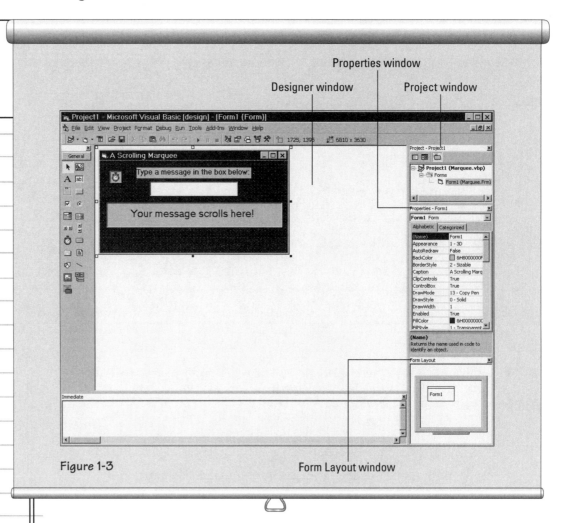

Figure 1-3

Loading a recently used Visual Basic program

Chances are that you'll work on the same project every day until you complete it. Rather than look all over your hard drive for the same file every day, you can look through the list of projects on the Recent tab of the New Project dialog box (the dialog box that you see every time you start Visual Basic) to find the file you want to work on. The following steps show you how to use this feature:

1 Click on the Recent tab of the New Project dialog box.

Visual Basic displays a list of recent projects like the one shown in Figure 1-4.

2 Click on the Marquee project and click on Open.

The Marquee project opens and the Visual Basic Marquee Project, Properties, and Form Layout windows change as shown in Figure 1-3.

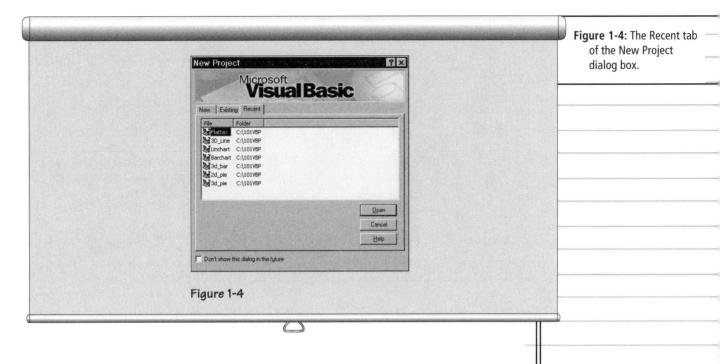

Figure 1-4

Figure 1-4: The Recent tab of the New Project dialog box.

Understanding the Parts of Visual Basic

Lesson 1-2

At first glance, Visual Basic may look a bit confusing because it contains so many windows and funny-looking icons, but don't worry. There's actually a purpose behind all those funny looking things you see on the screen. The seven main parts of Visual Basic are:

- ◗ The Project window
- ◗ The Designer window
- ◗ The Toolbox
- ◗ The Properties window
- ◗ The Form Layout window
- ◗ The Immediate window
- ◗ The Code window

The rest of this lesson gets you better acquainted with each of these seven important parts of the Visual Basic program.

Figure 1-5: The Visual Basic Code window for the Marquee.FRM file.

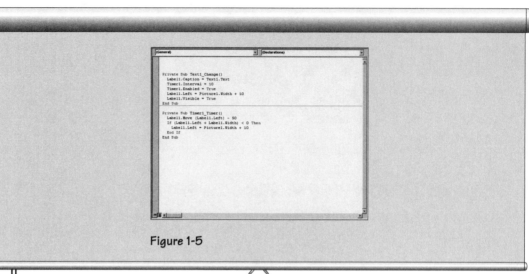

Figure 1-5

View Code
button

View Object
button

Toggle Folders
button

user interface =
what the user sees
when the program
is running

The Project window

The Project window acts like a road map, helping you find your way around a Visual Basic program by listing all the files that make up the program. In Figure 1-3, the Marquee program only consists of a single file called Marquee.FRM.

If you look carefully at Figure 1-3, you see three buttons directly above the Marquee.FRM Form file: View Code, View Object, and Toggle Folders. The View Code button lets you see the BASIC code that makes the Marquee.FRM file actually do something; the View Object button lets you see the user interface of the Marquee.FRM file.

Visual Basic normally groups like elements of your project together into folders. For example, all the form files appear in the Forms folder. If you want to look at your project files without the aid of folders, then click the Toggle Folders button. (There isn't any good reason to remove the folders because they help you organize your project.)

To learn a little about the wonderful things you can do with the Project window and how the window works, follow these steps:

1 **Click on and highlight the name of the Form file you want to view, Marquee.FRM.**

2 **Click on View Code.**

Visual Basic displays the Code window, shown in Figure 1-5, where you can type BASIC commands.

3 **Click on View Object.**

Visual Basic displays the Designer window, as shown in Figure 1-3.

heads up

Only one Project window can appear at any given time. In case the Project window disappears from view, you can make it appear again by doing one of the following:

- Pressing Ctrl+R
- Choosing <u>V</u>iew⇨<u>Pr</u>oject Explorer
- Clicking on the Project Explorer button in the Toolbar

The Designer window, the Toolbox, the Properties window, and the Form Layout window

on the test

The Designer window lets you design the way your program looks. Think of the Designer window as a blank canvas. To make your program show something on the screen, you have to draw objects in the Designer window. An object can be text, lines, boxes, buttons, or pictures to make your program look pretty.

To create an object, you have to click on the appropriate tool stored in the Toolbox. For example, to draw a command button, click on the Command Button icon in the Toolbox. After you choose a tool from the Toolbox, you can draw the object on your form.

After you place an object on a form, you can move, resize, or modify the object until it looks just the way you want. To modify an object already drawn on a form, you use the Properties window. The Properties window lists different characteristics about an object, such as its width, its color, and its position on the form.

Visual Basic also allows you to determine where your program starts in relation to the Windows 95 desktop. This is where the Form Layout window comes into play. You adjust a form's starting position by moving it around in the Form Layout window. This window also lets you coordinate the position of multiple forms if your program has more than one.

To get some experience using the Toolbox, the Properties window, and the Form Layout window to design a form, try the following exercise (make sure that you still have the Marquee project open):

1 **Press Ctrl+R to display the Project window (in case the window is hidden).**

2 **Click on View Object.**

Visual Basic displays the Designer window (refer to Figure 1-3).

3 **Click on the Command Button icon in the Toolbox.**

Doing so allows you to draw a command button.

Figure 1-6: Using the Command Button tool to draw a button in the Visual Basic Designer window.

Figure 1-7: The Visual Basic Code window.

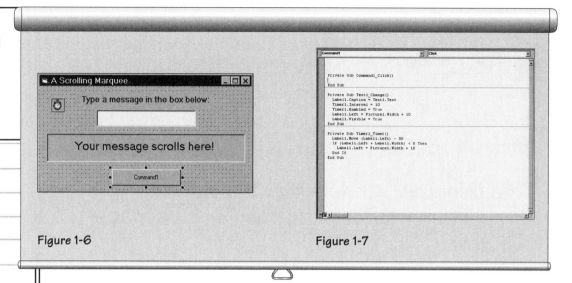

Figure 1-6   Figure 1-7

Notes:

4 **Move the cursor on the form (the cursor turns into a crosshair) to where you want to draw the object, hold down the left mouse button, and move the mouse.**

Visual Basic draws an outline showing the size and location of your object (a command button in this case).

5 **Release the mouse button so your Command1 command button looks like the one shown in Figure 1-6.**

6 **Press F4 to display the Properties window (in case the window is hidden).**

7 **Click on the Caption property.**

8 **Type** Exit **and press Enter.**

Notice that your command button now displays the caption Exit. By changing the Caption property of the command button, you make the button display something more descriptive than Command1. (This is purely optional, by the way.)

9 **Move the cursor to the Form1 box in the Form Layout window.**

The cursor turns into a quadruple arrow.

10 **Left click on Form1 and then move Form1 to the center of the display.**

Notice that moving the form in the Form Layout window doesn't affect its position in the Designer window. The Form Layout window only affects where the form gets drawn when you run the program.

In the next section, you'll write simple BASIC code to make this command button do something when the user clicks on it. In the process, you'll learn some valuable stuff about the Code window.

The Code window

on the test

When you click on an object such as a command button or check box drawn on a form, your program won't do anything until you write BASIC commands telling the program what to do. For example, the command button you just drew now displays Exit — but you haven't yet written any BASIC code to tell Visual Basic to end the program when someone clicks on the Exit button.

To enter BASIC commands into Visual Basic, you type them into the Code window. Of course, you can't randomly type BASIC commands into the Code window and expect them to work. Instead, you have to write BASIC commands that tell Visual Basic what to do when a certain *event* occurs with a certain object. For example, a command button can be an object and an event can be when the user clicks the mouse on the button. So, if you want your program to do something when the user clicks a command button, you have to write BASIC commands to tell your program what to do.

To get acquainted with typing BASIC code in the Code window, follow these steps:

1 Double-click on the Command Button object you just drew.

The Code window for your command button appears, as shown in Figure 1-7.

2 Type the word End (in bold) after Private Sub Command1_Click( ) in the Code window so it looks like this:

```
Private Sub Command1_Click()
End
End Sub
```

Although you can't tell just by looking at it, this BASIC code tells Visual Basic, "When someone clicks on the Command1 command button, end the program."

3 Click in the close box of the Code window (or press Alt+F4) to make the Code window go away.

Keep the Marquee.VBP program loaded for the next lesson, where you get to see the Marquee program work right before your eyes.

Recess

If you've made it this far, you deserve a break. In fact, in each unit in this book, when we think you've done enough work for one sitting, we tell you to take a recess and get away from Visual Basic for a while. After you've taken a short walk, had a soda, or watched a few minutes of the tube, feel free to sit back down and do the next lesson. When you've finished the next lesson, take the quiz and do the exercise at the end of this unit, just to make sure that you really did learn something and just didn't skim over the text, looking for answers that nobody cares if you memorized or not.

☑ Progress Check

If you can do the following, you've mastered this lesson:

❑ Call up the form by using the Project window.

❑ Call up the Code window by using the Project window.

❑ Draw a command button on a form, call up its Properties window, and give the button a new caption.

❑ Change the form's starting position on the Desktop using the Form Layout window.

❑ Assign BASIC commands to a command button by using the Code window.

Lesson 1-3

Running and Exiting a Visual Basic Program

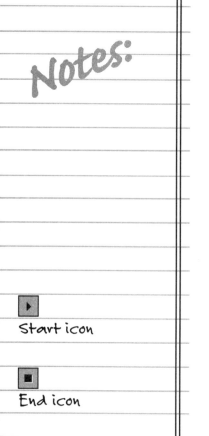

The whole purpose of running a Visual Basic program is to make sure that the program works before you sell or give away copies to unsuspecting friends or customers. When you run a program, you can test to see what parts need improving (and what parts actually work right).

To see an actual Visual Basic program run right before your eyes, load the Marquee.VBP program and follow these steps:

1 **Press F5 (or choose <u>R</u>un⇨<u>S</u>tart).**

The lifeless form of the program immediately springs to life on the screen, waiting for you to do something. Notice that the form appears in the position that you requested in the Form Layout window.

2 **Type a message.**

Visual Basic scrolls your message across the screen.

3 **Click on the Exit command button that you drew (refer to Figure 1-6).**

Visual Basic stops running your program.

heads up

You can run a Visual Basic program three ways: by pressing F5, by clicking on the Start icon in the Toolbar, or by choosing <u>R</u>un⇨<u>S</u>tart.

on the test

Likewise, you can stop a Visual Basic program in two ways: by clicking the End icon in the Toolbar, or by choosing <u>R</u>un⇨<u>E</u>nd.

heads up

Most (but not all) programs also provide an Exit command button (refer to Figure 1-6). If the program includes this button, you can click on it to stop a Visual Basic program.

No matter how much fun you may have using Visual Basic, you eventually have to exit it so you can turn your computer off and go to sleep. To exit Visual Basic, follow these steps:

1 **Choose <u>F</u>ile⇨E<u>x</u>it.**

A dialog box box appears, asking whether you want to save your changes to a specific file.

2 **Click on <u>Y</u>es to save your file.**

Visual Basic goes away.

heads up

Most of the time, clicking on Yes in step 2 to save any changes you may have made to your program is a good idea. However, if you changed your program and made some horrible mistakes, you may not want to save your changes. In that case, just click on No in step 2.

▶
Start icon

■
End icon

☑ **Progress Check**

If you can do the following, you've mastered this lesson:

❑ Run a Visual Basic program.

❑ Exit a Visual Basic program.

Unit 1 Quiz

For each of the following questions, circle the letter of the correct answer or answers. Just to keep you thinking, each question may have more than one correct answer. The answers can be found in Appendix A.

1. **How can you start Visual Basic?**

    A. You can't, unless you own the most expensive computer on the market, running at 900 MHz with 640MB of RAM and a 120 zigabyte hard disk.

    B. Click on the Start button, choose Programs, choose the Microsoft Visual Basic 5.0 folder, and then select Visual Basic 5.0.

    C. It's impossible for an adult to use Visual Basic. Everyone knows that the only people smart enough to program a computer are teenagers.

    D. Starting Visual Basic requires attaching jumper cables from your computer to your car battery.

    E. What's Visual Basic?

2. **How do the Designer window, the Toolbox, the Properties window, and the Form Layout window work together?**

    A. The Toolbox lets you choose an object to draw in the Designer window. Then the Properties window lets you modify the object's color, size, or height. The Form Layout window allows you to determine the form's starting position on the Windows 95 Desktop.

    B. The Designer and Properties windows usually completely cover the Toolbox so you can never find or use it when you need it. You use the Form Layout window to find the hidden Toolbox.

    C. The Toolbox lets you choose what type of weapon you want to smash your computer with, such as a hammer, a screwdriver, or a chain saw. The Designer, Properties, and Form Layout windows exist only to get in your way.

    D. The Designer window lets you erase anything you try creating in the Properties window with the Toolbox. The Form Layout window tells you when the program is completely erased.

    E. Hey, wait a minute! What program am I supposed to be learning?

3. **What does the Project window contain and how many Project windows can you display at any given time?**

    A. The Project window is something you stare out of when you should be working on your project at the office.

    B. You can have as many Project windows open as you want. The purpose of each Project window is to show you how far behind you've fallen in completing all of your projects.

C. The Project window contains a list of all the files that make up a single Visual Basic program. You can only display one Project window at a time.

D. The Project window contains top secret information from Microsoft that's more valuable than any of the secrets kept by the CIA.

E. You can display three Project windows at any given time, provided that they contain absolutely worthless information that makes it look like you're working when you're really daydreaming at your desk.

4. **What does the Code window do?**

A. The Code window lets you intercept and decipher secret codes passed back and forth between spies.

B. The Code window doesn't do anything until you type in the secret code to make it work.

C. The Code window lets you feel important by giving you a window where you can type gibberish while hoping something useful eventually will come out of it.

D. The whole purpose of the Code window is to cover up the Designer window so you can't see what you're doing.

E. The Code window lets you type BASIC commands to make your program do something, such as respond when the user clicks on a command button.

5. **How can you stop a program from running?**

A. Shoot it in the leg to cripple it before it can get away.

B. Make sure that you've tied its hands and feet securely.

C. Click on the End icon in the Toolbar.

D. Hire an overweight bodyguard to whack it on the knee when nobody's looking.

E. Choose Run⇨End.

Unit 1 Exercise

1. Start Visual Basic.

2. Load a Visual Basic program of your choice (you may want to look through the project files for this book).

3. Run the program to see what it looks like.

4. Exit Visual Basic.

Dissecting a Visual Basic Program

Prerequisites
- ▶ Starting Visual Basic and loading a program (Lesson 1-1)
- ▶ Knowing the parts of a Visual Basic window (Lesson 1-2)

 on the CD   ▶ Flattax.VBP

Objectives for This Unit

✓ Understanding Visual Basic projects

✓ Getting to know your Form files

✓ Using the Visual Basic Application Wizard

When you create a worksheet with a spreadsheet application, your spreadsheet program stores the worksheet in a single file. But when you write a program in Visual Basic, guess what? Visual Basic stores your program in two or more files.

Why does Visual Basic divide a single program into multiple files? Mostly to make it easy to organize a program. For example, storing one huge program in a single file is like storing the contents of your entire filing cabinet in one stack of paper on the floor. You can do it, but it makes it much harder to find anything later.

Speaking of filing cabinets, Visual Basic also uses folders to keep your files separate. Each kind of file appears in a different folder, such as the Forms folder used to store all your forms. Think of each folder as a drawer in the filing cabinet. Finding a file is easier when you can limit the number of places you have to look for it.

Visual Basic forces you to divide a single program into multiple files so each file can perform a specific purpose, and all the files work together to create a single Visual Basic program. Each kind of file can also appear in a separate folder unless you disable this feature by clicking the Toggle Folders button in the Project window.

Tip: Storing all the files of a single Visual Basic program in a separate directory is a good idea. That way you can't lose or mix up files.

Three of the most common types of Visual Basic files are

on the test

▶ **Project files:** A Project file contains a list of all the Form files used by a single Visual Basic program. Every Visual Basic program must have one Project file. When you load a Visual Basic program, you're actually loading its Project file.

▶ **Form files:** A Form file contains two items: the user interface of a program (such as windows, pull-down menus, and command buttons) and the BASIC code that tells the user interface what to do if the user clicks on a button, chooses a menu command, closes a window, and so on. Most Visual Basic programs contain at least one Form file.

▶ **Module files:** A Module file contains BASIC code to calculate some sort of result in most cases. You can also use them to store the required to do things like setup your printer or open a database file. Module files are completely optional but extremely useful for organizing your BASIC code.

In the first lesson in this unit, we want to get you better acquainted with Visual Basic Project files. Later in this unit, we talk about Form files and Module files for your viewing entertainment.

have separate directory for each Visual Basic program, and put all program files in program's directory

---

Lesson 2-1

Understanding Visual Basic Projects

Every Visual Basic program needs one (but only one) Project file. A Project file appears on your hard disk with the VBP file extension, which stands for *Visual Basic Project.*

on the test

The sole purpose of a Project file is to keep track of all the different files used by a single Visual Basic program. Although you can name a Project file anything you want, give the file a descriptive name so you can tell what the program is by just looking at the Project filename. For example, if you write a Visual Basic game about raiding and looting innocent people, you may give your Project file a name like "Pirates," "Viking Raid," or "Political Party."

on the CD

Just so you can identify the contents of a real live Visual Basic Project file, open the FlatTax Project file supplied with this book. Lesson 1-2 explains how to load a Visual Basic program, in case you've forgotten already.

Visual Basic Project filenames have VBP file extensions

use descriptive filenames

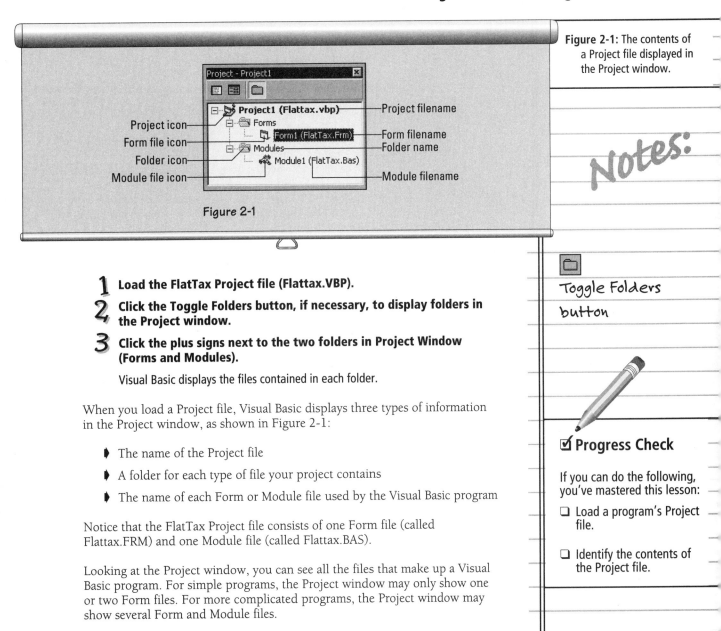

Project icon
Form file icon
Folder icon
Module file icon

Project filename
Form filename
Folder name
Module filename

Figure 2-1

Figure 2-1: The contents of a Project file displayed in the Project window.

Notes:

1 Load the FlatTax Project file (Flattax.VBP).

2 Click the Toggle Folders button, if necessary, to display folders in the Project window.

3 Click the plus signs next to the two folders in Project Window (Forms and Modules).

Visual Basic displays the files contained in each folder.

When you load a Project file, Visual Basic displays three types of information in the Project window, as shown in Figure 2-1:

- The name of the Project file
- A folder for each type of file your project contains
- The name of each Form or Module file used by the Visual Basic program

Notice that the FlatTax Project file consists of one Form file (called Flattax.FRM) and one Module file (called Flattax.BAS).

Looking at the Project window, you can see all the files that make up a Visual Basic program. For simple programs, the Project window may only show one or two Form files. For more complicated programs, the Project window may show several Form and Module files.

Toggle Folders button

☑ **Progress Check**

If you can do the following, you've mastered this lesson:

❏ Load a program's Project file.

❏ Identify the contents of the Project file.

Getting to Know Your Form Files

Lesson 2-2

on the test

A Form file lets your Visual Basic program display information on the screen and get information from the user. Most programs contain at least one Form file, and if you write a really complicated program, your program might require several hundred Form files.

Form files store the following two parts of a Visual Basic program:

- The user interface — how your program looks on-screen when running
- The BASIC code that makes the user interface do something

The user interface consists of items that let the user interact with the program, such as pull-down menus, command buttons, check boxes, and toolbars; and windows that let the user see what the program is doing or display information.

Of course, a user interface is useless by itself. If someone clicks on a command button or chooses a menu, the user interface has no idea what to do unless the Form file also contains BASIC code.

Viewing your user interface

The Project window lists all the Form files used by a Visual Basic program, but the user interface portion of a Form file won't always be visible. To see the user interface stored on a Form file, you have three methods to choose from:

- Highlight the Form file name in the Project window and then click View Object
- Right click the Form file name in the Project window and then select View Object from the context menu
- Double-click on the Form file name in the Project window

Using these three techniques always opens the Designer window to its full size. You can also use part of the Designer window area for one form and part for another by clicking the Restore window button on the Designer window and resizing the form as needed.

Another option is to display the Designer window at the bottom of the Designer window area as an icon.

To see the user interface of the FlatTax file, follow these steps:

1 Click on the FlatTax.FRM Form file and click View Object.

   Visual Basic displays the FlatTax Form file window in all its glory, as shown in Figure 2-2.

2 Click on the Restore Window button of the Designer window.

   Visual Basic displays a reduced size version of your form as shown in Figure 2-3. You can resize this copy of the Designer window as needed to fit more than one form on the screen at a time.

3 Click on the Minimize Window button of the Designer window.

   Visual Basic displays the Designer window as an icon at the bottom of the Designer window area.

Notes:

Restore Window
button

form displayed as
an icon

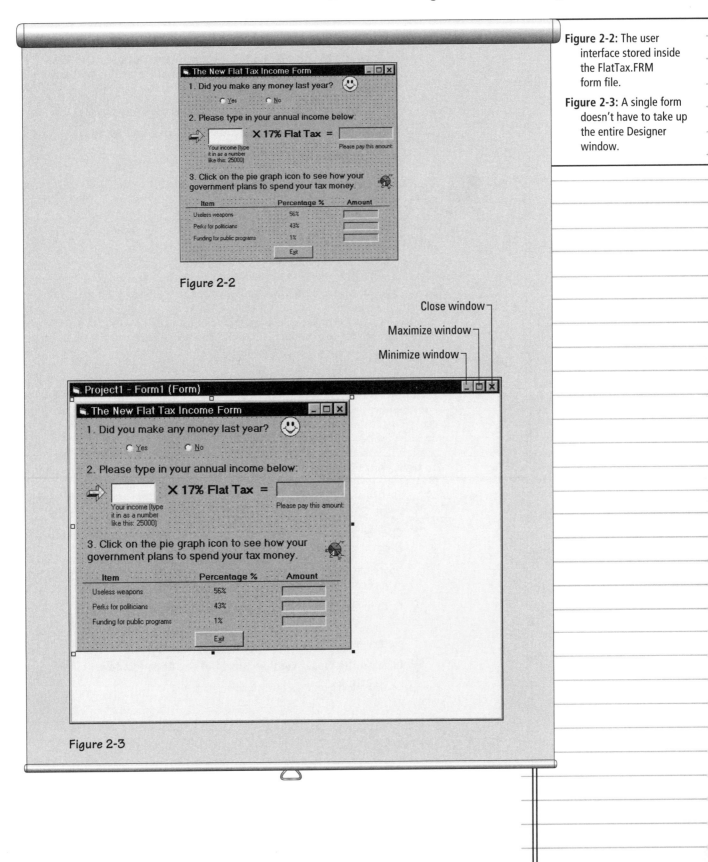

Figure 2-2

Figure 2-3

Figure 2-2: The user interface stored inside the FlatTax.FRM form file.

Figure 2-3: A single form doesn't have to take up the entire Designer window.

Close window

Maximize window

Minimize window

4 **Click on the Maximize Window button of the Designer window. (The Maximize Window button takes the place of the Restore Window button.)**

The FlatTax form takes up the entire Designer Window area again.

5 **Click on the Close Window button of the Designer window.**

Visual Basic tucks the Form file out of sight.

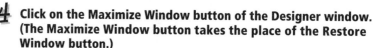

heads up

You can display as many Form files as you want, but the more you display, the more crowded your screen looks.

Viewing your code

Each Form file also contains BASIC code that tells the user interface how to act when a specific event occurs, such as when the user clicks on a command button or chooses a command from a pull-down menu. To see the BASIC code trapped inside a Form file, you have to open up the Code window. You'll learn more about writing basic code in Unit 11. For now, we just want you to get a glance at what some of this code looks like.

on the test

The Code window organizes BASIC code into mini-programs called *procedures*. Each procedure tells Visual Basic what to do when the user does something. For example, you need one procedure to tell Visual Basic what to do if the user clicks on a command button and another procedure to tell Visual Basic what to do if the user clicks on a check box.

To view a procedure, just click in the Object list box or click in the Procedure list box.

1 **Press Ctrl+R to make the Project window appear (if necessary).**

2 **Click on the FlatTax.FRM Form file in the Project window and then click on View Code to display the Code window.**

Notice that Visual Basic automatically places the cursor on the first line of code in the Command1_Click() procedure.

3 **Click in the Object list box and choose Image1.**

Visual Basic changes the cursor position to the Image1_Click() procedure. This procedure tells Visual Basic what to do if someone clicks on Image1.

4 **Click on the Close Window button of the Code window.**

Visual Basic makes the Code window go away.

Unit 11 explains more about writing BASIC code

Close Window button

☑ Progress Check

If you can do the following, you've mastered this lesson:

❏ Find the user interface of a Visual Basic program.

❏ Find the Code window of a Visual Basic Program.

All About Module (BAS) Files

Module files store special code used to do things such as calculate a result, set up a printer, or open a database file. Module files are strictly optional, but the more you use Visual Basic, the more likely you'll eventually use a Module file. Every Visual Basic program needs at least one Project file, but never needs to use a Module file. The sole purpose of a Module file is to store BASIC code.

So what's the difference between storing BASIC code in a Form file and storing BASIC code in a Module file? Good question. In general, BASIC code serves two purposes:

▶ To make the user interface work

▶ To calculate a result of some kind

You can store BASIC code in both Form and Module files, but here's the difference:

▶ Form files must contain BASIC code that makes the user interface work. Optionally, they can also contain BASIC code that calculates or manipulates data in some way.

▶ Module files only contain BASIC code that calculates or manipulates data in some way.

Although you can cram your Form files with BASIC code that makes the user interface work and calculates or manipulates data, doing so isn't always a good idea. One reason: If you cram too much BASIC code in a single form file, finding the specific procedure (BASIC code) that you want can be cumbersome — sort of like tossing all your clothes on the closet floor and then wondering why you can never find what you're looking for.

Another reason to use Module files is to share BASIC code between your Visual Basic programs. For example, suppose you wrote BASIC code to calculate the best way to make a million bucks by investing in the stock market. If you store this BASIC code in a Form file, you'd have to copy all this valuable BASIC code to a Form file in another Visual Basic program to use it again. But if you stored all the BASIC code in a Module file, then you could simply plug that Module into another Visual Basic program as easily as connecting building blocks together. (Code in a module is also available all the time, while code in a form is only available when that form is loaded.)

Code windows can only be displayed one at a time by a Form file

Notes:

Using the Visual Basic Application Wizard

Lesson 2-3

After you get to this point with Visual Basic, you're ready to start getting more productive with it. You know where all of the essential interface elements fit in, so take a look at one of the special ways that Visual Basic can help you write an application.

Sometimes the application is so unique that there isn't any other application like it. Fortunately, that's not going to happen most of the time. Most of the time, your application shares many of the same features as other programs that you've used or created. For example, just about every application you own has a File menu and an About Box.

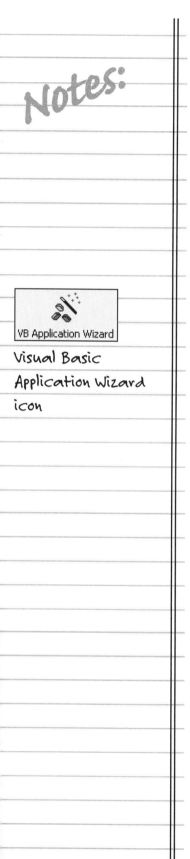

Visual Basic
Application Wizard
icon

on the test

Someone at Microsoft was actually thinking one day and happened upon a unique way to write programs. Why not have Visual Basic get all of the common program elements together for you before you even write one line of code? That's what the Visual Basic Application Wizard is all about.

You can use the Visual Basic Application Wizard to help you write applications that feature common program elements that we're all familiar with, such as the File menu. Not only does using the Wizard save you time, but it ensures that your application will look just like all those other great Windows applications. The Visual Basic Application Wizard creates a blank application (think of it like a blank form) for you, which you can then fill in with details.

Let's look at how you'd start writing an application using the Visual Basic Application Wizard:

1 Start Visual Basic.

You see the New Project dialog box.

2 Double-click on the VB Application Wizard icon.

The Visual Basic Application Wizard displays the Introduction page.

3 Click on Next.

The Interface Type window appears as shown in Figure 2-4. This is where you'll select the kind of application you want to create. A Multiple Document Interface (MDI) application works like your word processor. One main window holds all of the child (document) windows. A Single Document Interface (SDI) application is like the utility programs you use. Each form appears as a separate window. An Explorer Style application allows you to look for things by using the same interface that Explorer does. You may use this application type as part of a database search program.

4 Choose Multiple Document Interface (MDI) and then click Next.

You see a Menus window like the one shown in Figure 2-5. From this window, you can add the standard menus that you see in all Windows applications. Notice that the Application Wizard automatically selects the menus that it thinks everyone will want.

5 Click on Next.

The Resources window appears (see Figure 2-6), offering some options. A *resource string* can contain a variety of information, such as your company name and the version of the program. These strings always appear in an *RC file*. In most cases, you won't have a resource file to use unless you write programs for a living.

6 Click on Next.

Microsoft has added Internet capability to most of its programming languages, so it's no surprise that the Application Wizard includes the Internet Connectivity window shown in Figure 2-7. Selecting this option gives your application very simple Internet capabilities. The most important feature is a simple browser that the user can select from a menu in your application — all without any programming on your part! Normally you choose a starting address (URL) for your browser that points to your company page or a technical support site, but you can choose any starting location you wish.

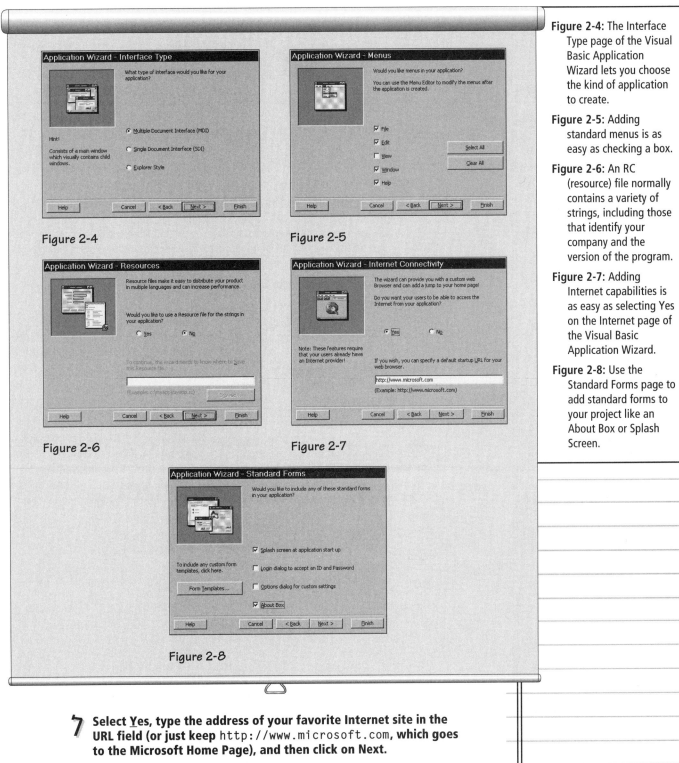

Figure 2-4

Figure 2-5

Figure 2-6

Figure 2-7

Figure 2-8

Figure 2-4: The Interface Type page of the Visual Basic Application Wizard lets you choose the kind of application to create.

Figure 2-5: Adding standard menus is as easy as checking a box.

Figure 2-6: An RC (resource) file normally contains a variety of strings, including those that identify your company and the version of the program.

Figure 2-7: Adding Internet capabilities is as easy as selecting Yes on the Internet page of the Visual Basic Application Wizard.

Figure 2-8: Use the Standard Forms page to add standard forms to your project like an About Box or Splash Screen.

7 **Select Yes, type the address of your favorite Internet site in the URL field (or just keep** `http://www.microsoft.com`, **which goes to the Microsoft Home Page), and then click on Next.**

You see a Standard Forms window like the one shown in Figure 2-8. This window works just like the Menu window. Of course, in this window, you can select standard forms, such as the About Box, instead of menus. The About Box is what you see when you choose Help⇨About on most programs. The splash

more about database access in Unit 15

☑ **Progress Check**

If you can do the following, you've mastered this lesson:

❑ Use the Visual Basic Application Wizard to start a program.

❑ Choose between various application interfaces depending on what kind of program you want to create.

❑ Decide on standard menus and dialog boxes that you want to include with your application.

❑ Add Internet capability to your application.

screen is what you see when you first start an application — it usually contains the name of the program and perhaps some registration information. The splash screen goes away when the program displays the main editing window.

8 **Check the About Box and splash screen options and then click on Next.**

Visual Basic displays the Data Access Forms window shown in Figure 2-9. This is where you'd create a standard data entry form if you were using a database. We'll talk about database access in Unit 15.

9 **Click on Next.**

You see the final window of the Visual Basic Application Wizard (signified by the nifty finish flag icon) as shown in Figure 2-10. In this window you can decide on a name for your application. You also have the choice of making the settings you just made permanent. The Summary Report displays a dialog box that tells you what to do next.

10 **Type** My Application **in the application name field and then click on Finish.**

The Visual Basic Application Wizard creates all of the forms required to build your application. These forms aren't quite complete, but at least they're started so that you won't need as much time to finish them. The Application Wizard also includes TO DO statements throughout the procedures in your application so that you know where to add code.

You could compile and run this application right now. The Web Browser feature would work. Clicking on most of the File menu options would do something, though not much in many cases. You'd also find that the About Box gets displayed when you choose Help⇨About. In essence, you'd have all of the common pieces required to create an application — if you wanted to make this into a fully-functional program, all you'd need to do is fill in the gaps. At this point you can discard the sample program you've created or save it to impress your friends.

Recess

Congratulate yourself for getting through this last lesson. As you can see, dissecting the contents of a typical Visual Basic program is a lot cleaner and less disgusting than dissecting a frog, which may explain why more people make their living by programming computers than by dissecting amphibians.

Before you rush outside to get a breath of fresh air, just remember that Visual Basic uses Form files to store the user interface, Module files to store BASIC code, and Project files to keep track of all the Form and Module files that make up a single Visual Basic program.

Enough thinking. Go outside and play now.

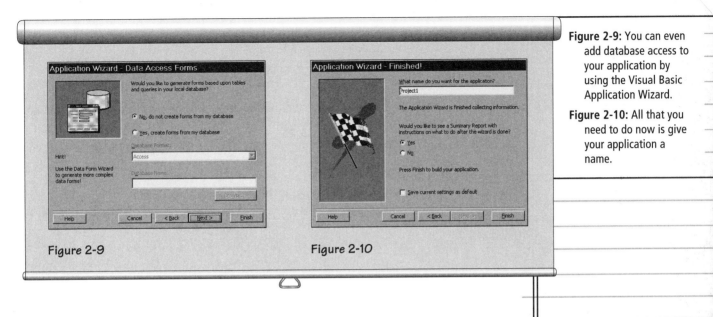

Figure 2-9

Figure 2-10

Unit 2 Quiz

For each of the following questions, circle the letter of the correct answer or answers. To force you to think, each question may have more than one correct answer.

1. **What is the purpose of the Project file and how can you view its contents?**

   A. The Project file contains all the projects that you never got around to doing. You can view this file by looking over your past New Year's resolutions.

   B. The Project file hides all important information out of sight so you can't use it. This is the reason why Visual Basic is so easy to use.

   C. The Project file is something you can steal from a competitor that contains top secret information. You can view its contents by using any word processor.

   D. There's no purpose for the Project file, its contents, or the existence of Visual Basic. Everything is meaningless, and then you die.

   E. The Project file contains a list of all the separate Form and Module files used to make up a single Visual Basic program. To view the contents of a Project file, just look at the Project window.

Notes:

2. **What does a Form file do?**

   A. Not much, which is why they're so expensive and so popular with governments all over the world.

   B. A Form file contains all the useless forms that you need to fill out so that you can sue somebody rich if something goes wrong.

   C. Form files contain the user interface portion of a Visual Basic program. Visual Basic programs usually contain one or more Form files.

   D. A Form file contains BASIC code that makes the user interface work. Optionally, a Form file can also contain BASIC code that calculates a result of some sort.

   E. Form files are used by large bureaucracies so that people can avoid responsibility. The less responsibility workers have, the less incentive they have for actually doing something useful.

3. **How can Form files and Module files work together to create a Visual Basic program?**

   A. The Form file contains the user interface of your program, while Module files can contain the BASIC code to calculate a result so that your program actually does something.

   B. Form files and Module files never get along. That's why your Visual Basic programs will never work.

   C. Form files take care of displaying information on the screen and retrieving data from the user. Module files take care of calculating a result or manipulating the data that comes from the Form file.

   D. You can design your Form files first so that you can see what your program will look like and how the program will interact with a user. After designing your user interface (Form files), you can write BASIC code and store it in Module files so your program will do something useful.

   E. Module files contain your user interface, while Form Files contain all the information your program needs to harass the user with an endless series of forms to fill out before your program will even begin to do any real work.

4. **What is a procedure?**

   A. A procedure is something written on paper that people in large corporations follow without questioning, because otherwise they may get fired.

   B. A procedure contains BASIC code telling Visual Basic what to do. A procedure may tell Visual Basic what to do if a user clicks on a command button, or a procedure may calculate a mathematical result.

C. Procedures are checklists that force people to do something that they may ordinarily forget to do.

D. A procedure is a noun, often tortured to function as a verb, as in, "Tell Bob to procedurize those instructions so people can understand why our cars keep catching on fire whenever you turn the ignition key."

E. Procedure is a word that starts to look and sound funny if you say it over and over again.

5. **Why would you ever need to use a Module file?**

A. You should always use a Module file and every other possible feature of Visual Basic because doing so gives others the impression that you actually know what you're doing.

B. A Module file lets you organize related procedures together for your convenience.

C. There's no reason to use a Module file. Microsoft offers Module files just to confuse you and make you think that Visual Basic is harder to use than it really is.

D. Module files let you store BASIC code that you can easily share between two or more Visual Basic programs.

E. Module files help you hide your BASIC code from others. That way not even you can figure out how your program really works.

6. **How can the Visual Basic Application Wizard help you?**

A. It can't help you because it's too busy casting magic spells at some imaginary castle.

B. Using the Application Wizard helps you write broken applications with lots of bugs without a lot of effort.

C. The Visual Basic Application Wizard can help you get all of the common elements for an application together, such as the File menu and About Box.

D. Never use the Application Wizard because it steals your thoughts and transmits them to Microsoft through the Internet.

E. The Application Wizard helps you finally figure out how to use that utility program you downloaded from the Internet last year.

Unit 2 Exercise

1. Start Visual Basic.

2. Load a Visual Basic program of your choice.

3. Choose a Form file at random from the Project window.

4. View the user interface stored on that form.

5. Restore and then minimize the form.

6. Open more than one form at once.

7. Close all the open forms.

8. Repeat steps 5 through 7 until you're completely dizzy.

9. Open the Code window for that Form file and view the procedures stored on that form.

10. Choose a Module file (if one exists) from the Project window.

11. Open the Code window for that Module file and look at all the pretty BASIC code.

12. Exit Visual Basic.

Form Essentials

Objectives for This Unit

✓ Using the Properties window

✓ Creating inviting forms

✓ Adding, deleting, and saving your forms

Prerequisites

▶ Starting Visual Basic and loading a program (Lesson 1-1)

▶ Knowing the parts of a Visual Basic window (Lesson 1-2)

▶ Flattax.VBP

on the CD

Just about every program you use displays one or more windows. Word processors display blank windows where you can type, spreadsheets display a grid in a window where you can type in numbers and formulas, and many games display monsters that you can shoot at in a window.

A window serves two purposes:

▶ To display information on the screen

▶ To allow the user to type or click in the window to give the program commands or information

Because enough confusion already exists between the generic term *windows* (used to describe a rectangular portion of the computer screen) and *Microsoft Windows* (used as a trademark to identify an operating system sold by Microsoft to dominate the world), Visual Basic refers to a window as a *form*. When you create a form, Visual Basic saves it in a special file called a *Form file*.

on the test

A Visual Basic form is what appears on the screen when someone uses your program, and it serves as a way for the user to communicate with your program and vice versa. Because almost every Visual Basic program uses at least one form, knowing how to create and modify your forms so they look the way you want is a good idea.

form = what appears on the screen when someone uses a Visual Basic program

Note: Before continuing with the rest of the exercises in this unit, make sure that you have loaded Visual Basic so a form appears on the screen. Choose the Flattax file in the New Project dialog box. If you need help, refer to Lesson 1-1.

Using the Properties Window

The Properties window lets you define the appearance of an object, such as its background color, caption, or size. Any time you want to modify an object (such as a form or a command button), you have to open its Properties window and change its property values.

To open the Properties window:

on the CD

1 Click on the Form1.FRM Form file entry in the Project window and then click the View Object button.

The Form1 form pops up on the screen for you to look at.

2 Press F4 to display the Properties window.

You see a Properties window like the one shown in Figure 3-1. (The default Visual Basic interface setup displays the Properties window at all times, but you can close it as needed to obtain additional work space.)

The left-hand column of the Properties window lists all the properties that define an object. The right-hand column lists all the values for each property. Some properties have numerical values, some have text values, and some display either True or False values. If you can't see all the properties for an object, either resize the Properties window by moving the mouse pointer over the edge of the window; holding the left mouse button and moving the mouse; or scroll up and down by clicking on the arrows at the top or bottom of the scroll bar along the right edge of the Properties window.

heads up

Visual Basic gives you four different ways to open the Properties window, so use the method that you like the best:

▶ Press F4

▶ Choose <u>V</u>iew⇨<u>P</u>roperties

▶ Click the right mouse button to display a context menu and choose Properties

▶ Click on the Properties button in the Toolbar

Modifying properties in the Properties window

After you open the Properties window for a particular object, you can change one or more of its property values. Properties have two purposes:

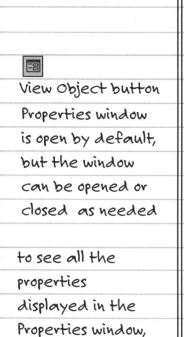

View Object button

Properties window is open by default, but the window can be opened or closed as needed

to see all the properties displayed in the Properties window, use vertical scroll bar to scroll up and down

Properties button

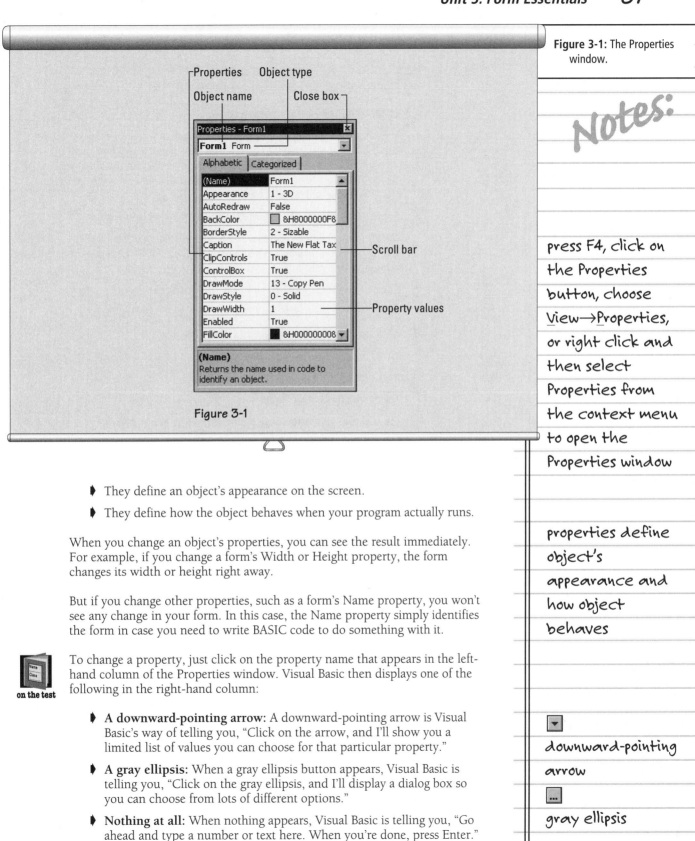

Figure 3-1: The Properties window.

Properties
Object type
Object name
Close box

Properties - Form1

Form1 Form

Alphabetic | Categorized

(Name)	Form1
Appearance	1 - 3D
AutoRedraw	False
BackColor	&H8000000F8
BorderStyle	2 - Sizable
Caption	The New Flat Tax
ClipControls	True
ControlBox	True
DrawMode	13 - Copy Pen
DrawStyle	0 - Solid
DrawWidth	1
Enabled	True
FillColor	&H000000008

Scroll bar

Property values

(Name)
Returns the name used in code to identify an object.

Figure 3-1

Notes:

press F4, click on the Properties button, choose View→Properties, or right click and then select Properties from the context menu to open the Properties window

properties define object's appearance and how object behaves

downward-pointing arrow

gray ellipsis

▶ They define an object's appearance on the screen.

▶ They define how the object behaves when your program actually runs.

When you change an object's properties, you can see the result immediately. For example, if you change a form's Width or Height property, the form changes its width or height right away.

But if you change other properties, such as a form's Name property, you won't see any change in your form. In this case, the Name property simply identifies the form in case you need to write BASIC code to do something with it.

on the test

To change a property, just click on the property name that appears in the left-hand column of the Properties window. Visual Basic then displays one of the following in the right-hand column:

▶ **A downward-pointing arrow:** A downward-pointing arrow is Visual Basic's way of telling you, "Click on the arrow, and I'll show you a limited list of values you can choose for that particular property."

▶ **A gray ellipsis:** When a gray ellipsis button appears, Visual Basic is telling you, "Click on the gray ellipsis, and I'll display a dialog box so you can choose from lots of different options."

▶ **Nothing at all:** When nothing appears, Visual Basic is telling you, "Go ahead and type a number or text here. When you're done, press Enter."

Notes:

title bar is
highlighted on
selected form

▼
downward-pointing
arrow

✓ **Progress Check**

If you can do the following,
you've mastered this lesson:

❏ Open the Properties
window.

❏ Change a property.

❏ Close the Properties
window.

To get a feel for how Visual Basic uses these different types of property option boxes, follow these steps:

1 Click anywhere in the Form1 form.

Visual Basic highlights the title bar of a form when you have chosen the form. This is Visual Basic's way of saying, "This form is the object you want to choose, okay?" (You'll also see a set of sizing handles surrounding the selected object. The sizing handles look and function just like the ones you've used in lots of Windows programs.)

2 Press F4 (if necessary) to open the Properties window.

The Properties window appears. The left-hand column of the Properties window lists all the properties that define an object. The right-hand column lists all the values for each property.

3 Click in the left-hand column on the BorderStyle property.

Visual Basic displays a downward-pointing arrow in the right-hand column.

4 Click on the downward-pointing arrow.

Visual Basic displays a menu of acceptable options for the BorderStyle property.

5 Press Esc.

The pop-up menu goes away.

6 Click in the left-hand column on the Font property.

Visual Basic displays a gray ellipsis (...) button in the right-hand column.

7 Click on the ellipsis.

A dialog box pops up, showing you the multiple options you have for changing the Font property.

8 Press Esc.

The Font dialog box goes away.

9 Click in the left-hand column on the Caption property.

Notice that Visual Basic doesn't display either a gray downward-pointing arrow or a gray ellipsis in the right-hand column. This is Visual Basic's way of telling you that you can type anything in the right-hand column.

Opening and closing the Properties window

No matter how useful the Properties window is, you may want to tuck it out of sight once in a while. Of course, that means you'll eventually need to open it back up again. Let's look at how you can do both:

1 Close the Properties window by clicking the Close box (see Figure 3-1).

The Properties window disappears.

2 Right click the Exit button on Form1.

You'll see a context menu similar to the one shown in Figure 3-2. (Notice that the sizing handles now surround the Exit button instead of Form1.)

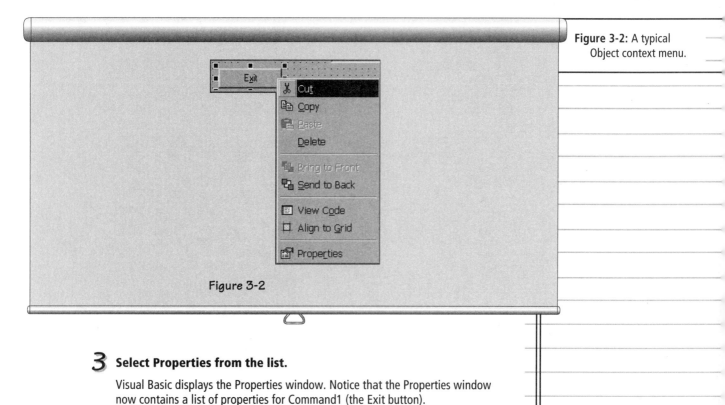

Figure 3-2: A typical Object context menu.

Figure 3-2

3 **Select Properties from the list.**

Visual Basic displays the Properties window. Notice that the Properties window now contains a list of properties for Command1 (the Exit button).

Making Your Forms Look Nice

Lesson 3-2

By itself, a blank form has all the charm and popularity of cooked turnips. To give your form some character, you'll have to change its properties using the Properties window. Some of the more obvious ways to make a form look nice are to change the caption, border, background color, or whether the Minimize and Maximize buttons appear or not.

Figure 3-3 shows the different parts of a form that you can change and other important items.

Using the caption to describe your program

A form's *caption* is the text that appears in the title bar. The caption can be blank, or it can contain a string of up to 255 characters. Of course, if you create a long caption — such as This is the caption of Jonathan Smith Jacob's form — then the caption will appear cut off if your form isn't wide enough.

Ideally, you want a form's caption to be short but descriptive. A caption can display the name of your program (such as PC-Embezzle), the purpose of the form (such as Main Menu), or a message to the user (such as Reactor meltdown, evacuate now). Some programs also include the name of the current document in the caption so the user knows what file she's working on.

Figure 3-3: The visible properties of a typical form.

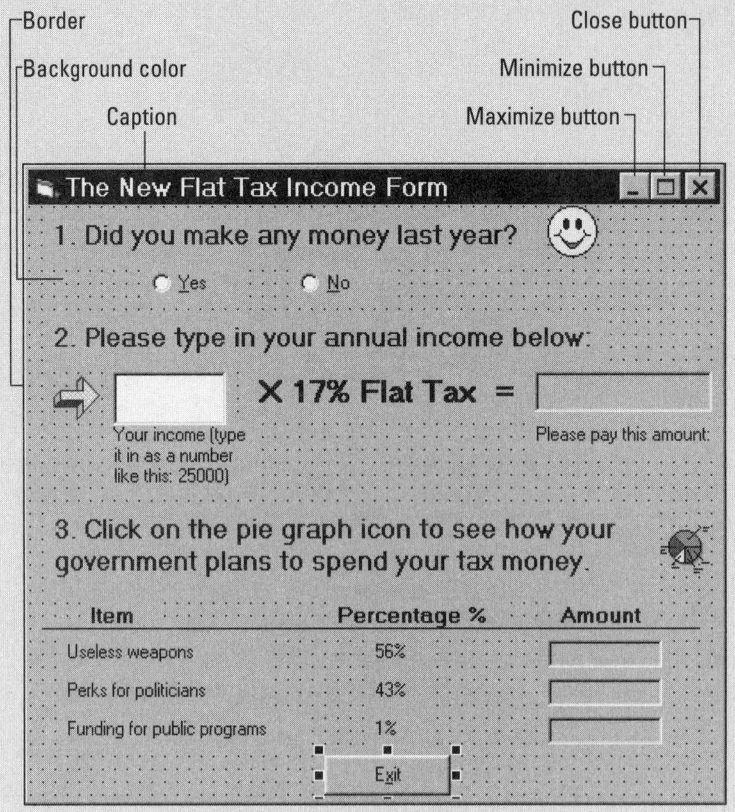

Figure 3-3

press Ctrl+R to
display the Project
window

right click and
then select
Properties on the
context menu
that appears to
see the Properties
window

select View Object
from a form's
context menu to
display the form

Unless you specify otherwise, Visual Basic gives your forms a boring caption like Form3 or Form82. If you grow tired of Visual Basic's lack of imagination, you can change a form's caption by following these steps:

1 Press Ctrl+R to display the Project window.

2 Right click on the Form1 form and select Properties from the context menu to open the Properties window.

3 Right click on the Form1 form and select View Object from the context menu to display the form.

4 Click on the Caption property (in the left-hand column) to highlight it.

5 Click in the Caption box (in the right-hand column).

6 Type a new caption (such as Form2) and press Enter.

You can use the arrow keys and the Backspace or Delete keys to edit an existing caption instead of wiping out the current caption completely. Visual Basic displays your new caption in the form's title bar as you type.

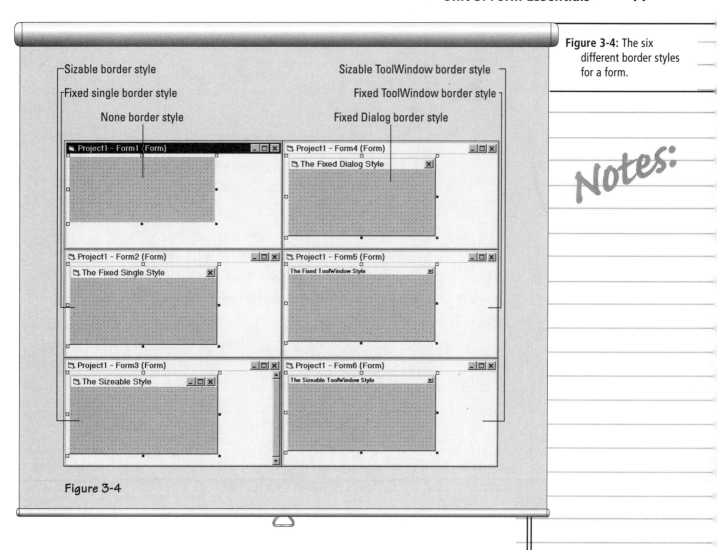

Figure 3-4: The six different border styles for a form.

Figure 3-4

Designing pretty borders

To add some spice to the appearance of your forms, you can choose from six different types of borders, as shown in Figure 3-4. The six different border styles are:

> ◆ **None:** Displays no borders or title bar
>
> ◆ **Fixed Single:** Refuses to let the user resize, minimize, or maximize the form
>
> ◆ **Sizable:** Allows the user to resize, minimize, or maximize the form
>
> ◆ **Fixed Dialog:** Refuses to let the user resize, minimize, or maximize the form
>
> ◆ **Fixed ToolWindows:** Refuses to let the user resize, minimize, or maximize the form
>
> ◆ **Sizable ToolWindows:** Only allows the user to resize the form

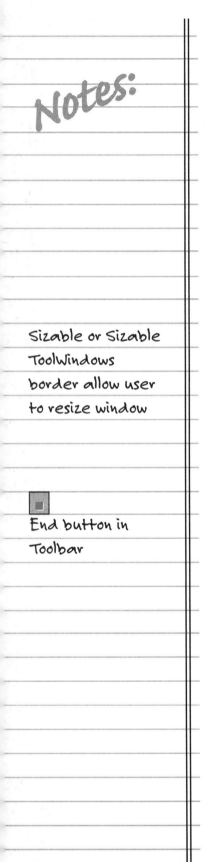

Notes:

Sizable or Sizable
ToolWindows
border allow user
to resize window

End button in
Toolbar

on the test

If you want to give users the option of resizing your form, choose Sizable or Sizable ToolWindows. If you don't want the user to be able to resize your form, choose the None, Fixed Single, Fixed Dialog, or Fixed ToolWindows border style.

To change a border style, follow these steps:

1 Click on the form displayed on your screen.

Visual Basic highlights the title bar of the form.

2 Press F4.

The Properties window appears.

3 Click in the BorderStyle property in the left-hand column.

A downward-pointing arrow appears in the right-hand column.

4 Click on the downward-pointing arrow and choose one of the following:

- 0 - None
- 1 - Fixed Single
- 2 - Sizable
- 3 - Fixed Dialog
- 4 - Fixed ToolWindows
- 5 - Sizable ToolWindows

5 Press F5.

Visual Basic shows you what the form looks like with your new border style.

6 Click on the End button in the Toolbar.

7 Repeat steps 4 through 6 using a different border style.

When you're bored with this exercise, skip to step 8.

8 Go to the next section to learn more about forms.

Changing a form's background color

Visual Basic, being a mindless computer program, always assumes that the background of every form should be battleship gray. While nothing's wrong with a gray background, you may want to choose a different color to make your forms prettier. Follow these steps to change the background color:

1 Click on the form and press F4.

Visual Basic displays the Property window.

2 Click on the BackColor property in the left-hand column.

Visual Basic displays a downward-pointing arrow in the right-hand column.

3 **Click on the downward-pointing arrow in the right-hand column.**

A palette of different colors pops up.

4 **Click on a color.**

Visual Basic provides instant gratification by changing the background color you chose on the form.

5 **Repeat steps 3 and 4 each time you want to change the background color, just to convince yourself that it really works.**

When you settle on a color that you like, stop and reward yourself with a cookie.

Recess

Time to take another break, whether your boss lets you or not. Get up, stretch, go to the bathroom, and try to remember all the programs you've ever used in your life, such as Microsoft Flight Simulator, Lotus 1-2-3, Myst, WordPerfect, Harvard Graphics, CorelDRAW, Microsoft Paint, or America Online.

How many different windows did these programs use? Don't worry about being accurate. Just try to get a rough idea how other programs worked so you can see what you liked and what you didn't like about each program. That way you can write Visual Basic programs that work the way you like best.

Okay, enough thinking. Start the next lesson, or else your mind may turn to mush.

when a different form background color is chosen, Visual Basic changes it instantly

☑ **Progress Check**

If you can do the following, you've mastered this lesson:

❑ Change a form's caption.

❑ Change a form's border style.

❑ Change a form's background color.

Adding, Deleting, and Saving Forms   Lesson 3-3

When you first start Visual Basic, a blank form appears so you can draw your user interface. But unless you're writing a really simple program that only needs to display one window (such as a game like chess or poker), your program will probably need additional forms.

heads up

Most programs include at least two forms. The first is for the main window, the second is for the *About Box*. An About Box is important because it identifies who wrote a program and tells the user about any copyright or registration information. Some About Boxes include other information as well, like the amount of system memory available for running applications.

You can add a new form to your Visual Basic program at any time— and delete a form just as easily. Because adding and deleting forms is so easy, feel free to experiment with your Visual Basic program until it looks absolutely perfect.

add or delete forms at any time

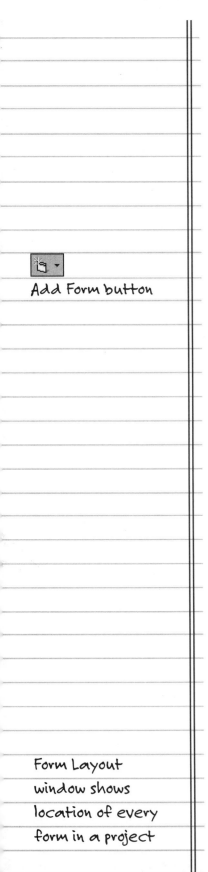

Add Form button

Form Layout
window shows
location of every
form in a project

Adding a new form

Because Visual Basic only gives you one form to work with when you create a new program, you'll have to add additional forms yourself. This section assumes that you have Visual Basic started with the Flattax.VBP project loaded.

To add a form at any time, choose one of the following:

▶ Choose Project⇨Add Form

▶ Right click anywhere in the Project window and then choose Add Form from the context menu

▶ Click on the Add Form button on the Toolbar

Note: You'll find a down arrow next to the Add Form button on the Toolbar. Clicking the down arrow displays a list of the objects you can add to your project. If you select one of these other objects, the Add Form button changes to whatever you select. For example, you can change your Add Form button into an Add User Control button.

When you choose either of these methods, Visual Basic displays a new form on the screen with an unimaginative caption, such as Form2. After you create a new form, you can start putting objects on the form, such as command buttons, labels, and text boxes.

To create a new form, follow these steps:

1 Choose Project⇨Add Form (or click the Add Form button on the Toolbar).

You'll see an Add Form dialog box like the one shown in Figure 3-5.

2 Highlight Form and then click Open.

Visual Basic displays a new form with the generic name of Form2.

3 Press Ctrl+R to display the Project window (if necessary).

Notice that the new form appears in the Project window.

Visual Basic provides a wealth of standard forms in addition to the generic form that you just saw. If you look again at Figure 3-5, you'll see that it includes an About Box form along with many others. The VB Data Form Wizard allows you to create a form based on the contents of a database. You can also grab a form that you used in a previous project by clicking the Existing tab and then selecting a file from a past project (you'll use a standard File Open dialog box to do so).

Saving a form

on the test

After you add a new form, you need to save it on disk as a Form file. To show you which Form files haven't been saved yet, the Project window displays the Form file name without the FRM file extension, as shown in Figure 3-6. Notice also that the Form Layout window shows both forms. You can use the Form Layout window to position the two windows in any way that you need them to appear when in use.

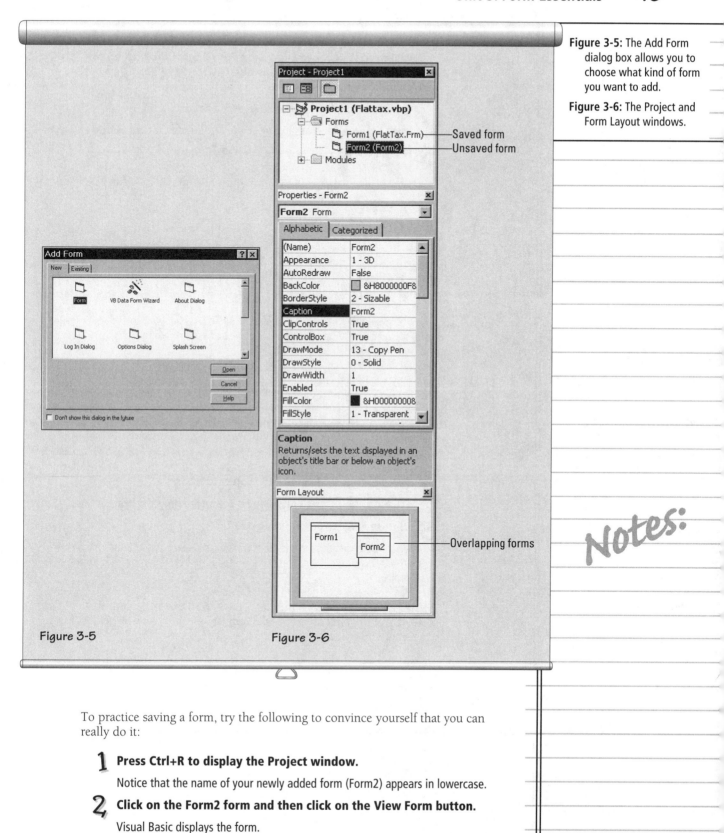

Figure 3-5: The Add Form dialog box allows you to choose what kind of form you want to add.

Figure 3-6: The Project and Form Layout windows.

Figure 3-5

Figure 3-6

To practice saving a form, try the following to convince yourself that you can really do it:

1 Press Ctrl+R to display the Project window.

Notice that the name of your newly added form (Form2) appears in lowercase.

2 Click on the Form2 form and then click on the View Form button.

Visual Basic displays the form.

3 Press Ctrl+S, choose File⇨Save Form2, or right click on the Form2 entry in the Project window and choose Save Form2 from the context menu.

Visual Basic displays a Save File As dialog box.

4 Type a name for your form in the File name box and click on Save.

5 Press Ctrl+R to display the Project window.

Notice that your newly saved file now appears with the FRM file extension.

Removing a form

After adding a form to your Visual Basic program, you may decide that you don't need the form after all. If this ever happens, simply remove the form from your Visual Basic Project file.

When you remove a form from a Visual Basic project file, you're essentially telling Visual Basic, "See that Form file? I don't want to include it in my Visual Basic program anymore."

on the test

If you remove a form that you haven't saved, then the form disappears for good. However, if you remove a form that you have already saved as a Form file, then Visual Basic removes the form from the Project window, but leaves the Form file intact on your hard disk, in case you ever want to use it again. To wipe a Form file off your hard disk permanently, delete the form by using the Windows Explorer. To remove a form from a Visual Basic program:

1 Press Ctrl+R to display the Project window.

2 Click on the Form2 Form file so it appears highlighted.

3 Choose Project⇨Remove Form2.

Visual Basic removes the form. If you haven't saved any changes to the form, Visual Basic asks if you want to save the form before removing it from the project.

Tip: You can also right click on the form entry in the Project window for the form that you no longer want. Click Remove <Form Name> to remove the form from the project.

☑ Progress Check

If you can do the following, you've mastered this lesson:

❑ Add a new form to a project.

❑ Save a new form.

❑ Remove a form from a project.

Unit 3 Quiz

For each of the following questions, circle the letter of the correct answer or answers. Each question may have more than one correct answer, so don't give up too soon.

1. **What is a form?**

   A. A form is a combination of artistic and technical skills that all ice skaters must master if they hope to win a gold medal at the next Winter Olympics.

   B. A form is a window that your program can use to display information or retrieve information from the user.

   C. A form is a worthless piece of paper that corporations value highly, even though nobody knows what forms are and nobody cares.

   D. A form is a printed piece of paper that companies use to pigeonhole employees so the workers don't have to be thought of as individuals anymore.

   E. A form is something that governments require their citizens to fill out, even though filling the form out doesn't change anything.

2. **When a downward-pointing arrow appears in the right-hand column of the Property window, what does that mean?**

   A. It means you just made a horrendous mistake and Visual Basic is about to punish you for your incompetence.

   B. The downward-pointing arrow is Visual Basic's polite way of telling you that you should drop your computer the next time it doesn't work properly.

   C. The gray downward-pointing arrow means Visual Basic is telling you that your shoelaces are untied.

   D. The gray downward-pointing arrow displays a list of options you can choose for that particular property.

   E. It doesn't mean anything. People are always trying to apply their own belief system to explain random events.

3. **Which of the border styles provided by Visual Basic allow the user to resize the form?**

   A. You can always resize the form. Anyone who tells you something different is merely trying to confuse the issue.

   B. The Sizable or Sizable ToolWindows border styles allow the user to resize the form.

   C. It's one of those phase of the moon things. No one knows in advance whether you can resize a form.

   D. Huh?

   E. You have no reason to resize the form, because you'll have it sized perfectly the first time.

Notes:

4. **How can you tell if you have saved a newly created form?**

   A. Ask your boss and see if he knows what you're even talking about.

   B. Pray for three straight hours and wait until the answer comes to you in a dream.

   C. Forms have sinned enough that they can never be saved, no matter how much religious fervor they may express.

   D. Open the Project window, and if the form's name appears without the FRM file extension, it hasn't been saved yet.

   E. You can always tell saved forms by the way they sneer at other forms, as if to say, "I'm better than you."

5. **When you remove a form using the Project⇨Remove <Form Name> command, what happens to the form?**

   A. When you remove a form, the form seeks revenge by wiping out everything on your hard disk.

   B. When you use the Project⇨Remove <Form Name> File command, you take the form out of your Visual Basic project. However, the form file still physically exists on your hard disk, in case you ever want to use it again.

   C. Removing a form is mathematically impossible, because that would violate the integrity of the third law of thermodynamics.

   D. Removing a form causes the form to experience a sense of confusion, despair, and loss of love, driving it to the brink of total desperation.

   E. A form can only be removed through patient surgical techniques that are much too advanced for this book.

Unit 3 Exercise

1. Start Visual Basic.

2. Load a Visual Basic program of your choice.

3. Choose a form at random from the Project window.

4. Resize the form by using the sizing handles.

5. Open the Properties window for the form.

6. Change a few properties of the form at random, just to see what happens.

7. Run the program so you can see how you may have changed the way the form looks on the screen.

8. Exit Visual Basic without saving the program.

Playing with Objects

Prerequisites
▶ Loading Visual Basic
(Lesson 1-1)
▶ Resizing and moving a
form (Lesson 3-1)
▶ Opening the Properties
window (Lesson 3-2)

Objectives for This Unit

✓ Drawing objects on a form

✓ Naming objects

✓ Selecting objects

✓ Changing the size of an object

✓ Moving objects around

✓ Deleting objects

When you create a standard form, it appears as a blank window on the screen when your program runs. If you want that type of effect, you can stop reading right now and close this book. However, creating blank windows won't make your program useful, so after you create a form you have to add objects to it.

Tip: Visual Basic provides the Form icon in the Add Form dialog box so that you can define your own user interface. Don't forget to use the predefined forms like the About Box or Splash Screen when you can.

on the test

Objects make up the parts of your user interface. Some common objects are command buttons, check boxes, radio buttons, list boxes, and combo boxes, as shown in Figure 4-1.

One of the most important things to remember about objects is that you can view them just like anything in the real world. For example, an apple allows you to perform actions like biting, throwing, and smelling. An apple also has characteristics like color and taste. Likewise, all objects that you use in Visual Basic provide actions (Microsoft calls these *methods*) and characteristics (Microsoft calls these *properties*). A pushbutton has a Move method that allows you to change its position on the form. You can also use the Move method to change the size of the pushbutton. One of the pushbutton properties is Caption, which defines the text you see printed on the pushbutton face.

Figure 4-1: The objects of a typical user interface.

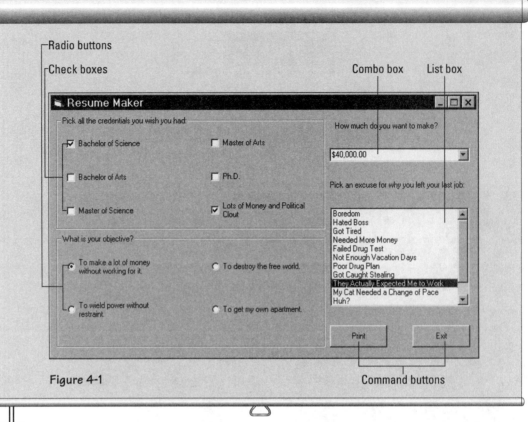

Figure 4-1

all objects have methods and properties

right-clicking an object always displays context menu that tells Visual Basic specific things that can be done to object

Every object in Visual Basic has a context menu. A context menu changes to meet the *current object context* — just a fancy way of saying that it shows you the general things you can do with the object. A right-click on an object always displays the context menu. The context menu always shows Visual Basic the specific things that you can do to the object like cutting, pasting, or viewing the object's properties.

Lesson 4-1 · Drawing Objects on a Form

The blank form displayed when you select Standard EXE in the New Project dialog box when you start Visual Basic for the first time is Visual Basic's way of saying, "Okay, here's a blank canvas. Start drawing the parts of your user interface." Just as painters have a palette containing different colors the artists can choose from, so Visual Basic provides a Toolbox containing icons representing tools. Selecting a Toolbox icon tells Visual Basic, "This is the type of object I want to draw." The Toolbox provides everything you need to create a user interface for your Visual Basic programs.

heads up

Any time that you have no clue as to what an icon represents in the Toolbox, move the mouse pointer over the icon and wait a few seconds. If you're patient enough, Visual Basic displays a little message letting you know what the icon represents.

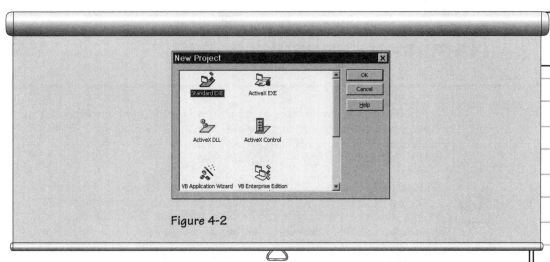

Figure 4-2

Figure 4-2: The New Project dialog box.

To give yourself some real-life experience drawing an object on a form, start Visual Basic, and then follow these steps:

1 **Choose File⇨New Project.**

A New Project dialog box like the one shown in Figure 4-2 appears. Notice that this New Project dialog box looks different than the one you see when you first start Visual Basic.

2 **Double-click on the Standard EXE icon.**

A blank form appears.

3 **Click on the Command Button icon in the Toolbox.**

Notice that the Command Button icon appears depressed in the Toolbox, which is Visual Basic's way of telling you what object you're about to draw.

4 **Move the mouse over the form.**

Notice that when the mouse pointer appears over a form, the mouse pointer turns into a crosshair.

5 **Hold down the left mouse button and drag the mouse.**

Visual Basic draws a white outline on the form, showing you the size of your object if you release the left mouse button. Notice that Visual Basic also provides a pop up dialog box showing the size of the object in pixels. This dialog box helps you make every one of your objects a consistent size.

6 **Release the left mouse button.**

Your object (in this case a command button) appears on the form. A simple task, isn't it?

heads up

To draw an object quickly on a form, just double-click on the object's icon in the Toolbox. Visual Basic draws the chosen object automatically. You can resize an object later; Lesson 4-4 will show you how.

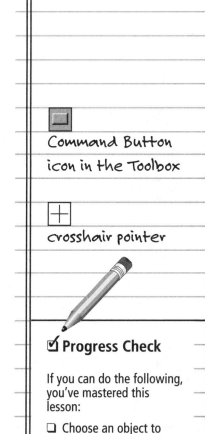

Command Button icon in the Toolbox

crosshair pointer

☑ **Progress Check**

If you can do the following, you've mastered this lesson:

❏ Choose an object to draw using the Toolbox.

❏ Draw an object on a form.

Lesson 4-2

Naming Your Objects

name = what
Visual Basic knows
an object by

caption = label
placed on an
object that the
user sees

Notes:

Visual Basic automatically names your objects for you. Unfortunately, Visual Basic lacks any imagination and just uses generic names like Form2, Command1, or Option4. As a result, you should take the time to give each object a name, just to give the object a unique identity.

heads up

The purpose of using names is to help you identify your objects. For example, if you have command buttons with names like Command12 or Command7, finding which command button exits the program can be difficult. But if you name one command button cmdExit and another one cmdPrint, the descriptive names make it much easier to identify what your different command buttons actually do.

The name of any object can be up to 40 characters long, but can't include spaces or punctuation marks. To give your objects a consistent name, Microsoft recommends that all command button names begin with the cmd prefix, such as cmdStop, cmdOK, or cmdCallYourMother. Table 4-1 shows Microsoft's recommended prefixes for naming your objects.

Table 4-1	Recommended Object Prefixes	
Type of Object	*Prefix*	*Example*
Check box	chk	chkYourMail
Combo box	cbo	cboNation
Command button	cmd	cmdExitOrDie
Directory list box	dir	dirChoice
Drive list box	drv	drvMeHome
File list box	fil	filUpTheGasTank
Form	frm	frmAStraightLine
Frame	fra	fraTheButler
Horizontal scroll bar	hsb	hsbVolumeControl
Image	img	imgMirage
Label	lbl	lblWarning
Line	lin	linEdges
List box	lst	lstGroceries
Menu	mnu	mnuGreenEggsAndHam
Radio button	opt	optRockOrCountry
Picture box	pic	picXRated
Shape	shp	shpStrangeObject
Text box	txt	txtRansomMessage
Vertical scroll bar	vsb	vsbRadiationLevel

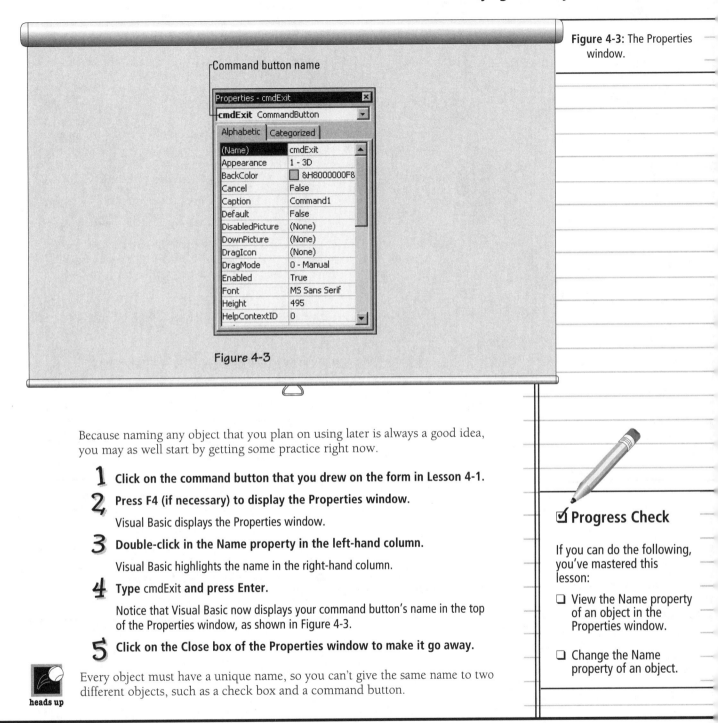

Command button name

Figure 4-3: The Properties window.

Figure 4-3

Because naming any object that you plan on using later is always a good idea, you may as well start by getting some practice right now.

1 **Click on the command button that you drew on the form in Lesson 4-1.**

2 **Press F4 (if necessary) to display the Properties window.**

Visual Basic displays the Properties window.

3 **Double-click in the Name property in the left-hand column.**

Visual Basic highlights the name in the right-hand column.

4 **Type cmdExit and press Enter.**

Notice that Visual Basic now displays your command button's name in the top of the Properties window, as shown in Figure 4-3.

5 **Click on the Close box of the Properties window to make it go away.**

Every object must have a unique name, so you can't give the same name to two different objects, such as a check box and a command button.

heads up

☑ **Progress Check**

If you can do the following, you've mastered this lesson:

❑ View the Name property of an object in the Properties window.

❑ Change the Name property of an object.

Selecting Objects

Lesson 4-3

Drawing objects on a form is the first step to creating a user interface, but until you change the objects' properties or write BASIC code for them, the objects will just sit there doing nothing, like a bunch of teenagers on a Saturday afternoon.

Before you can do anything to an object, you have to select it, which tells Visual Basic, "See that object right there? That's the one I want to modify."

To select an object, just click on it with the mouse. To show you which object you've selected, Visual Basic highlights the object with black rectangles around its outline. Just to give you a new term to memorize, these black rectangles are called *sizing handles* (or just handles depending on whom you talk to).

on the test

If you want to select more than one object, you have to get a little fancy and use one of the following two techniques:

♦ Hold down the Ctrl key and click on each object with the mouse.

♦ Hold down the left mouse button, drag the mouse to enclose all the objects you want to select, and then release the left mouse button. Visual Basic draws a black dashed line around the objects you select as you drag the mouse.

Because experience is the best teacher, follow these steps to practice selecting multiple objects:

1 **Draw two or more command buttons anywhere on your form.**

2 **Click on one command button. Then click on the other command button.**

Notice that when you click on the second object, Visual Basic assumes that you don't want to select the first object any more.

3 **Hold down the Ctrl key and click on one of the command buttons. Keep holding down the Ctrl key and click on the second button.**

Notice that when you hold down the Ctrl key and click on multiple objects, Visual Basic assumes you want to select all the objects you've clicked on. To show you all your selected objects, Visual Basic displays them with gray handles around the sides.

margin notes

hold down the CTRL key and click on objects to select more than one object

☑ **Progress Check**

If you can do the following, you've mastered this lesson:

❏ Select an object by clicking on it.

❏ Select two or more objects by using the Ctrl key and the mouse.

❏ Select two or more objects by dragging the mouse pointer over them.

Lesson 4-4   Changing the Size of an Object

use handles to resize an object

You can select any object on a form and change its size, making it taller, shorter, wider, or skinnier. Because you can always change the size of an object after drawing it, feel free to experiment with objects until they appear exactly the way you want.

Whenever you click on an object, black handles magically appear around the object as quickly as mold on leftovers in your refrigerator. Depending on which handle you choose, you can make the object bigger or smaller:

♦ Drag handles on the top and bottom to make an object taller or shorter.

♦ Drag handles on the sides to make an object wider or skinnier.

♦ Drag corner handles to simultaneously resize an object vertically and horizontally.

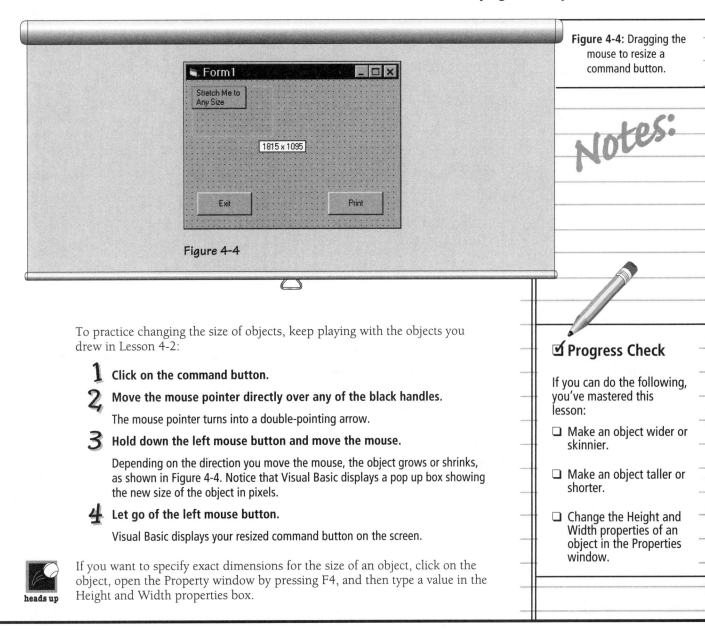

Figure 4-4: Dragging the mouse to resize a command button.

Figure 4-4

Notes:

To practice changing the size of objects, keep playing with the objects you drew in Lesson 4-2:

1 Click on the command button.

2 Move the mouse pointer directly over any of the black handles.

The mouse pointer turns into a double-pointing arrow.

3 Hold down the left mouse button and move the mouse.

Depending on the direction you move the mouse, the object grows or shrinks, as shown in Figure 4-4. Notice that Visual Basic displays a pop up box showing the new size of the object in pixels.

4 Let go of the left mouse button.

Visual Basic displays your resized command button on the screen.

heads up

If you want to specify exact dimensions for the size of an object, click on the object, open the Property window by pressing F4, and then type a value in the Height and Width properties box.

☑ **Progress Check**

If you can do the following, you've mastered this lesson:

❑ Make an object wider or skinnier.

❑ Make an object taller or shorter.

❑ Change the Height and Width properties of an object in the Properties window.

Moving Objects Around

Lesson 4-5

Before you can move an object, you have to select it. After you select an object (or objects), move the mouse pointer to the middle of the object, hold down the left mouse button, and move the mouse. The object appears wherever you move the mouse. When you're happy with the object's new location, release the left mouse button, and you're done.

1 Click on the command button; handles appear around the object's edges.

2 Move the mouse pointer inside the command button, hold down the left mouse button, and move the mouse.

Figure 4-5: Moving an object.

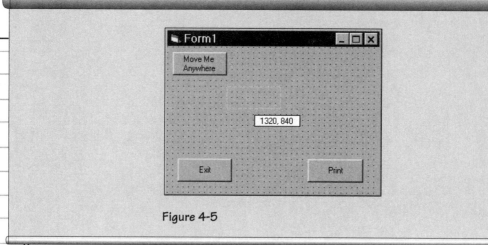

Figure 4-5

☑ Progress Check

If you can do the following, you've mastered this lesson:

❏ Move an object on a form.

❏ Select two or more objects and move them as a group.

Notice that wherever you move the mouse, Visual Basic displays an outline of the object to show you its location if you release the left mouse button, as shown in Figure 4-5. It also displays a pop up box showing the coordinates of the upper-left corner of the object.

3 **Release the left mouse button when you're happy with the new location of the object.**

heads up

If you've selected two or more objects (see Lesson 4-3), you can move all of your selected objects at once.

Recess

Congratulations! Get up, stretch, and congratulate yourself for getting this far in the book.

Lesson 4-6   Deleting Objects

☑ Progress Check

If you can do the following, you've mastered this lesson:

❏ Delete an object from a form.

❏ Recover an object that you just deleted.

Everyone changes his mind, which explains the rise and fall of disco, polyester leisure suits, and pet rocks. Fortunately, when you change your mind in Visual Basic, you don't have to suffer any subsequent embarrassment for your actions.

When you draw an object on a form, Visual Basic kindly gives you the option of deleting that object at any time. To delete an object, you must first select it, and then choose one of the following methods:

   ▶ Press the Delete key (disguised on some keyboards as the Del key).

   ▶ Right-click on the object and select Cut from the context menu.

   ▶ Choose Edit➪Cut (or press Ctrl+X).

1 **Draw a command button on a form.**

Black handles appear around the command button.

2 **Press the Delete key.**

The command button immediately disappears off the face of the earth (and the face of your form as well).

on the test

To recover an object you just deleted, choose Edit⇨Undo or press Ctrl+7.

Unit 4 Quiz

Circle the letter of the correct answer or answers for each of the following questions. Some questions may have more than one correct answer, so read all answers carefully or you may miss something really important.

1. What are objects?

A. Objects are abstract items that exist only in philosophy.

B. Objects are those unidentified flying things that look like saucers.

C. An object is something that makes up your program's user interface. Typical objects include command buttons, radio buttons, check boxes, and pull-down menus.

D. In English grammar, an object can either be a direct object or an indirect object.

E. Object! is something that lawyers say constantly when they're afraid someone may tell the truth and blow their case wide open, such as, "Your Honor, I object!"

2. How can you select more than one object on a form?

A. Hold down the Ctrl key and click on each object that you want to select.

B. Drag the mouse so it encloses all the objects you want to select.

C. Press the Delete key rapidly with one hand while typing DELETE with the other hand.

D. Point to the object and state in a loud, clear voice, "I want you!"

E. Objects are like cats. You don't select them; they select you.

3. If you delete an object, how can you retrieve it?

A. You can't, but at least you can feel better if you blame the computer.

B. If you wiggle it in front of your dog's nose before deleting it, you can train your dog to retrieve your objects for you at any time.

C. No way to retrieve objects exists, so feel free to delete all of them from your coworkers' programs on your last day at a dead end job.

D. If you look inside your keyboard, you can often find lost objects tucked away in there.

E. Choose Edit➪Undo or press Ctrl+Z.

4. **What are handles and why do they exist?**

A. Handles exist for carrying objects conveniently by hand. That's why the invention of the handle was such a revolution for the luggage industry.

B. Handles usually appear around the waist of any object that has a tendency to eat too much. Some people call them love handles, but because computers aren't supposed to evoke emotions, Visual Basic uses the official computer term of calling them just handles.

C. Handles are little black rectangles that appear whenever you select an object. You can use handles to resize an object.

D. A Handle is the popular misspelling of the famous composer Handel's last name.

E. Handles exist for the sole purpose of letting you open doors so you can get out of the room whenever you get sick of programming in Visual Basic.

5. **What are the two ways to change the size of an object on a form?**

A. Dope up its food with growth hormones and antibiotics.

B. If you only drew your objects correctly the first time, you wouldn't have to worry about changing the size of them later.

C. Click on an object to display its black handles and then drag the handles using the mouse. Or open the Property window and type in values for the desired width and height of the object.

D. Put it next to a defective microwave oven and hope the leaking radiation will mutate the object and cause it to grow uncontrollably.

E. No way exists to change anything without cooperation from the object.

Unit 4 Exercise

1. Load a Visual Basic program of your choice.

2. Select two or more objects and move them to a different location on the form.

3. Delete the selected objects.

4. Press Ctrl+Z (or Ctrl+V) to retrieve your deleted objects.

5. Press F5 to run the program.

6. Press Tab to see the order in which Visual Basic highlights the objects on the form.

7. Exit Visual Basic without saving the program.

Part I Review

Unit 1 Summary

▶ **Loading Visual Basic:** Click on the Start button on the Taskbar, click on Programs, click on the Visual Basic 5.0 folder, and then click on Visual Basic 5.0.

▶ **Loading a Visual Basic Project:** Click on the Open Project icon on the Toolbar.

▶ **Project window:** Lists all the files used to make up a single Visual Basic project. Project window can also categorize files by type and place them in separate folders. Press Ctrl+R to display the Project window.

▶ **Design window:** The window where you design your program's user interface. Right-click on the object's entry in the Project window and choose View Object from the context menu, press Shift+F7, or click on the View Object button in the Project window to open the Design window.

▶ **Toolbox:** Displays all the objects you can draw on a Form window. Choose <u>V</u>iew⇨Toolbox to open the Toolbox.

▶ **Properties window:** The window that lets you customize the objects drawn in a Form window. Press F4 to open the Properties window.

▶ **Form Layout window:** Allows you to see where your program will appear on the Desktop when you start it. Choose <u>V</u>iew⇨Form Layout Window to open the Form Layout window.

▶ **Code window:** The window where you write BASIC code. Press F7, right-click the object and choose View Code from the context menu, or click on the View Code button to open the Code window.

▶ **Running a Visual Basic program:** Press F5 or choose <u>R</u>un⇨<u>S</u>tart.

▶ **Exiting a Visual Basic program:** Choose <u>F</u>ile⇨E<u>x</u>it.

Unit 2 Summary

▶ **Project file:** A single file containing a list of all the files used to make up a single Visual Basic program. Project files always end with the VBP file extension.

▶ **Form file:** A file containing the user interface of a program and BASIC code to make the user interface work. Form files always end with the FRM file extension.

▶ **Module files:** An optional file containing only BASIC code. Module files always end with the BAS file extension.

▶ **Two parts of a Visual Basic program:** The user interface and the BASIC code that makes the program work.

▶ **Procedures:** Miniprograms that tell Visual Basic what to do when the user does something.

▶ **Visual Basic Application Wizard:** Use the special VB Application Wizard icon in the New Project dialog box if you want Visual Basic's help in starting a new application.

Unit 3 Summary

▶ **Opening the Properties window:** Press F4, choose <u>V</u>iew⇨Propertie<u>s</u>, right-click on an object, and choose Properties from the context menu, or click on the Properties button in the Toolbar.

▶ **Modifying a form:** The most common properties to change on a form are its Caption property, BorderStyle property, and BackColor property.

Part I Review

- **Adding a form:** Choose Insert⇨Form, right-click in the Project window and select Add⇨Form from the context menu, or click on the Form button on the Toolbar.

- **Saving a form:** Press Ctrl+S, right-click on the form's entry in the Project window and choose Save <Form Name> from the context menu, or choose File⇨Save File.

- **Removing a form:** Right-click on the form's entry in the Project window and choose Remove <Form Name> from the context menu or choose File⇨Remove File.

- **Multiple Form Positioning:** All your open forms appear in the Form Layout window. You can simply move them around as needed to change their starting position on screen.

Unit 4 Summary

- **Drawing an object on a form:** Click on the object's icon on the Toolbox, move the mouse pointer to the form, hold down the left mouse button, drag the mouse pointer, and release the left mouse button.

- **Naming an object:** Change the Name property of an object in the Properties window.

- **Selecting an object:** Click on an object. To choose two or more objects, hold down the Ctrl key and click on two or more objects. Or hold down the left mouse button, drag the mouse over two or more objects, and release the left mouse button.

- **Changing the size of an object:** Click on an object, move the mouse pointer over one of the object's black handles, hold down the left mouse button, drag the mouse, and release the left mouse button. Or change the Height and Width properties of the object in the Properties window.

- **Moving objects on a form:** Click on an object, hold down the left mouse button, drag the mouse, and release the left mouse button. Or change the Left and Top properties of the object in the Properties window.

- **Deleting objects from a form:** Click on an object and press Delete or press Ctrl+X.

- **Size pop up:** Visual Basic always displays a pop-up menu when you draw or resize an object. The two numbers tell you the current size of the object (Height and Width properties).

- **Coordinate pop up:** Visual Basic displays another pop-up menu when you move an object. This menu tells you the coordinates of the upper-left corner of the object (Top and Left properties).

- **Object Terminology:** Every object provides properties, which tell you about the object itself. Methods tell you how to interact with the object.

Part I Test

The questions on this test cover material presented in Part I, Units 1, 2, 3, and 4. The answers are in Appendix A.

True False

T   F   1. The Project window lists all the files used to make up a single Visual Basic project.

T   F   2. A Design window is a window without shape, form, or direction.

T   F   3. The Toolbox contains objects you can draw on a Design window.

T   F   4. Right-clicking on an object causes the computer to blow up and creates a terrible mess on your desk.

T   F   5. Pressing F5 will cause your Visual Basic program to leave the room at a high rate of speed.

T   F   6. The two parts of a Visual Basic program are its user interface and its BASIC code.

T   F   7. A procedure is a miniature program that tells Visual Basic how to work.

T   F   8. To save a Form file and a Project, you must pray for 40 days.

T   F   9. You should give each object a unique name.

T   F   10. The Form Layout window allows you to print all your forms in the order the user will see them, unless it's Tuesday, when they get printed in reverse order.

Multiple Choice

For each of the following questions, circle the correct answer or answers. Some questions may have more than one right answer, so read all the answers carefully.

11. **What are the two ways you can select an object on a form?**

    A. You can select two or more objects on the Form window by dragging the mouse over the objects or holding down the Ctrl key while clicking on the objects.

    B. Point to the object with your finger and proclaim in a loud voice, "I want you!"

    C. There is no way to select an object on a form. Who told you that you can?

    D. Put a paper bag over the object's head while it's not looking, or grab the object by the hand and run before anyone sees you.

    E. You can only select an object after you have written 100,000 lines of BASIC code first.

12. **What does the Properties window do?**

    A. It gets in the way when you're trying to write BASIC code or design your user interface.

    B. It holds all the deeds necessary to conquer the real estate world on your own.

    C. The Properties window does windows, unlike many cleaning services you can hire for your home.

    D. The Properties window lets you change the properties of an object, such as its name, caption, height, or position on the form.

    E. It gets dirty very easily despite its small size.

Part I Test

13. How can you use the Form Layout window to improve your application?

A. The Form Layout window is a myth spread around by jealous C programmers.

B. It allows you to arrange multiple forms in such a way that the user can see them all.

C. You use it see huge boulders rumbling down the side of a mountain toward your computer.

D. The Form Layout window allows you to adjust the starting position of a single form with respect to the entire Desktop.

E. Actually, it's the Form Wayout window and it's used to create '60s era displays.

14. How can you change the size of an object?

A. Click on the object and then press Delete until the object goes away.

B. Wait until the object gets old enough to grow on its own.

C. Click on the object, move the mouse pointer over a black handle surrounding the object, hold down the left mouse button, drag the mouse, and release the left mouse button.

D. Use your mind and concentrate for long periods of time.

E. Change the Height and Width properties of the object in the Properties window.

15. What are object methods used for?

A. Discerning the evil that men do.

B. Figuring out the madness in front of them.

C. Methods tell you how to interact with the object and define what kinds of things you can do with it.

D. Don't call them objects — they're pieces parts.

E. What do objects have to do with Visual Basic anyway?

16. How can you draw an object on a form?

A. Hire a costly freelance artist.

B. Click on the Properties window, click on the Project window, and then click on the Toolbar until you realize this answer isn't getting you any closer to the truth.

C. Use a pencil and paper and then tape the object to your monitor.

D. Click on an object in the Toolbox and then drag the mouse pointer across the form to draw your chosen object.

E. Double-click on an object in the Toolbox. Visual Basic will then draw your object on the form automatically.

Part I Test

Matching

17. **Match the file extension with the correct file type.**

    A. FRM   1. A Project file

    B. VBP   2. A Module file

    C. BAS   3. A Form file

    D. XXX   4. The first three letters of the alphabet

    E. ABC   5. A triple-X-rating

18. **Match the object name with the correct object type.**

    A. cmdExit   1. A label

    B. chkToilet   2. A command button

    C. optRadio   3. A text box

    D. txtState   4. A check box

    E. lblNaughty   5. A radio or option button

19. **Match the window with its purpose.**

    A. Code window   1. Contains objects you can draw on a form

    B. Properties window   2. Shows the position of forms on the Desktop

    C. Project window   3. Displays the properties of an object

    D. Form Layout window   4. Lists the files contained in a Project

    E. Toolbox   5. Where you write BASIC code

20. **Match the adjectives that best describe the following.**

    A. Your boss   1. A swell person around your review time

    B. Your significant other   2. Caring, friendly, joyful

    C. Your pets   3. Cute and cuddly

    D. A pit bull   4. Vicious and unpredictable

    E. A plate of prime rib   5. Delicious with red wine

Part I Lab Assignment

This is the first of many lab assignments you'll find at the end of each part in this book. These lab assignments give you a chance to practice your Visual Basic skills and knowledge using real-life examples.

Unlike the exercises provided in each unit, lab assignments provide more general instructions. Instead of telling you exactly which keys to press or which icons to click on, lab assignments tell you what task to accomplish. If you have trouble finishing a lab assignment, that's a clue that you may need to review one or more units in this book to learn how to perform specific commands.

In this lab assignment, you get to play around with an existing Visual Basic program and experiment with modifying the way it looks.

Step 1: Load any of the sample programs provided with Visual Basic

Choose any program at random, as long as you select a Project file (one with a VBP extension). You can choose any file you want, because you're going to modify it anyway.

Step 2: Change the appearance of the program's forms

Some of the properties of a form you can change include its caption, size, background and foreground colors, and border style.

Step 3: Change the look of the objects that appear on the forms

Try modifying the appearance of the existing objects on a form. Then try adding your own objects to a form, such as a command button or check box.

Step 4: Change the form's starting position

Use the Form Layout window to change the starting position of your form on screen.

Step 5: Run the program

After making as many changes as you want, run the program to see how it looks with the changes you've made. When you're done, exit Visual Basic without saving your modified program. (If you want to save your program, save it under a different name so you can always return to the original version of the program at a later time.)

Designing Your User Interface

In this part ...

Face it: No matter how powerful, feature-packed, and elegantly written your program is, nobody will want to use it if the program is ugly-looking and confusing. The user interface of your program is the first impression people get when they use your program, and if that impression isn't a good one, no one may try your program ever again.

To keep your program from degenerating into the realm of the ugly and useless, this part of the book explains all the different ways to create your program's user interface using command buttons, check boxes, pull-down menus, dialog boxes, list boxes, and combo boxes. By making your program easy to use, you increase the chances that people will like your program and (possibly) even pay you big bucks for the privilege of owning their own copy.

We'll also look at some of the ways that Visual Basic helps make your program interesting to look at. For example, you can use colors and fonts to enhance the appearance of your program. You can also use pictures in place of words with some controls like command buttons, check boxes, and radio buttons.

Command Buttons

Objectives for This Unit

✓ Changing a command button caption

✓ Defining how your command buttons work

✓ Writing BASIC code for your command buttons

Prerequisites

▶ Using the Toolbox to draw objects on a form (Lesson 4-1)

▶ Opening the Properties window to change the values of properties (Lesson 3-1)

▶ Message.VBP

on the CD

*C*ommand buttons are referred to by a wealth of names, depending on whom you talk to and what they're used for. Some people call them push buttons, because you push a command button to get it to do something. A command button on a toolbar is called a *speed button* because it allows you to do something faster than a menu can. We'll use command button throughout the book to refer to this control.

Visual Basic performs a specific task, such as exiting a program, printing a report, or starting the program over again, whenever you click on a command button. To help users determine what happens when they click on a command button, most programs include captions that explain what the button does, such as Yes, OK, No, or Cancel, as shown in Figure 5-1.

on the test

Lesson 4-1 showed you how to draw a command button. But after you draw a command button, guess what? A click on the button does absolutely nothing until you write BASIC code in the button's Code window telling Visual Basic what to do. After you write code for a button — which you learn how to do in Lesson 5-3 — Visual Basic follows your instructions whenever someone clicks on that button.

clicking on
command button
makes Visual Basic
perform task
defined by
button's BASIC
code

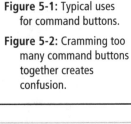

Notes:

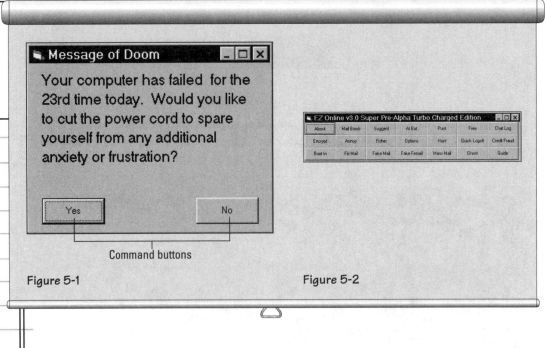

Figure 5-1

Figure 5-2

Command buttons

heads up

Command buttons are best used sparingly. If you cram too many command buttons together, finding the command button you need can be difficult, as shown in Figure 5-2.

How do you draw a command button? The same way you draw other objects, using the Toolbox. Refer back to Lesson 4-1 if you need a refresher.

Lesson 5-1 — Changing a Command Button Caption

A caption is the text that appears on a command button and — ideally — identifies what the button does when you click on it. When you first create a command button, its default caption is something boring like Command2 or Command9.

on the test

caption = text
that appears on an
object

name = how you
refer to an object
when writing BASIC
code

Don't get confused between a command button's name and its caption. The *name* identifies the command button only if you're writing BASIC code for it. The *caption* is the text that you can see on the command button. For example, a command button may be named cmdExit but its caption can be something like Exit, Quit, Go Away, or Leave. If you look at a command button on your screen, you can easily see its caption, but you have to open up the Properties window to see its name.

Changing the captions on your command buttons so that you can identify their functions is a good idea. Some common examples of command button captions include Exit, Yes, or No (refer to Figure 5-1). Of course, you can always make up totally nonsensical captions if you really want, but that just makes your program harder to use.

Captions can be up to 255 characters long and may include spaces (such as in the caption Click Me) and punctuation marks (like in the caption Exit?). Just remember that if you make your captions really long, the words may not all be completely visible unless your button is extra wide.

on the test

As a special bonus, you can also use the ampersand (&) character to create something called a *hot key,* a keyboard shortcut that activates a command button. When your program is running, the user can choose the command button either by clicking on the command button or simultaneously pressing Alt and the hot key.

When you place the ampersand character in front of a letter in your caption, Visual Basic underlines that letter and crowns it as the reigning hot key for that command. For example, suppose that you create a command button and type the caption **E&xit** in the Properties window:

The command button displays the caption Exit; the letter x is underlined and represents the hot key. The user can either choose the command by pressing the hot key (Alt+X) or by clicking on the command button.

heads up

You can use only one ampersand (&) character in each caption because you can only create one hot key for each command button.

Tip: What if you want to use the ampersand as part of the caption? For example, you may want to make the command button caption Save & Exit. All you need to do is type two ampersands in the caption property like this: **Save && Exit**. (No, you can't type three ampersands to create an underlined ampersand.)

on the CD

To experiment with a command button's caption, follow these steps:

1 Load the Message.VBP project file.

2 Draw a command button on the form next to the Display message button.

If you need a refresher on how to draw a command button, refer back to Lesson 4-1.

3 Click on the command button that you drew on the form.

Visual Basic displays black handles around the command button.

4 Press F4 to display the Properties window.

5 Double-click in the Caption property in the left-hand column.

Visual Basic highlights the caption in the right-hand column.

6 Type E&xit and press Enter.

Notice that Visual Basic now displays your command button with Exit as its caption. You'll also see that the "x" in Exit is underlined.

Margin notes:

button captions, unlike button names, can include spaces

handles show which object is selected

☑ **Progress Check**

If you can do the following, you've mastered this lesson:

❑ Change the caption of a command button.

❑ Include a hot key in your caption.

Lesson 5-2

Defining How Your Command Buttons Work

After taking time to write descriptive captions for your command buttons, you may want to define the following two additional features of your command buttons before writing BASIC code for the buttons:

▶ The default button

▶ The cancel button

Choosing a default button

default button = button user selects just by pressing Enter or Return

If you have more than two buttons on a form, you may want to make one of them the *default button*, which is the button that you expect users to choose most often. For example, in the Font dialog box in Figure 5-3, the default button is the OK button, because most users will usually click on OK after making font selections. The default button appears with a dark border around its edge.

on the test

You can designate only one command button as the default button on a form. You do not have to define a default button if you don't want to. You may not always want to create a default button if your program displays two or more buttons that the user may be equally likely to choose. For example, many database programs contain lists of names and addresses, both of which the user may use equally.

To let you experience the joy and excitement you can get from defining the default button, try the following exercise:

1 **Click on the command button that you drew on the Message.VBP form in Lesson 5-1.**

Visual Basic displays black handles around the command button.

2 **Right-click on the Exit button and choose Properties from the context menu to display the Properties window.**

3 **Double-click on the Name property in the left-hand column.**

4 **Type cmdExit and press Enter.**

5 **Click in the Default property in the left-hand column.**

Visual Basic displays a downward-pointing arrow in the right-hand column.

6 **Click on the downward-pointing arrow and choose True from the list.**

7 **Double-click on the Exit button displayed on the form.**

The Code window appears, as shown in Figure 5-4.

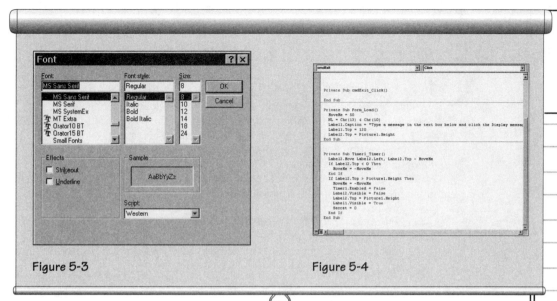

Figure 5-3

Figure 5-4

Figure 5-3: The Font
dialog box.

Figure 5-4: The Code
window for the cmdExit
button.

Notes:

8 **Type** End **(entered in bold below so you know where to type it) so
the code appears as follows:**

```
Private Sub Command1_Click ()
  End
End Sub
```

9 **Press F5 to start the program.**

Notice that your default button now appears with a slightly darker border
around its edges. Congratulations! You've just created a default button. Now to
see it actually work, try the next step.

10 **Press Enter.**

Visual Basic automatically chooses the default command button, which in this
case is the Exit button that stops your program from running.

11 **Close the Code window by clicking on the Close box.**

When you run this program, you can mindlessly choose the default button just
by pressing Enter — without touching the mouse. That's the whole purpose of
choosing a default button — to let people choose the button as easily as
possible.

heads up

Pressing Enter chooses the default button only when the program runs and the
user hasn't touched certain keys or the mouse. The moment the user presses
Tab or any of the cursor keys ($\leftarrow$, $\uparrow$, $\rightarrow$, $\downarrow$), Visual Basic highlights a different
object. Then if the user presses Enter, Visual Basic chooses whatever object
happens to be highlighted, which most likely won't be the default button.

▼

downward-pointing
arrow

Notes:

Choosing a cancel button

A cancel button works similar to a default button. To choose the default button without thinking, all you do is press Enter. Likewise to choose the cancel button without thinking, all you do is press Esc.

The cancel button is often the command button that lets you escape from a dialog box or cancel a previous command. Cancel buttons are used to tell Visual Basic, "See all the commands or options I just chose? I'm now changing my mind, and I don't want them anymore."

Cancel buttons aren't always necessary. For example, many dialog boxes just display a simple message such as "Printer not working." If the dialog box didn't let you choose any commands, there's no reason to have a cancel button.

However, if you have a dialog box that gives the user an option to erase the entire hard disk, defining a button with the caption NO! as the cancel button is a good idea. That way a user could choose the NO! button just by pressing Esc.

To show you how to designate your very own cancel button, try the following:

1 Click on the Exit command button that you drew on the form.

Visual Basic displays black handles around the Exit command button.

2 Press F4 to display the Properties window if it's not already on screen.

3 Double-click on the Cancel property in the left-hand column.

Notice that Visual Basic changes the value of the property from False to True. In most cases, you can simply double-click on a property to toggle it between two states. Setting the Cancel property to True designates the Exit button as your cancel button.

4 Double-click in the Default property in the left-hand column.

Notice that the value of the Default property changes from True (where it was set in the previous exercise) to False.

5 Click in the TabIndex property in the left-hand column.

6 Type 5 in the right-hand column and press Enter.

7 Press F5.

Notice that because the Exit command button is no longer the default button, the Exit button doesn't appear highlighted when you run the program.

8 Press Esc.

By pressing Esc, you're telling Visual Basic to choose the cancel button. You now simply exit the program.

☑ **Progress Check**

If you can do the following, you've mastered this lesson:

❏ Double-click on a property to toggle it between True and False.

❏ Define a default button.

❏ Define a cancel button.

Writing BASIC Code for Your Command Buttons

After you draw your command buttons and make them look pretty with fancy fonts and (hopefully) descriptive captions, you can make your command buttons do something worthwhile.

for more about
BASIC programming,
see Unit 11

To make your command button do something when the user clicks on it, you have to write *BASIC code,* which is nothing more complicated than one or more instructions written by using the BASIC programming language.

Whenever you write BASIC code to make part of your user interface do something, Visual Basic stores that BASIC code in a short program called an *event procedure.* An event procedure is a short program that tells Visual Basic what to do when a certain event occurs on a certain object.

So what's an event? An *event* is anything that happens to your program, such as the user clicking (the event) on a command button (the object). The moment the user clicks on the mouse, Visual Basic quickly identifies the event and says to itself, "Ah ha! The event that just occurred was a mouse click." Then Visual Basic frantically tries to identify the object where the mouse click occurred (such as on a command button). The moment Visual Basic can identify the object where the event occurred, it follows the instructions stored in that object's event procedure.

To write BASIC code for a command button, all you have to do is open the Code window and write your instructions in the command button's event procedure.

If you have successfully completed the steps in Lesson 5-2, you can jump immediately to the following steps to get a taste of writing BASIC code for a command button:

on the CD

1 **Double-click on the Display message command button on the Message.VBP form.**

Visual Basic displays the Code window.

2 **Add** Label2.Caption = Text1.Text **(which appears in bold below so you know where to type it) so the entire event procedure looks like this:**

```
Private Sub cmdDisplay_Click ()
  Timer1.Interval = 50
  Timer1.Enabled = True
  NL = Chr(13) & Chr(10)
  Label1.Visible = False
  Label2.Visible = True
  Label2.Caption = Text1.Text
End Sub
```

Figure 5-5: The Message.VBP program running.

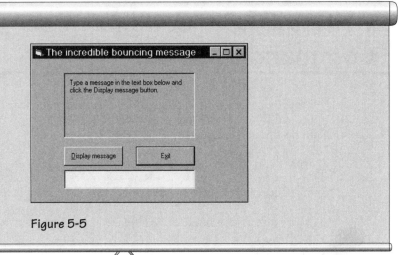

Figure 5-5

You'll learn more about BASIC programming in Unit 11, but for now, remember that the line you just typed in instructs Visual Basic to take whatever text a user enters and display it on the program form.

3 Press F5 to start the program.

Visual Basic runs your program, which looks like Figure 5-5.

4 Type a message in the text box that appears underneath the Display message and Exit command buttons.

5 Click on the Display message button.

Your message scrolls up and down above the two command buttons.

6 Click on Exit.

By writing BASIC code for a command button and clicking on that button when the program runs, you can see how Visual Basic follows your BASIC code instructions.

Recess

Command buttons are the easiest way your program can provide choices for the user, because ignoring huge gray rectangles that are staring you in the face is difficult. Now that you understand this concept and how to create command buttons in Visual Basic, take a break and think about all the wonderful programs you can create after you finish using this book.

☑ **Progress Check**

If you can do the following, you've mastered this lesson:

❑ Open the Code window for a command button.

❑ Write simple BASIC code.

❑ Run a Visual Basic program and click on a command button to see what it does.

Unit 5 Quiz

Circle the letter of the correct answer or answers for each of the following questions. To keep you on your toes, each question may have more than one correct answer.

1. **What are the two steps to create a command button?**

   A. First, you need to decide what a command button is, and then you need to decide why anyone bothered to create such a long-winded term in the first place.

   B. First, you have to draw your command button and make it look pretty. Then you have to write BASIC code to make the button do something useful.

   C. Command buttons can't be created in Visual Basic. This is a trick question.

   D. First, you must decide what you want your command button to do. Then you have to figure out why you wanted to learn programming in the first place when you could be outside instead.

   E. Command buttons are so difficult to create and use that you really need at least 59 steps to create just one.

2. **What's the difference between the name and the caption of a command button?**

   A. Name is spelled N-A-M-E; caption is spelled C-A-P-T-I-O-N.

   B. The name is the official label of a command button while a caption is the button's nickname.

   C. The caption is what appears underneath the command button's name and is used to help people who need subtitles.

   D. The name of a command button is for your convenience in identifying the button. The caption is the text that actually appears on the command button.

   E. No difference exists between the name and caption of a command button. That's why this answer is obviously wrong.

3. **What's a *hot key*?**

   A. A hot key is a special key on your keyboard that melts if you leave a cigarette burning too close to it.

   B. Hot keys are special keys that you can press to make your computer overheat and blow up, thereby preventing you from doing any more work on your computer for the day.

   C. A hot key is a character that appears underlined in the caption of a command button. You can create a hot key by using the ampersand character (&) in the caption, such as E&xit.

   D. A hot key lets you choose a command button by pressing the Alt key plus another key. For example, if the caption of a command button appeared as Exit, you could choose the button by pressing Alt+X.

   E. A hot key is the original Old English pronunciation of a game that's known today as *hockey*.

Notes:

4. **What's the difference between a default button and a cancel button?**

    A. Other than the fact that default buttons work differently than cancel buttons, no difference exists at all.

    B. A default button is a command button that you can create when you don't feel like doing anything else. The cancel button is a special button that shuts down your computer right before you get so frustrated that you want to throw the whole thing through the window.

    C. The cancel button erases anything the default button does.

    D. There's no reason to concentrate on differences. The world would be a better place if we all just focused on our similarities instead.

    E. The user can choose the default button by pressing Enter or choose the cancel button by pressing Esc.

5. **What happens when a user clicks on a command button?**

    A. The command button breaks.

    B. Nothing. Command buttons exist for decorative purposes only.

    C. The command button immediately follows the instructions written in BASIC code, which is stored in its event procedure.

    D. The monitor may explode, so wear goggles whenever you work on your computer.

    E. If you cut the cord to the mouse, the user won't be able to click on anything at all. So there.

Unit 5 Exercise

1. Load a Visual Basic program of your choice.

2. Choose a form at random from the Project window.

3. Click on one of the form's command buttons.

4. Open the Properties window for the command button and examine its Caption properties.

5. Close the Properties window.

6. Open the Code window for the command button and examine the BASIC code stored in its event procedure.

7. Run the program and click on the command button you examined, just so you can see how the command button works.

Check Boxes and Radio Buttons

Objectives for This Unit

✓ Framing check boxes and radio buttons

✓ Making check boxes, radio buttons, and frames look pretty

✓ Setting and getting values from check boxes and radio buttons

Prerequisites

♦ Using the Toolbox to draw objects on a form (Lesson 4-1)

♦ Opening the Properties window to change a property (Lesson 3-1)

♦ Writing captions for buttons (Lesson 5-1)

on the CD   ♦ Vote.VBP

*C*heck boxes and radio buttons let your program provide multiple options for users to choose from, as shown in Figure 6-1. The main difference between the two: Users can choose any or all of the available check boxes, but they can only choose one radio button in a group.

on the test

Check boxes are meant to work like an on/off switch. You either select an option or you don't. They're also stand alone — one check box doesn't affect others around it.

Radio buttons allow you to create a menu of choices. They're always placed in groups. Selecting one radio button in a group automatically excludes all of the other radio buttons in that group.

heads up

Instead of using the term radio buttons, Visual Basic calls them *option buttons*. However, many people still use the term radio button because it's more descriptive.

radio buttons always appear in groups

Figure 6-1: Typical uses for check boxes and radio buttons.

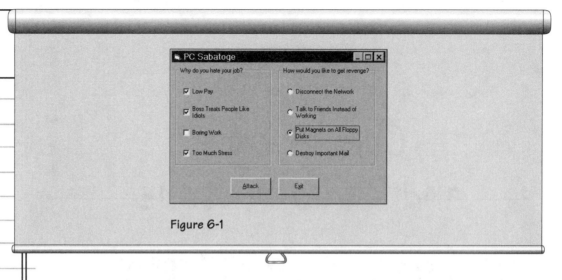

Figure 6-1

Radio buttons are so named because you can only tune in to one radio station at a time. Because car radios let you switch stations by pressing buttons, the term radio button has stuck. When you say something is similar to a radio button, most people know what you're talking about, but when you call something an option button, does anyone understand?

Lesson 6-1

Framing Check Boxes and Radio Buttons

Although you can draw check boxes and radio buttons anywhere on a form, you're better off grouping your buttons within framing boxes so all your choices are easily seen at once. Framing check boxes organizes them for the user's convenience. The framing box only organizes the check boxes, it doesn't change how they work.

on the test

use frames to organize check boxes and radio buttons

Framing radio buttons is necessary if you want the user to be able to choose two or more radio buttons on a form at a time. Visual Basic knows that if it sees a framing box containing radio buttons, all those buttons belong to the same group. You can use two or more framing boxes to create two or more groups of radio buttons on a form.

For example, if you don't frame your radio buttons, as shown in Figure 6-2, you can only choose one radio button on a single form. Any time you need to display two or more separate groups of radio buttons, you should enclose each group within a frame, as shown in Figure 6-3.

When you want to frame check boxes or radio buttons, you must draw the frame first and then draw the check boxes or radio buttons inside the frame. Try it yourself and gain wisdom from the following exercise:

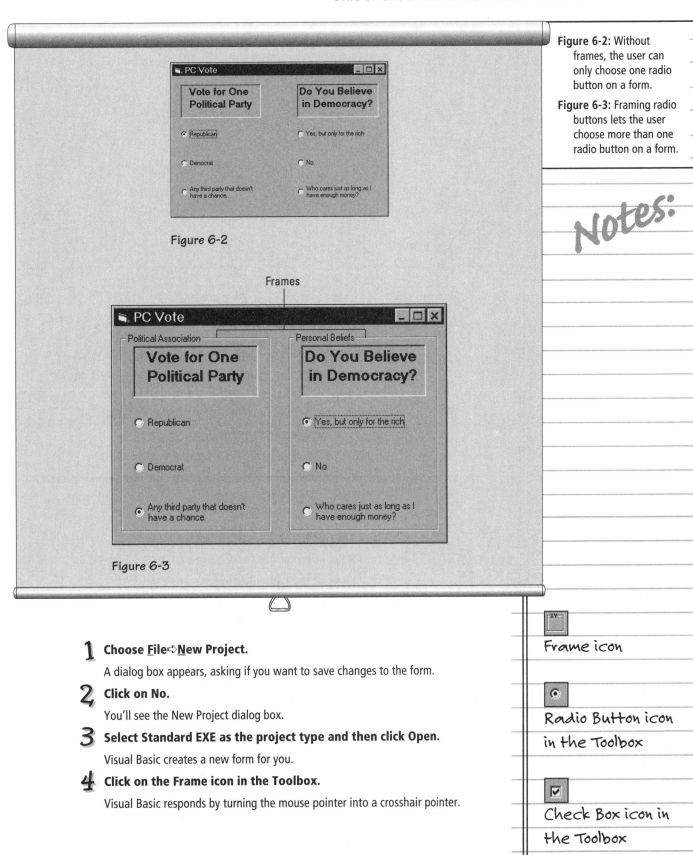

Figure 6-2

Frames

Figure 6-3

Figure 6-2: Without frames, the user can only choose one radio button on a form.

Figure 6-3: Framing radio buttons lets the user choose more than one radio button on a form.

Notes:

1 Choose File⇨New Project.

A dialog box appears, asking if you want to save changes to the form.

2 Click on No.

You'll see the New Project dialog box.

3 Select Standard EXE as the project type and then click Open.

Visual Basic creates a new form for you.

4 Click on the Frame icon in the Toolbox.

Visual Basic responds by turning the mouse pointer into a crosshair pointer.

Frame icon

Radio Button icon in the Toolbox

Check Box icon in the Toolbox

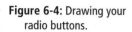

Figure 6-4: Drawing your
radio buttons.

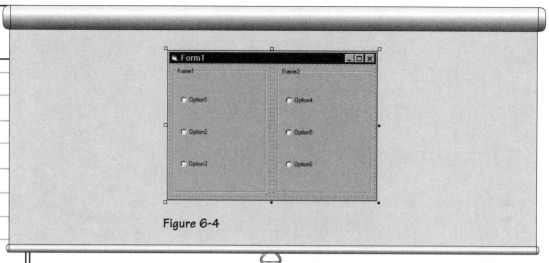

Figure 6-4

☑ Progress Check

If you can do the following,
you've mastered this lesson:

❏ Draw a frame and put
check boxes or radio
buttons inside it.

❏ Understand how a frame
separates groups of radio
buttons.

❏ Move a frame to
automatically move any
check boxes or radio
buttons inside.

5 **Position the mouse where you want the frame to appear, hold
down the left mouse button, and move the mouse.**

Visual Basic draws a white outline of your frame to show you its size.

6 **Release the left mouse button when you're happy with the
frame size.**

Visual Basic draws a frame with the generic caption of Frame1.

7 **Draw a second frame on the form.**

Visual Basic draws a frame with the generic caption of Frame2.

8 **Draw three radio buttons inside Frame1 and three more in Frame2,
as shown in Figure 6-4.**

9 **Press F5 to run your program.**

10 **Click on any of the radio buttons inside Frame1.**

Notice that you can only choose one radio button inside Frame1.

11 **Click on any of the radio buttons inside Frame2.**

Notice that you can only choose one radio button inside Frame2. Also important
is that your selection in Frame2 doesn't affect your previous selection in
Frame1. The radio buttons are totally independent.

12 **Click on the End button in the Toolbar.**

heads up

After you've drawn a check box or radio button inside a frame, you won't be
able to move the check box or radio button outside of the frame. If you move
the frame, the frame automatically moves any check boxes or radio buttons
inside it as well. (And if you delete a frame, you also delete any objects inside
the frame, so watch out!)

Tip: Placing an object inside a frame doesn't mean that the object is there
forever. Visual Basic will allow you to select the object, cut it to the clipboard,
and then paste it outside the frame. Make sure that you select the form before
pasting, though, or the object will end up back in the frame when you paste it.

Making Check Boxes, Radio Buttons, and Frames Look Pretty

After drawing check boxes, radio buttons, and frames, you may want to take a little extra time to make them look pretty by using different colors and/or alignments. You don't have to make your check boxes, radio buttons, or frames look different, but doing so gives your program an added touch of class that can mean the difference between selling your program for $19.95 or $149.95.

extra credit

> ## Captioning a common property
>
> Command boxes, check boxes, radio buttons, and frames may have different uses and different traits, but the objects are similar when it comes to captions.
>
> You can use the Caption property in the Properties window to change captions, change fonts, change type sizes, and add hot keys to captions for all four types of
>
> objects. (But because users rarely need to click on a frame, you probably wouldn't want to add a hot key to a frame's caption.)
>
> Also remember that the caption limitations placed on one type apply to all. To learn more about captions, turn back to Lesson 5-1 in Unit 5.

Changing colors

Visual Basic tends to create everything with the same dull, battleship gray that would be perfect if you were trying to camouflage your program in an ocean fog. Because gray may not be your favorite color, you can change both the background and foreground colors of check boxes, radio buttons, and frames.

The foreground color affects the caption. The background color changes (what else?) the background that the caption appears against, as shown in Figure 6-5. By default, the foreground color is black and the background color is gray.

on the test

You can define color selections in two ways when using Visual Basic. The first is to choose a custom color. Using a custom color ensures that the user sees the same colors every time she uses your application.

The second method of setting a color is to choose a system color. Using a system color means that the colors of your application will change to match the colors that the user has chosen for Windows, which means that the user can customize your application to suit her tastes.

Play around with different colors until you find a combination that appeals to your sense of beauty.

custom colors
remain consistent,
system colors
change to match
user's Windows
setup

Figure 6-5: Identifying the foreground and background colors for radio buttons and frames.

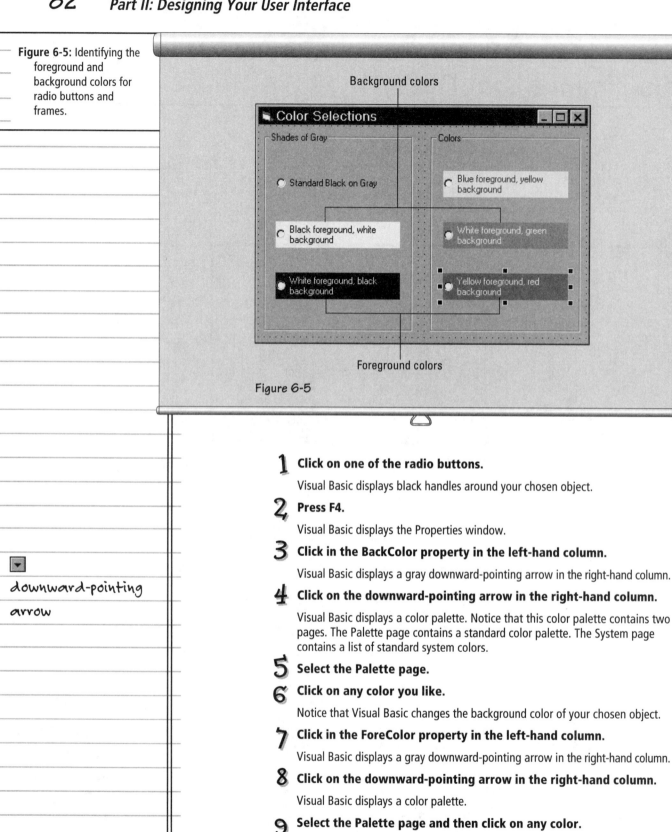

Figure 6-5

downward-pointing arrow

1 **Click on one of the radio buttons.**

Visual Basic displays black handles around your chosen object.

2 **Press F4.**

Visual Basic displays the Properties window.

3 **Click in the BackColor property in the left-hand column.**

Visual Basic displays a gray downward-pointing arrow in the right-hand column.

4 **Click on the downward-pointing arrow in the right-hand column.**

Visual Basic displays a color palette. Notice that this color palette contains two pages. The Palette page contains a standard color palette. The System page contains a list of standard system colors.

5 **Select the Palette page.**

6 **Click on any color you like.**

Notice that Visual Basic changes the background color of your chosen object.

7 **Click in the ForeColor property in the left-hand column.**

Visual Basic displays a gray downward-pointing arrow in the right-hand column.

8 **Click on the downward-pointing arrow in the right-hand column.**

Visual Basic displays a color palette.

9 **Select the Palette page and then click on any color.**

Notice that Visual Basic changes the foreground color of your chosen object, which affects the check box's caption.

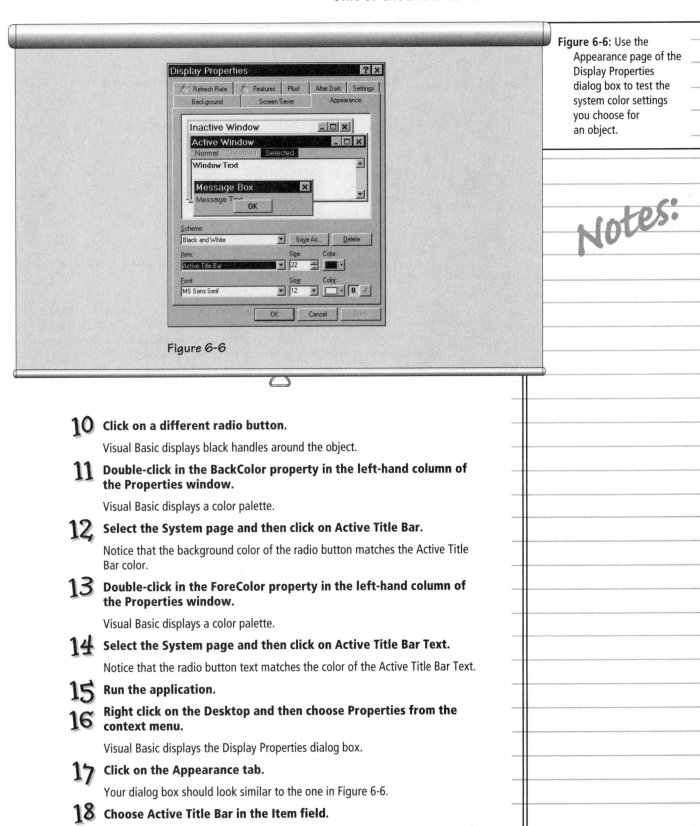

Figure 6-6

Notes:

10 **Click on a different radio button.**

Visual Basic displays black handles around the object.

11 **Double-click in the BackColor property in the left-hand column of the Properties window.**

Visual Basic displays a color palette.

12 **Select the System page and then click on Active Title Bar.**

Notice that the background color of the radio button matches the Active Title Bar color.

13 **Double-click in the ForeColor property in the left-hand column of the Properties window.**

Visual Basic displays a color palette.

14 **Select the System page and then click on Active Title Bar Text.**

Notice that the radio button text matches the color of the Active Title Bar Text.

15 **Run the application.**

16 **Right click on the Desktop and then choose Properties from the context menu.**

Visual Basic displays the Display Properties dialog box.

17 **Click on the Appearance tab.**

Your dialog box should look similar to the one in Figure 6-6.

18 **Choose Active Title Bar in the Item field.**

19 **Change the colors shown in the two Color fields (the upper Color field changes the background, the lower Color field the foreground).**

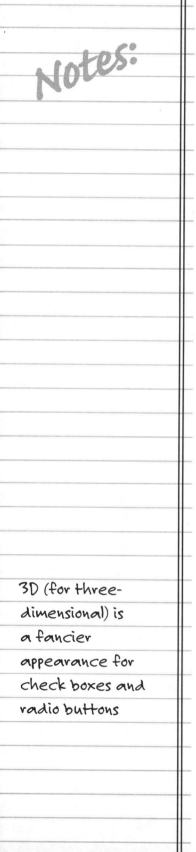

Notes:

20 **Click on Apply.**

Notice that the colors used by the second radio button change, but the colors in the first don't.

Repeat these steps for any other object you want until you get bored and decide to move to the next part of this lesson.

heads up

Be careful not to get too creative with background and foreground colors. Different color combinations can look annoying on the screen, and if you choose the wrong background and foreground colors, you may make the text hard to read. For example, text on a dark gray foreground with a black background is nearly impossible to read.

Changing alignment

Visual Basic gives you two choices for aligning your check boxes and radio buttons: Left Justify or Right Justify. Left-justified check boxes and radio buttons are displayed to the left of their captions, while right-justified boxes and buttons are displayed to the right of their captions, as shown in Figure 6-7.

Most people expect to see left-justified check boxes and radio buttons, but just so you know how to right-justify something, try the following steps.

1 **Click on any radio button on your form.**

Visual Basic displays black handles around the radio button.

2 **Press F4 to display the Properties window.**

3 **Double-click in the Alignment property in the left-hand column.**

Notice that your right-aligned radio button appears on the form, looking rather peculiar.

Changing appearance

on the test

You can display check boxes and radio buttons in two ways: 3D or Flat. As shown in Figure 6-8, a 3D appearance gives your check boxes and radio buttons a fancier look, as if the boxes and buttons are chiseled out of stainless steel. A Flat appearance makes your check boxes and radio buttons look plain and dull, as if it the boxes and buttons are printed on a piece of white paper.

To change the appearance of check boxes or radio buttons, try the following:

1 **Click on any radio button on your form.**

Visual Basic displays black handles around the radio button.

2 **Press F4 to display the Properties window.**

3 **Click in the Appearance property in the left-hand column.**

Visual Basic displays a downward-pointing arrow in the right-hand column.

3D (for three-dimensional) is a fancier appearance for check boxes and radio buttons

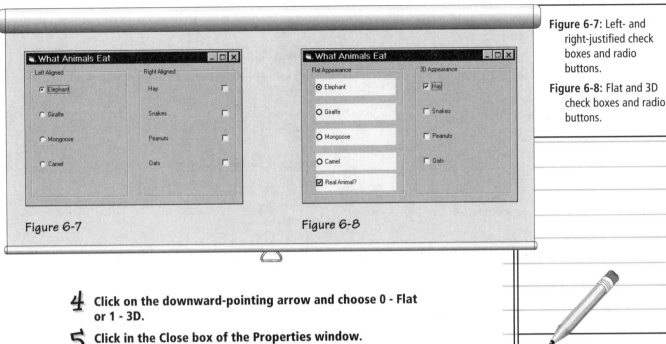

Figure 6-7

Figure 6-8

Figure 6-7: Left- and right-justified check boxes and radio buttons.

Figure 6-8: Flat and 3D check boxes and radio buttons.

4 **Click on the downward-pointing arrow and choose 0 - Flat or 1 - 3D.**

5 **Click in the Close box of the Properties window.**

Notice that your check box appears on the form with a flat appearance, which looks pretty boring. Now you know why the default appearance of check boxes and radio buttons is 3D.

As you may have already decided, the Flat appearance is dull. That's why Visual Basic always assumes that you want to use the 3D appearance until you specify otherwise. Unless you have a really good reason to use the Flat appearance, using the 3D appearance is probably a good idea.

Recess

Now that you've had a chance to play around and see the differences between check boxes and radio buttons, you can see how they're pretty handy to have around. Just remember the crucial rule of thumb: If you want the user to choose multiple choices, use check boxes. If you only want the user to choose just one choice, use a radio button. If you don't want to give your users any choice at all, force them to use only Microsoft products. Now go outside and see if you can find some radio buttons and check boxes in the clouds.

☑ Progress Check

If you can do the following, you've mastered this lesson:

❏ Change the background and foreground colors of a check box, radio button, and frame.

❏ Define the difference between custom and system colors.

❏ Alter the alignment of a check box or radio button.

❏ Modify the appearance of a check box or radio button.

Setting and Getting Values from Check Boxes and Radio Buttons

Lesson 6-3

When you draw a check box, the check box appears empty. Likewise, when you draw a radio button, the radio button appears blank. When the user clicks in a check box or radio button, the user is telling Visual Basic, "See that choice represented by that check box or radio button? That's the choice I want to pick."

Figure 6-9: The three possible appearances of check boxes and the two possible appearances of radio buttons.

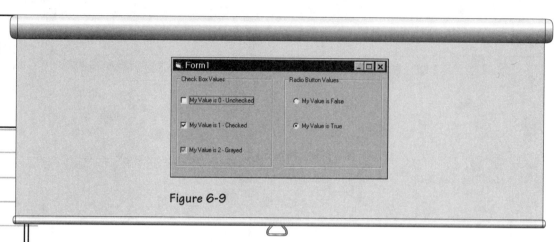

Figure 6-9

How does Visual Basic tell which check box or radio button the user picks? By examining the box or button's Value property.

The Value property of a check box can hold one of three different values, as shown in Figure 6-9:

- ◆ 0 - Unchecked
- ◆ 1 - Checked
- ◆ 2 - Grayed

The Checked value means that a user has clicked on the box. The Unchecked value means the box is still unchecked. And Grayed is an option that the user cannot access, but that you can define by using BASIC code — although practically no reasons exist to do so. (Some installation programs use a grayed check box to show that you've selected some, but not all, of the installation options for an application.)

Similarly, the Value property of a radio button can hold one of two different values:

- ◆ False (the radio button appears empty)
- ◆ True (the radio button appears with a black dot in it)

If you change the Value property of a check box or radio button using the Properties window, you can make a check box or radio button appear checked when your program runs.

Remember: You can only choose one radio button in a group to appear checked.

To see how the Value property works for both check boxes and radio buttons, try the following steps and see what amazing new discoveries you may uncover in your quest for Visual Basic knowledge and enlightenment.

1 **Load the Vote.VBP project file.**

Notice that the <u>C</u>onservative radio button appears checked.

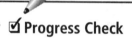

☑ Progress Check

If you can do the following, you've mastered this lesson:

❑ Explain the two different ways you can change the Value property of a check box or radio button.

❑ Change the Value property of a check box or radio button through the Properties window.

❑ Explain what happens to the Value property of a radio button the moment a user clicks on it.

2 **Click on the Conservative radio button.**

Visual Basic displays black handles around the radio button.

3 **Press F4 to display the Properties window.**

4 **Click in the Value property in the left-hand column.**

Notice that the Value property is True, which is why this radio button appears checked.

5 **Click on the Liberal radio button on the form.**

6 **Click in the Value property in the left-hand column.**

Notice that the Value property is False, which is why this radio button does not appear checked.

If you ran this program (by pressing F5), you could click on a different radio button, such as Fanatical. The moment you click on the Fanatical radio button, Visual Basic would set the Fanatical radio button's Value property to True. Because only one radio button in a group can be *chosen* (have its Value property set to True), the Conservative radio button's Value property would be set to False, and the black dot would disappear from that button.

Unit 6 Quiz

Circle the correct answer or answers for each of the following questions. Again, each question may have more than one correct answer. The answers for each question are in Appendix A.

1. **What is the difference between a check box and a radio button?**

   A. Radio buttons let you tune in to your favorite radio stations through your computer. Check boxes let you check to make sure that your computer is working correctly.

   B. A check box requires more RAM, hard disk space, and processing power than a radio button. So use check boxes sparingly.

   C. Users can only choose one radio button in a group but can choose more than one check box.

   D. Check boxes are rectangular in shape while radio buttons resemble radios.

   E. Radio buttons are just another name for check boxes. Some people refer to check boxes as option buttons, while others just refer to them using four-letter words.

Notes:

2. **Why is framing radio buttons important?**

   A. Because if you don't frame them, you may not have enough evidence alone to convict them.

   B. So you can hang them on the wall over the fireplace.

   C. Framing radio buttons lets you organize radio buttons into logical groups. Frames also make choosing more than one radio button easy, as long as they are enclosed inside different frames.

   D. Framing keeps radio buttons from escaping, much in the same way that you need to corral cows to keep them from escaping.

   E. The only reason to frame a radio button is to make your program even more confusing for people to use. Everyone knows the harder you make your software, the more likely you'll gain market share.

3. **What are the two ways that you can use to set colors for an object in Visual Basic?**

   A. You can use a system color if you want your application to use standard Windows system colors.

   B. Visual Basic never lets you set the colors for your application, so why try?

   C. Custom colors allow you to choose a specific color for your application that the user can't change without help.

   D. There's only one way, the Microsoft way.

   E. Never set the colors of an object in Visual Basic because that's what people expect.

4. **What is the difference between a Flat and a 3D appearance for your check boxes or radio buttons?**

   A. The Flat appearance tends to look dull and boring. The 3D appearance is prettier and more pleasing to the eye.

   B. They are exactly identical. In Swahili, the word Flat translates into the term 3D.

   C. No difference exists between a Flat and a 3D appearance. Anyone who tells you otherwise is crazy.

   D. The 3D appearance makes finding your check boxes or radio buttons on the screen easier for the user. The Flat appearance simply makes check boxes or radio buttons look dull.

   E. A Flat appearance can be adjusted using a kaleidoscope, thus creating a more visually stunning 3D effect.

5. **What two things can you do to allow users to choose your check boxes and radio buttons just by using the keyboard and not the mouse?**

   A. Nothing. If users aren't going to use the mouse, then they're probably not worth catering to in the first place.

   B. You can make your check boxes appear in really ugly colors to discourage nonmouse users from daring to use your program at all.

   C. You can display hot keys in your check box or radio button captions.

   D. Users who still prefer the keyboard need to break antiquated habits, so you'll be doing these people a favor by forcing them to choose your check boxes or radio buttons with a mouse instead.

   E. The two ways you can help keyboard users are to use MS-DOS instead of Windows and to throw away your mouse so they have no choice but to use the keyboard.

6. **What is the value of any check box or radio button clicked on by a user?**

   A. A check box that is checked has a value of 1 (Checked). A radio button that is chosen has a value of 1 (True).

   B. If a user clicks on a check box or radio button, nothing happens because Visual Basic doesn't work anyway.

   C. If you click too hard on a check box or radio button, you may push the mouse pointer right through the screen.

   D. Clicking on a radio button changes the station on your radio whether you're listening to it or not.

   E. The value of check boxes and radio buttons cannot be determined. Suffice to say that their value is priceless.

Unit 6 Exercise

on the CD

1. Load the Vote project (Vote.VBP).

2. Press F5.

   Visual Basic runs your program. The user interface appears. On the left side you'll see a row of radio buttons, the right side contains a row of check boxes. At the bottom of the form you'll see two buttons: Vote and Exit.

3. Click on any radio button in the Choose a political affiliation group.

4. Click in one or more check boxes in the Choose a platform group.

5. Click on the Vote button.

   A message box appears. The title bar of the message box displays the radio button you chose in step 3. The middle of the message box displays the check boxes you chose in step 4.

6. Click on OK.

7. Click on Exit.

8. Press F7 to display the Code window.

9. Scroll through the list of procedures to find the cmdVote_Click() procedure.

   You'll see the following BASIC code:

```
Private Sub cmdVote_Click()
Dim Message As String
Dim Platform As String
Dim NL As String
NL = Chr(13) & Chr(10)
If optConservative.Value = True Then Message = "Conser-
        vative"
If optLiberal.Value = True Then Message = "Liberal"
If optFanatical.Value = True Then Message = "Fanatic"
If optAnarchist.Value = True Then Message = "Anarchist"

If chkTaxes.Value = 1 Then Platform = "Cut taxes for the
        rich" & NL & Platform
If chkDeficit.Value = 1 Then Platform = "Increase the
        deficit" & NL & Platform
If chkReward.Value = 1 Then Platform = "Reward big busi-
        ness" & NL & Platform
If chkAbolish.Value = 1 Then Platform = "Abolish democ-
        racy" & NL & Platform

MsgBox Platform, 48, Message
End Sub
```

Don't worry too much about what this BASIC code means. Just be aware that this mass of BASIC code determines which radio buttons and check boxes a user chooses. For example, the following line checks to see if the user chose the optLiberal radio button:

```
If optLiberal.Value = True Then Message = "Liberal"
```

Text Boxes and Labels

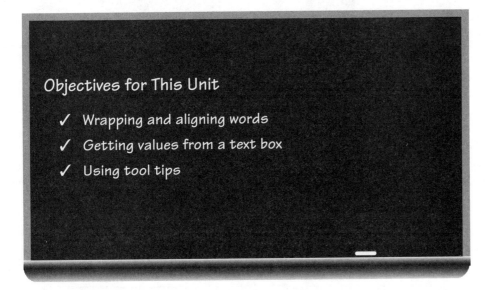

Objectives for This Unit

✓ Wrapping and aligning words

✓ Getting values from a text box

✓ Using tool tips

Prerequisites
▶ Using the Toolbox to draw objects on a form (Lesson 4-1)
▶ Changing foreground and background colors (Lesson 6-2)
▶ Changing property values through the Properties window or through simple BASIC code (Lesson 3-1)

▶ Gossip.VBP

on the CD

Many times your program needs to display messages or instructions on the screen for the user. The two simplest ways to display text with a Visual Basic program area are to use text boxes or labels.

on the test

A *label* does nothing more exciting than display letters or numbers on the screen. A *text box* is a little fancier. A text box displays text on the screen and lets the user type in text. In this way, a text box can get information from the user.

heads up

As a general rule of thumb, use a label when you only want to display text on the screen. Use a text box when you want to display text and give the user the option of typing text into your Visual Basic program. For example, if your program asks the user for a name, address, or part number, your program can display a text box where the user could type in that information. Figure 7-1 shows typical uses for labels and text boxes.

use a label to only display text on screen

use a text box to give the user the option of typing text into your program

Figure 7-1: Typical uses for text boxes and labels.

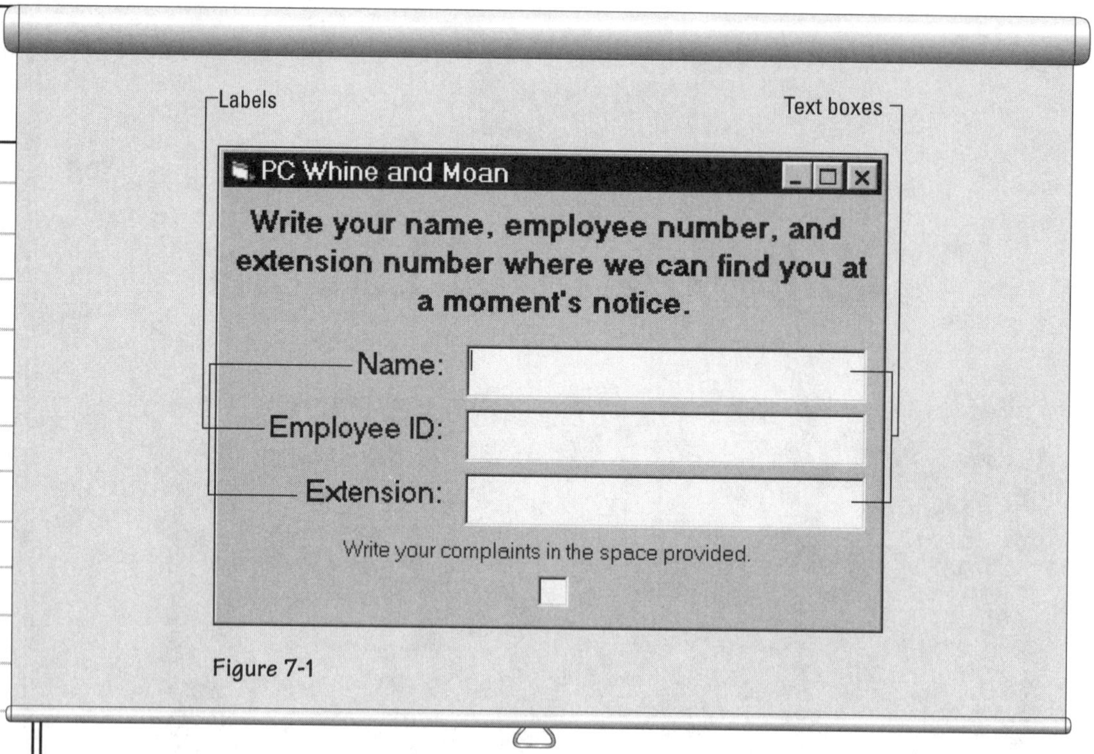

Figure 7-1

Notes:

Lesson 7-1

Alignment and Word-Wrapping

At some point in your Visual Basic programming career, you'll probably want to display multiple lines of text within a label or text box. In that case, you may want to align your text, provide word-wrapping, or display horizontal or vertical scroll bars to help the user view all the text trapped inside a text box.

For example, you may want a text box where users can type in some comments about how well (or how poorly) your company treats its customers. In that case, you can draw a really big text box to hold all the text someone might type in. But using word-wrapping in your text box so the angry customer can type as much as he (or she) wants without regard to the physical size of the text box is a better solution.

Aligning text

Visual Basic gives you three ways to align text inside a label or text box:

▶ Left justified
▶ Centered
▶ Right justified

Aligning text in a label involves modifying the label's Alignment property.

1 **Start Visual Basic, choose a Standard EXE in the New Project dialog box, draw a label and text box anywhere on the form, and then click on the label that you drew.**

Visual Basic displays black handles around your chosen object.

2 **Press F4 to display the Properties window (if necessary).**

3 **Click in the Alignment property in the left-hand column.**

Visual Basic displays a downward-pointing arrow in the right-hand column.

4 **Click on the downward-pointing arrow.**

A drop-down list appears.

5 **Choose one of the following:**

- 0 - Left Justify
- 1 - Right Justify
- 2 - Center

Visual Basic shows you how your text appears aligned.

on the test

Aligning text in a text box also involves modifying the Alignment property, but first you must change the MultiLine property.

1 **Click on the text box you drew on the form.**

2 **Press F4 to display the Properties window.**

3 **Double-click in the MultiLine property if it has a value of False.**

Visual Basic sets the value of the MultiLine property to true.

4 **Double-click in the Alignment property to cycle between the following values:**

- 0 - Left Justify
- 1 - Right Justify
- 2 - Center

Visual Basic shows how your text appears aligned within your text box.

Displaying multiple lines of text with word-wrapping

on the test

If you've ever used a word processor, you know that when you type a long string of text, the word processor automatically wraps your text around to the next line. That way you can keep typing without worrying if you're getting too close to the edge of the page, which is something you have to worry about when using a typewriter. Obviously, word-wrapping is useful if you have multiple lines of text. If you're only displaying a single line of text, you don't need word-wrapping.

---

change the Alignment property to change how text is aligned in a label

downward-pointing arrow

for a refresher on how to draw an object on a form, look back at Lesson 4-1

change the MultiLine property to True, and then change the Alignment property to change how text is aligned in a text box

double-click in the Alignment property to change its value

to word-wrap in a label, set AutoSize and WordWrap properties to True

to word-wrap in a text box, set MultiLine property to True

on the test

You can use word-wrapping in two ways in a label: Draw a really big label or set the AutoSize and WordWrap properties to True. If you have a large enough label and type a really long caption, the label is smart enough to word-wrap automatically. The problem with this approach is that you must make the label large enough to display your entire caption, but not so large that space is wasted. In case you want to make the label adjust its height automatically while using word-wrapping, you have to set the AutoSize and WordWrap properties to True.

Using word-wrapping with text boxes is different. (So what else is new?) By itself, a text box is too stupid to use word-wrapping. To make a text box use word-wrapping, you must set its MultiLine property to True.

To see the wonders of word-wrapping in a label, try the following steps:

1 **Click on the label you drew on the form.**

2 **Press F4 to display the Properties window.**

3 **Double-click in the Caption property in the left-hand column.**

4 **Type a really long caption and press Enter when you're done.**

   If your label isn't tall enough, the caption may appear cut off.

5 **Double-click on the WordWrap property in the left-hand column to set its value to True.**

6 **Double-click on the AutoSize property in the left-hand column to set its value to True.**

7 **Double-click in the Caption property.**

8 **Type a really long caption (make this one even longer than the one you typed in step 4).**

   You'll see that the label automatically adjusts its height to display the entire caption, no matter how long it may be.

Making a text box do word-wrapping is just as easy as making a label do word-wrapping. Try the following, in case you're one of those types who never believes anything he reads:

1 **Click in the text box you drew on the form and press F4.**

   The Properties window appears.

2 **Double-click in the Text property.**

3 **Type a really long text string and press Enter.**

   Notice that if you type a long text string, part of it may get cut off by the text box.

4 **Double-click in the MultiLine property in the left-hand column to set its value to True.**

   Notice that now your text box uses word-wrapping.

to word-wrap in a text box, set MultiLine property to True

Adding scroll bars to a text box

If you set a text box's MultiLine property to True, the box displays multiple lines by using word-wrapping. However, your text box may not be big enough to show all of the text trapped inside of it. To let the user see all of the text inside a text box, use scroll bars.

Horizontal scroll bars let you scroll side to side. *Vertical scroll bars* let you scroll up and down. If you have both horizontal and vertical scroll bars, then you can scroll up and down or right and left. Follow these steps to add scroll bars to a text box:

1 **Click on the text box that you drew on the form.**

2 **Press F4.**

The Properties window appears.

3 **Click in the Scroll Bars property in the left-hand column.**

4 **Choose one of the following:**

- 1 - Horizontal
- 2 - Vertical
- 3 - Both

5 **Double-click in the Text property in the left-hand column.**

A box appears where you can type text.

6 **Type a lot of text in this box. To move the cursor to the next line, press Ctrl+Enter.**

7 **Click on the Close box of the Properties window.**

Notice how the scroll bars work with multiple lines of text in a text box.

Recess

Text boxes offer two-way communication with the user. They can display text and accept new text that the user may type in. Labels offer one-way communication, only displaying text.

Now that you know the two ways to display text within a Visual Basic program, all you have to do is write programs that people think are worth using and, hopefully, worth paying for. Get a cup of coffee and think about all the money you'll make as a programmer.

Notes:

☑ **Progress Check**

If you can do the following, you've mastered this lesson:

❏ Align text within a label or text box.

❏ Add word-wrapping to a label or text box.

❏ Display scroll bars in a text box.

Lesson 7-2

Getting Values from a Text Box

Displaying text in a text box is simple enough, but what happens when the user types something into a text box? Because your program can use a text box to ask for information, your program needs to know how to retrieve any data that someone may type in a text box.

For example, your program may ask a user to type a name in a text box. But until you write BASIC code to retrieve that information, your program won't have any idea what the user just typed inside the text box.

on the test

When a user types something in a text box, Visual Basic stores those characters in the Text property of the text box. If someone types in the string "Hello, all you rabid Visual Basic programmers" in a text box named txtMessage, Visual Basic stores this string in the Text property of the txtMessage text box.

To see how an actual Visual Basic program retrieves data from a text box, try the following steps:

on the CD

1 **Load the Gossip project (Gossip.VBP).**

2 **Press Ctrl+R to display the Project window.**

3 **Click on the Gossip.FRM Form file and click on View Form.**

4 **Double-click on the View answers command button.**

The Code window appears and displays the following BASIC code:

```
Private Sub cmbView_Click ()
  MsgBox "My boss did this: " & txtAct.Text, 48,
         "Unusual thoughts of " & txtName.Text
End Sub
```

This code simply tells Visual Basic, "When the user clicks on the View answers command button, yank out any data stored in the Text properties of the txtAct and the txtName text boxes and display it on screen."

5 **Press F5 to run your program.**

6 **Type a name in the text box next to the label Name of your boss you want to schmooze:.**

7 **Type anything in the text box next to the label What interesting thoughts does your boss have? Please be very descriptive.**

8 **Click on View answers.**

A message box appears, showing the name and text that you typed in the two text boxes.

9 **Click on OK.**

10 **Click on Exit.**

☑ Progress Check

If you can do the following, you've mastered this lesson:

❏ Identify the property that stores any text the user types into a text box.

❏ Understand how you can use BASIC code to retrieve data stored in the Text property of a text box.

Using Tool Tips

Several Windows 95 programs use *tool tips* now. They're the little balloons like the one shown in Figure 7-2 that appear when you hold the mouse cursor over a button, text box, or other object. Visual Basic allows you add tool tips to any object that you can create.

Tool tips are a very valuable form of help when the user needs just a little information to perform a task. You may add just the word Open as a tool tip for a File Open speed button on the Toolbar of your application. A data entry form may have a tool tip for each blank so the user can get expanded information about what you want typed in it.

on the test

You don't want to use tool tips in some places, even though Visual Basic allows you to do so. For example, adding a tool tip like "This is a Label" to a label that the user can't interact with won't accomplish much. Normally, you attach a tool tip to an object that the user can work with.

on the CD

Just to see how you can add tool tips to your next application and delay its release by at least a week, try the following steps:

1 Load the Gossip project (Gossip.VBP).

2 Press Ctrl+R to display the Project window.

3 Click on the Gossip.FRM Form file and click on View Form.

4 Click on the View answers command button.

5 Double-click in the ToolTipText property in the Properties window.

6 Type "Displays an interesting dialog box." and then press Enter.

7 Press F5 to run your application.

8 Move the mouse over the View answers command button.

You'll see the tool tip.

9 Click on Exit.

☑ Progress Check

If you can do the following, you've mastered this lesson:

❑ Define what a tool tip is.

❑ Describe when to use tool tips.

❑ Add a tool tip to a Visual Basic object.

Figure 7-2: Tool tips are just another form of help.

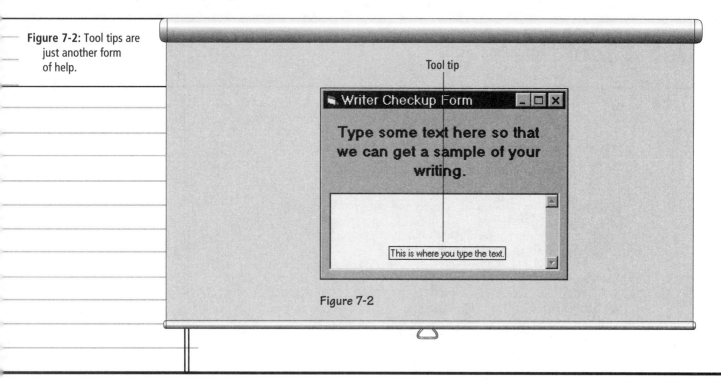

Figure 7-2

Unit 7 Quiz

For each of the following questions, circle the letter of the correct answer or answers. Unlike high school tests, some questions may have two or more correct answers. That forces you to think rather than guess at the answer for each question.

1. **What is the difference between a text box and a label?**

    A. Labels are used to pigeonhole complex ideas into simplistic terms, something politicians do all the time when they label a candidate liberal, conservative, or a loser. Text boxes have nothing to do with politics, much like 80 percent of the American people.

    B. A text box can only contain text. A label can only contain pictures of embarrassing moments from family vacations.

    C. A text box can display text or allow the user to type in text. A label can only display text.

    D. Text boxes are simply bigger versions of labels. Labels, on the other hand, are absolutely useless, so use text boxes all the time.

    E. A text box is where highly literate children go to play. A label is what highly ignorant adults use to identify large groups of people they don't understand, such as "Those bleeding-heart liberals" or "Those right-wingers."

2. **What is word-wrapping?**

   A. Word-wrapping is something that literate rap musicians use to get their message across in a song.

   B. Word-wrapping lets text flow or wrap around from one line to the next.

   C. Word-wrapping means that you can't see the contents of your text boxes or labels until you unwrap them first.

   D. Word-wrapping erases all of your text and keeps you from typing it into your computer ever again.

   E. This question is unimportant, and thus I refuse to answer it on the grounds that it may reveal my ignorance.

3. **If you want to align text in a text box, what two properties must you change?**

   A. You cannot change properties until they want to change.

   B. You set the MultiLine property to True and then you can set the Alignment property to Left Justify, Center, or Right Justify.

   C. Text boxes don't align themselves with anything. Just like Sweden and Switzerland, they try to stay neutral so that they can sell supplies to both sides.

   D. What's a text box?

   E. If you want to align text in a text box, you must align two properties that do something important, although I'm not quite sure what those two properties may be. But they're crucial.

4. **What happens if you set a label's AutoSize property to True and its WordWrap property to True?**

   A. You cannot set the AutoSize or WordWrap properties until you file the proper papers and forms at your local government office first.

   B. Catastrophic changes occur on the molecular level.

   C. The label word-wraps and adjusts its height automatically to accommodate the entire size of its caption.

   D. The AutoSize property means that the label will adjust its height automatically when you type in a really long caption. The WordWrap property means that text will word-wrap within the width of the label.

   E. Setting the AutoSize property to True makes sure that all your computer-related papers take up just enough space on your desk to look like a mess.

Notes:

5. **In which property does a text box store and display text? In which property does a label store and display text? In which of these questions do you get bombarded by more than one question?**

   A. Both the label and text box store text in the BorderStyle property. That's why giving your labels and text boxes pretty borders is important — so you can mask your text as hieroglyphics.

   B. Text boxes can hold text? Does that mean labels can only hold labels?

   C. The two most important properties on the Monopoly board are Park Place and Boardwalk. This has nothing to do with text boxes and labels, but it's important to know.

   D. The text box stores text in a label. Likewise, a label stores text in a text box. Because this is a circular reference, you'll never have to worry about the location of text ever again.

   E. The text box stores text in its Text property. The label stores text in its Caption property. (And question number five asks three questions.)

6. **You normally won't use tool tips with this object:**

   A. You normally won't use tool tips with labels, because the user can't interact with them.

   B. Tool tips aren't usable by any object, you have to force them to work.

   C. Visual Basic is too old and out of date to support a modern feature like tool tips.

   D. Most people won't find tool tips on a computer; they'll find them on PBS do-it-yourself shows instead.

   E. Only the Shadow knows what secrets lurk in the heart of your program.

Unit 7 Exercise

on the CD

1. Load the Gossip project (Gossip.VBP).

2. Press Ctrl+R to display the Project window.

3. Click on the Gossip.FRM Form file and click on View Form.

4. Click on the text box that appears next to the label What interesting thoughts does your boss have? Please be very descriptive.

5. Press F4 if necessary to display the Properties window.

6. Click in the ScrollBars property and change the setting to 1 - Horizontal.

7. Press F5.

8. Type text in the text box that appears next to the label. What interesting thoughts does your boss have? Please be very descriptive. Notice how the text box acts differently with horizontal scroll bars.

Making Menus

Objectives for This Unit

✓ Studying the basic elements of a pull-down menu bar

✓ Creating pull-down menus

✓ Writing BASIC code for your menu commands

Prerequisites

◆ Captioning command buttons (Lesson 5-1)

◆ Writing simple BASIC commands (Lesson 5-3)

◆ Wordfake.VBP

Users must choose different command options to make most programs do something. For example, if you're using a word-processing program, one command option checks your spelling, another prints your document, and another changes fonts.

Naturally, you can't make your program read users' minds. Instead, your program needs a way for the user to tell the program what to do next. For simple programs, big, fat command buttons plastered on the screen work, but if you have many commands to choose from, stuffing the commands into organized menus is easier for the user.

Nearly every Windows program uses *pull-down menus,* a list of which appears across the top of the screen. Click on the menu title, and a list of menu commands appears.

To make sure that your Visual Basic programs look just like the professional programs sold by large corporations, add pull-down menus and their close cousins, submenus and pop-up menus. Just like everything else with Visual Basic, designing menus for your program is simple, painless, and easy.

menu = on-screen display listing available command options

pull-down menu = list of command options you can access at the top of the screen

Lesson 8-1

Studying the Basic Elements of a Pull-Down Menu

Before you start designing your own pull-down menus, take some time to study the basic elements found in a typical pull-down menu. First, examine the elements in the menu bar at the top of the screen in Figure 8-1:

on the test

♦ **Menu captions:** Captions are the menu titles that appear on the screen and organize menu commands into logical categories. For example, all editing commands appear under the Edit menu title in Visual Basic. (The menu name, on the other hand, is how you refer to a menu when writing BASIC.)

♦ **Menu caption hot keys:** These let you choose a menu by pressing the Alt key plus the menu caption hot key. For example, in Visual Basic you can choose the File menu caption by pressing Alt and then pressing F.

Each individual menu can contain five more elements:

♦ **Menu commands:** These provide the actual commands you can choose to make the program do something.

♦ **Menu command hot keys:** Hot keys let you choose a menu command by typing its hot key. For example, after displaying the File menu, you can choose the Print command by typing **P**.

♦ **Menu command keystroke shortcuts:** Shortcuts display an alternate keystroke you can press to avoid using the pull-down menus. For example, pressing Ctrl+S to save your file means you don't have to use the File menu and choose the Save File command.

♦ **Separator bars:** These horizontal lines divide menu commands into logically organized groups within a pull-down menu.

♦ **Check marks:** These show which command is currently chosen.

heads up

Not all of these features are used in every pull-down menu. For example, some pull-down menus don't use check marks, while others won't display keystroke shortcuts for different menu commands. Check marks are mostly used only to show when a particular menu command is already selected, such as the currently selected form in the Window menu. Keystroke shortcuts are used only for those commands that you use often, such as Ctrl+S for the Save File command in the Visual Basic File menu.

☑ Progress Check

If you can do the following, you've mastered this lesson:

❑ Identify menu hot keys and explain what they do.

❑ Identify check marks or separator bars on a pull-down menu.

❑ Identify keyboard shortcuts for a menu command.

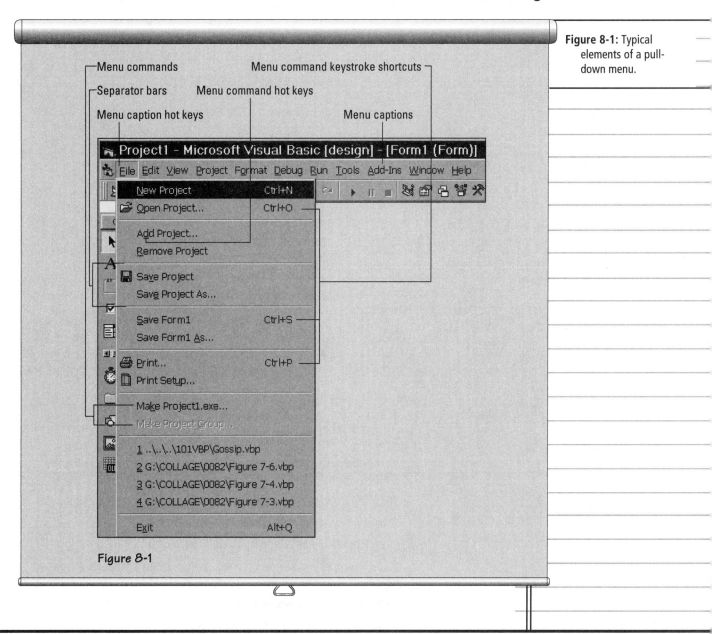

Figure 8-1: Typical elements of a pull-down menu.

Menu commands

Menu command keystroke shortcuts

Separator bars

Menu command hot keys

Menu caption hot keys

Menu captions

Project1 - Microsoft Visual Basic [design] - [Form1 (Form)]

File Edit View Project Format Debug Run Tools Add-Ins Window Help

New Project   Ctrl+N
Open Project...   Ctrl+O
Add Project...
Remove Project
Save Project
Save Project As...
Save Form1   Ctrl+S
Save Form1 As...
Print...   Ctrl+P
Print Setup...
Make Project1.exe...
Make Project Group...
1 ..\..\..\101VBP\Gossip.vbp
2 G:\COLLAGE\0082\Figure 7-6.vbp
3 G:\COLLAGE\0082\Figure 7-4.vbp
4 G:\COLLAGE\0082\Figure 7-3.vbp
Exit   Alt+Q

Figure 8-1

Creating Pull-Down Menus

Lesson 8-2

Use the Menu Editor to create pull-down menus for your Visual Basic programs. Just to keep you from getting bored, Visual Basic gives you four different ways to start the Menu Editor:

♦ Press Ctrl+E

♦ Choose Tools➪Menu Editor

Menu Editor can be started in four different ways

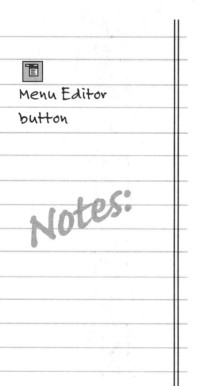

Menu Editor
button

▶ Right-click on the form and choose Menu Editor from the context menu

▶ Click on the Menu Editor button on the Toolbar

Any of the methods brings up the Menu Editor dialog box, shown in Figure 8-2.

When creating pull-down menus, you must define

▶ The menu caption

▶ The menu name

on the test

The *menu caption* is what the user sees on the screen. The *menu name* is never seen on the screen, but is how you refer to a particular menu when writing BASIC code for it. Captions and names are typed into their respective boxes on the Menu Editor dialog box.

heads up

Use the ampersand (&) character to define a hot key. For example, to create a File menu where F is the hot key, you type in **&File** for your menu caption.

Microsoft recommends that you use the mnu prefix plus the caption of your menu when naming a menu. For example, Microsoft recommends that the name of the Edit menu be mnuEdit and the name of the File menu be mnuFile.

Follow these steps to practice creating some common menus and a menu bar:

1 **Start Visual Basic. Select Standard EXE from the New Project dialog box, and then click on Open.**

2 **Right-click on the form and select the Menu Editor entry on the context menu.**

The Menu Editor dialog box appears.

3 **Type &File in the Caption box and press Tab.**

4 **Type mnuFile in the Name box and press Enter.**

Visual Basic displays &File in the menu control list box and moves the cursor back to the Caption box.

5 **Type &Edit in the Caption box and press Tab.**

6 **Type mnuEdit in the Name box and press Enter.**

7 **Type &View in the Caption box and press Tab.**

8 **Type mnuView in the Name box and press Enter.**

9 **Type &Window in the Caption box and press Tab.**

10 **Type mnuWindow in the Name box and press Enter.**

11 **Type &Help in the Caption box and press Tab.**

12 **Type mnuHelp in the Name box and press Enter.**

13 **Click on OK.**

Visual Basic displays your newly created menu bar, as shown in Figure 8-3.

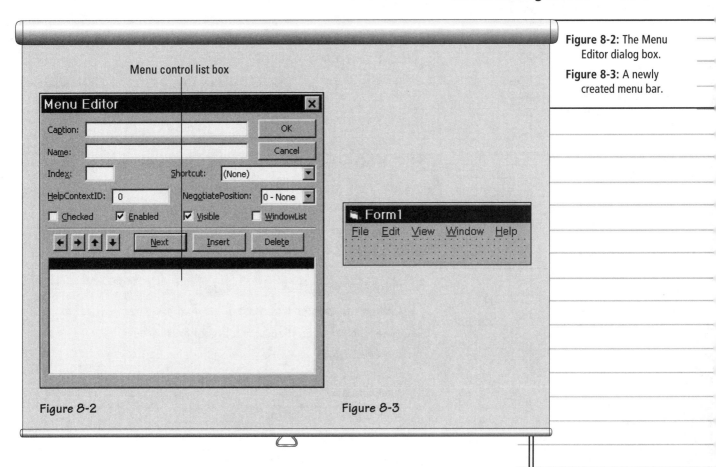

Menu control list box

Figure 8-2

Figure 8-3

Figure 8-2: The Menu Editor dialog box.

Figure 8-3: A newly created menu bar.

Creating menu commands

After you've created the menu titles to appear on your menu bar (see Figure 8-3), the next step is to create menu commands that appear in a list underneath each menu. For example, underneath the File menu you may have commands such as Open, Save, Print, and Exit.

Tip: Look at other applications to get a good idea of how to structure your menus. Larger applications like Microsoft Word or CorelDRAW! provide a wealth of ideas.

try to group menu commands into their logical categories

When naming menu commands, Microsoft recommends that you use the `mnu` prefix followed by the menu title plus the menu command. For example, the Open command underneath the File menu would be named `mnuFileOpen`.

Creating menu commands involves typing in the menu control list box, the big white area shown at the bottom of Figure 8-2. To create menu commands, follow these steps:

Menu command names = mnu prefix plus menu title plus menu command

1 Click on the Menu Editor button in the Toolbar.

The Menu Editor dialog box appears.

2 Click on &Edit to highlight it in the Menu Control list box.

Notes:

3 **Click on Insert.**

Visual Basic creates a blank line underneath the &File entry in the Menu control list box.

4 **Click on the right arrow.**

Visual Basic displays four dots, as shown in Figure 8-4.

5 **Click in the Caption box, type** &Open, **and press Tab.**

6 **Type** mnuFileOpen **in the Name box and press Enter.**

7 **Click on Insert.**

Visual Basic creates a blank line underneath the &Open entry in the Menu control list box.

8 **Click on the right arrow.**

Visual Basic displays four dots (see Figure 8-4).

9 **Click in the Caption box, type** &Save, **and press Tab.**

10 **Type** mnuFileSave **in the Name box and press Enter.**

11 **Click on Insert.**

Visual Basic creates a blank line underneath the &Save entry in the Menu control list box.

12 **Click on the right arrow.**

Visual Basic displays four dots (see Figure 8-4).

13 **Click in the Caption box, type** E&xit, **and press Tab.**

14 **Type** mnuFileExit **in the Name box.**

15 **Click on OK.**

16 **Click on the File menu title.**

The menu commands Open, Save, and Exit appear underneath the File menu, as shown in Figure 8-5.

Adding keystroke shortcuts

on the test

Pulling down a menu and choosing a command over and over again can be tedious. To provide a shortcut, many programs allow you to press a keystroke combination, such as Ctrl+C, thereby letting you choose a specific command without pulling down a single menu.

Tip: You'll reduce the learning curve for your program if you use the same keyboard shortcuts that other applications do. For example, use Ctrl+S for the File⇨Save menu command.

To help people remember the keystroke shortcuts for a specific command, you can assign a keystroke shortcut to any menu command and have that shortcut appear right next to the menu command.

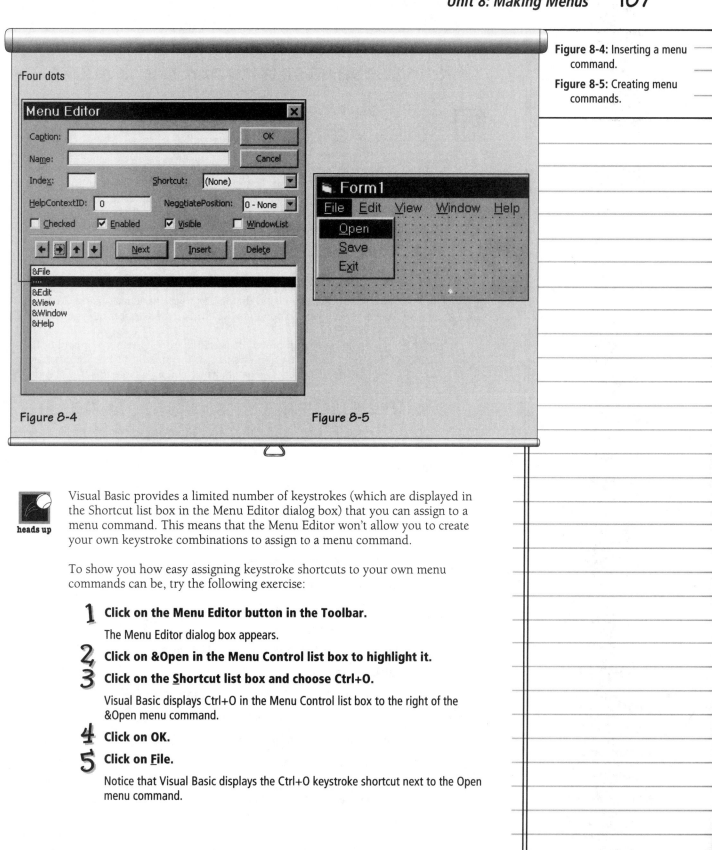

Four dots

Figure 8-4

Figure 8-5

Figure 8-4: Inserting a menu command.

Figure 8-5: Creating menu commands.

Visual Basic provides a limited number of keystrokes (which are displayed in the Shortcut list box in the Menu Editor dialog box) that you can assign to a menu command. This means that the Menu Editor won't allow you to create your own keystroke combinations to assign to a menu command.

To show you how easy assigning keystroke shortcuts to your own menu commands can be, try the following exercise:

1 Click on the Menu Editor button in the Toolbar.

The Menu Editor dialog box appears.

2 Click on &Open in the Menu Control list box to highlight it.

3 Click on the Shortcut list box and choose Ctrl+O.

Visual Basic displays Ctrl+O in the Menu Control list box to the right of the &Open menu command.

4 Click on OK.

5 Click on File.

Notice that Visual Basic displays the Ctrl+O keystroke shortcut next to the Open menu command.

Adding separator bars and check marks

on the test

Separator bars and check marks are also important menu elements. Separator bars allow you to group related commands together and avoid overwhelming your users with long lists of menu commands.

Check marks serve a different need. When you choose some menu commands, the command chosen is obvious from the resulting action. For example, when you choose E̲xit, a program ends. However, other menu commands simply turn on (or turn off) a certain feature, such as a command to display the toolbar or ruler. To show the user which commands are turned on (or off), you can have check marks appear next to a menu command. That way a user can see, at a glance, whether a particular command is turned on or not.

heads up

You can make check marks appear next to a menu command in two ways. The first way is to use the Menu Editor dialog box to specify check marks. The second way is to use BASIC code to make check marks appear or disappear.

In case you want to add or remove check marks from a menu command by using BASIC code, you have to know the menu command name. For example, to put a check mark next to the Open command, you would use this BASIC code:

```
mnuFileOpen.Checked = True
```

To remove a check mark, you would use this BASIC code:

```
mnuFileOpen.Checked = False
```

To see how to create check marks next to menu commands using the Menu Editor dialog box, try the following:

Menu Editor button

1 **Click on the Menu Editor button in the Toolbar.**

The Menu Editor dialog box appears.

2 **Click on &Save in the Menu Control list box to highlight it.**

3 **Click in the Checked check box.**

Visual Basic displays a check mark.

4 **Click on E&xit in the Menu Control list box.**

5 **Click on I̲nsert.**

6 **Type a dash (—) in the Caption box and press Tab.**

This step creates the separator bar for your menu.

7 **Type mnuBar in the Na̲me box and click on OK.**

8 **Click on the F̲ile menu.**

Notice that Visual Basic displays a check mark next to the S̲ave command and a separator bar between the S̲ave and the E̲xit commands.

using separator bars and check marks in a pull-down menu

Rearranging menu titles and commands

In case you haven't noticed by now, menu commands appear indented underneath menu titles in the Menu Control list box. If you want, you can rearrange menu titles and commands in the Menu Control list box.

heads up

If you move menu titles or commands around, you may want to change the name of your menu commands. For example, if the Exit command appears underneath the File menu, name the command mnuFileExit. But if you suddenly decide to move the Exit command underneath the Edit menu, change the menu name to mnuEditExit.

You can rearrange items listed in the Menu Control list box with four different commands:

- ▶ **Up:** Moves menu titles to the left of the menu bar or menu commands to the top of the pull-down menu
- ▶ **Down:** Moves menu titles to the right of the menu bar or menu commands to the bottom of the pull-down menu
- ▶ **Right:** Indents items to appear as menu commands
- ▶ **Left:** Unindents items to appear as menu titles

To see how easy rearranging menu titles and menu commands is, follow these steps:

1 **Click on the Menu Editor button in the Toolbar.**

The Menu Editor dialog box appears.

2 **Click on &Save in the Menu Control list box to highlight it.**

3 **Click in the Checked check box to clear it.**

4 **Click on the Left arrow button, shown in Figure 8-6, and then click on OK.**

Notice that the Save command appears as a menu title sandwiched between the File and the Edit menu titles.

5 **Press Ctrl+E.**

The Menu Editor dialog box appears.

6 **Click on &Save in the Menu Control list box to highlight it.**

7 **Click on the Right arrow button once, click on the Down arrow once, and then click on OK.**

8 **Click on the File menu.**

Notice that the Save command appears sandwiched between the separator bar and the Exit command.

9 **Press Ctrl+E.**

The Menu Editor dialog box appears.

Notes:

Figure 8-6: The four buttons for rearranging a menu item.

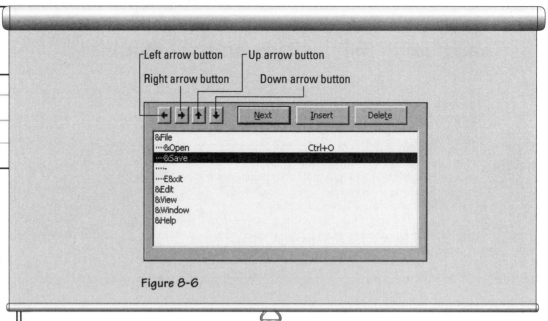

Figure 8-6

☑ Progress Check

If you can do the following, you've mastered this lesson:

❑ Create a menu command to appear underneath a menu title.

❑ Make a check mark appear next to a menu command.

❑ Add a keyboard shortcut to represent a menu command.

❑ Add separator bars within a pull-down menu.

❑ Rearrange menu titles and menu commands.

10 Click on &Save in the Menu Control list box to highlight it.

11 Click on the Up arrow button and click on OK.

Recess

If you're creating simple programs, you won't need to use pull-down menus. But if you're creating fairly complicated programs, then pull-down menus can organize commands so users can find them easily — theoretically.

The next time you're using your word processor or spreadsheet, dig through its pull-down menus and see if you like the way they're arranged. If the answer is no, then you'll know better ways to design your own pull-down menus in Visual Basic.

Lesson 8-3

Writing BASIC Code for Your Menu Commands

learn more about writing really powerful BASIC code in Units 11 through 15

After designing your pull-down menus, guess what? They do absolutely nothing until you write BASIC code to tell them how to work. To write BASIC code for a menu command, you have to pull down the menu containing the menu command that you want to write BASIC code for. Then click on that menu command to display the Code window.

To show you how simple writing BASIC code for your pull-down menus can be, try the following exercises:

1 Click on the <u>F</u>ile menu in the menu bar that you created in the previous lessons.

2 Click on the <u>O</u>pen command that appears underneath the File menu.

The Code window for the <u>O</u>pen command appears.

3 Type so the entire event procedure looks like the following:

```
Private Sub mnuFileOpen_Click ()
 MsgBox "You chose the Open command", 48, "Open
           Command"
End Sub
```

This BASIC code tells Visual Basic, "When the user chooses the Open command underneath the File menu, display a message box on the screen."

4 Click in the Object list box in the Code window and choose **mnuFileExit.**

A new event procedure appears.

5 Type so the entire event procedure looks like the following:

```
Private Sub mnuFileExit_Click ()
 End
End Sub
```

6 Press F5.

7 Click on the <u>F</u>ile menu and choose <u>O</u>pen.

The message dialog box that you created in step 3 appears.

8 Click on OK.

9 Press Ctrl+O.

Notice that the dialog box that you saw in step 7 appears again.

10 Click on OK.

11 Click in the <u>F</u>ile menu and choose E<u>x</u>it.

Visual Basic stops the program.

12 Click in the close box of the Code window to make it go away.

Notes:

☑ **Progress Check**

If you can do the following, you've mastered this lesson:

❑ Open the Code window to write BASIC code for a menu command.

❑ Understand why you need to write BASIC code to make your menu commands do something.

Notes:

extra credit

Submenus and pop-up menus

Besides creating pull-down menus, Visual Basic also lets you create submenus and pop-up menus. A *submenu* acts like a miniature pull-down menu. To access a submenu, you have to display a pull-down menu first (such as from the File or Edit menu) and then choose the submenu. Because submenus require you to wade through one or more menus just to find a command, many programs avoid using submenus.

A pop-up menu tends to be more popular because it pops up a tiny menu every time you click on the right mouse button. For those of you using Windows 95, click on the right mouse button while pointing the mouse anywhere on the screen and you'll see a tiny menu pop-up menu next to the mouse pointer.

Pop-up menus provide the most common commands you're likely to use at the moment. Submenus provide advanced commands that few people ever need.

Unit 8 Quiz

Circle the letter of the correct answer for each of the following questions. Some questions may have more than one correct answer.

1. **What does a menu hot key do?**

   A. A hot key describes a cheap keyboard where the keys rub off if you strike them too often.

   B. Hot keys are used to keep people from using commands they're not competent enough to use without supervision. If they try to touch the wrong key, the computer burns their fingers.

   C. A hot key lets you use your keyboard to choose a command from a pull-down menu.

   D. A hot key simply looks good but doesn't do anything important, like many of today's politicians.

   E. Hot keys are the keys on your keyboard that someone has stolen. That's why they're called hot keys.

2. **What is the difference between a menu caption and a menu name?**

   A. The menu caption displays subtitles for users who don't understand English.

   B. The menu caption appears on the screen. The menu name simply identifies the menu command for writing BASIC code.

   C. A menu caption and a menu name are two different words for the same thing. Just look it up in a thesaurus.

   D. The menu caption is purely decorative and can display an under-lined hot key. The menu name identifies the menu command and usually begins with the prefix mnu, such as `mnuFileSave`.

   E. Menu captions and menu names don't get along and spend most of their time trying to eradicate one another from your computer.

3. **What do separator bars do in a menu?**

   A. They keep menu commands from moving around and confusing you.

   B. They help make the program easier to use, because anything with the word "bar" in it is sure to attract the attention of underage drinkers.

   C. Separator bars divide related commands in a pull-down menu so viewing them all is easier.

   D. They separate the appetizers from the entrees.

   E. Separator bars help keep your program from slipping off your hard disk and escaping into the wild.

4. **Why would you want to assign a keystroke shortcut to a menu command?**

   A. Just to give you something to do and make you feel like you're being productive.

   B. A keystroke shortcut lets users choose a command by pressing keys such as Ctrl+O without bothering to use the pull-down menus.

   C. Keystroke shortcuts are used to make finding and using a command buried inside a pull-down menu even harder.

   D. You would want to assign a keystroke shortcut to a menu command when you can't figure out any other way to make your program look more complicated than it really is.

   E. There is no reason to assign a keystroke shortcut to a menu com-mand. This is a trick question designed to make you feel like you're back in high school, taking tests that will have no relevance whatsoever to the rest of your life.

5. What are the advantages of a pop-up menu over a submenu?

A. Submenus are a lower form of menus that have not yet evolved thumbs or broken off their tails. Pop-up menus are thus genetically superior to submenus from an evolutionary point of view.

B. A pop-up menu appears on top of anything else displayed on your screen. A submenu appears underneath anything displayed on your screen. Thus, you can never see a submenu without turning off your computer first.

C. A pop-up menu is easier to use because it appears when you click on the right mouse button. A submenu is harder to use because you have to dig through several menus just to display it.

D. You can put a pop-up menu in your toaster but submenus can only be used underwater.

E. A submenu buries commands in another layer of menus and is harder for the user to find. A pop-up menu avoids pull-down menus completely and just displays a simple menu when you click on the right mouse button.

Unit 8 Exercise

on the CD

1. Load the WordFake project (WordFake.VBP).

2. Press Ctrl+R to display the Project window.

3. Right click on the Edit.FRM Form file and choose View Object from the context menu.

4. Right-click on the form and select Menu Editor from the context menu to display the Menu Editor dialog box.

5. Scroll through the Menu Control list box to see how the menus and submenus appear.

6. Click on OK to close the Menu Editor dialog box.

7. Press F5.

8. Click in the Settings menu to see how submenus look.

9. Type some text.

10. Move the mouse pointer in the middle of the form and click on the right mouse button to see a pop-up menu appear.

11. Choose File⇨Exit in the WordFake program to exit the program.

Displaying Dialog Boxes

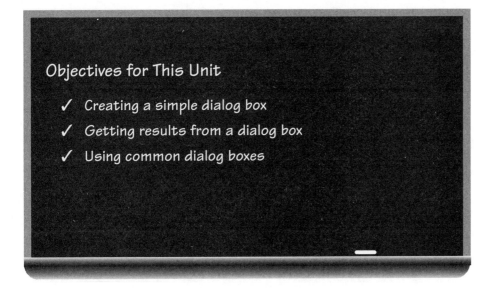

Objectives for This Unit

✓ Creating a simple dialog box

✓ Getting results from a dialog box

✓ Using common dialog boxes

Prerequisites

▶ Using the Toolbox (Lesson 1-2)

▶ Opening the Code window (Lesson 1-2)

▶ Writing simple BASIC commands (Lesson 5-3)

▶ Common.VBP

▶ Dialog.VBP

on the CD

on the test

Most times when you interact with the computer, you press a key or click on the mouse to tell the computer what you want the machine to do, and then the computer responds by either obeying your command or (more likely) displaying a cryptic error message that makes absolutely no sense whatsoever.

But when the computer needs to display a message or ask you for more information, a small window known as a *dialog box* is typically displayed. Dialog boxes are so named because when you use a computer, you carry on a dialogue with the machine, at least in the imagination of computer scientists. The dialog box is your computer's way of saying, "Hey, I don't know what to do next, so tell me." Then you type or click in the dialog box and the computer cheerfully obeys your command.

Not surprisingly, Visual Basic makes creating dialog boxes for your programs an easy task, as you will discover in this unit.

dialog box = an on-screen message box that conveys information or requests information from the user

Lesson 9-1 Creating a Simple Dialog Box

on the test

When creating a simple dialog box, you need to define three elements, as illustrated in Figure 9-1:

▶ A message

▶ A dialog box title

▶ An eye-catching, descriptive icon

All dialog boxes require some kind of response mechanism so that the user can converse with the computer. Simple dialog boxes normally provide one or more command buttons, such as the OK button shown in Figure 9-1. Even though the OK button is included automatically, you can tell Visual Basic to include other kinds of buttons, such as Cancel.

Just so you can see how amazingly simple creating a dialog box is, try the following (this exercise assumes you have Visual Basic open with a Standard EXE on screen):

1 Double-click on the Command Button icon in the Toolbox.

Visual Basic draws a command button on the form.

2 Double-click on the command button you just drew.

Visual Basic displays the Code window.

3 Type MsgBox **right below Command1_Click() and then press Space.**

Visual Basic displays a *Quick Info pop up* like the one shown in Figure 9-2. The Quick Info pop up is Visual Basic's way of telling you what kind of information it needs. You can always see the Quick Info pop up by right-clicking on the function name in the Code window and then choosing Quick Info from the context menu.

4 Type so the entire command button event procedure looks like this:

```
Private Sub Command1_Click()
 MsgBox "Turn in your two-week notice", 16, "What to
             do if you win the lottery"
End Sub
```

This BASIC code tells Visual Basic, "Display a dialog box on the screen with the phrase 'What to do if you win the lottery' in the title bar of the dialog box; the phrase 'Turn in your two-week notice' in the middle of the dialog box; and a Critical Message icon (represented by a value of 16)."

5 Press F5 to start the program.

6 Click on your command button.

Visual Basic displays your dialog box (see Figure 9-1).

7 Click on OK and then click on the End button in the Toolbar.

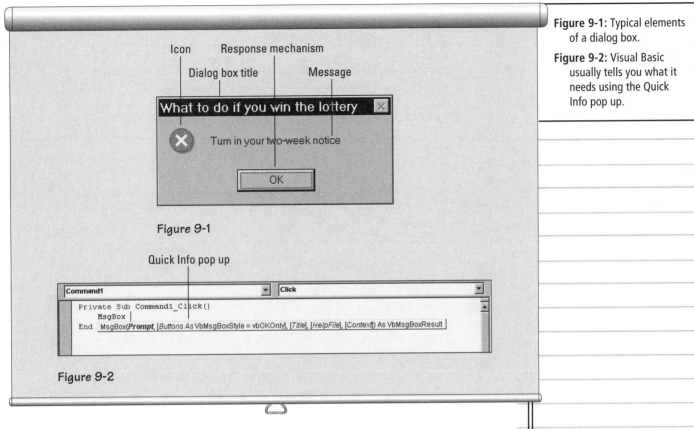

Icon Response mechanism

Dialog box title Message

What to do if you win the lottery

Turn in your two-week notice

OK

Figure 9-1

Quick Info pop up

```
Command1                                    Click
    Private Sub Command1_Click()
        MsgBox |
    End   MsgBox(Prompt, [Buttons As VbMsgBoxStyle = vbOKOnly], [Title], [HelpFile], [Context]) As VbMsgBoxResult
```

Figure 9-2

Figure 9-1: Typical elements of a dialog box.

Figure 9-2: Visual Basic usually tells you what it needs using the Quick Info pop up.

8 **Right-click on the 16 that you typed in the Code window and then choose List Constants from the context menu.**

Visual Basic displays the List Constants pop up shown in Figure 9-3. A *constant* is a human readable form of a number. It allows you to see what a particular value will do without having to remember a lot of strange numbers. Constants represent numbers; they don't replace them — that's a very important thing to remember.

9 **Double-click on the vbCritical entry of the List Constants pop up.**

Visual Basic replaces the number 16 in your code with vbCritical.

10 **Press F5 to start the program.**

11 **Click on your command button.**

Visual Basic displays the same dialog box that it did before (see Figure 9-1).

12 **Click on OK and then on the End button in the Toolbar.**

heads up

Visual Basic lets you display four different kinds of icons in a dialog box. You tell Visual Basic which of the four icons you want by typing in a number in the MsgBox part of the command button event procedure. The number 16 displays the Critical Message icon; 32 displays the Warning Query icon; 48 displays the Warning Message icon; and 64 displays the Information Message icon.

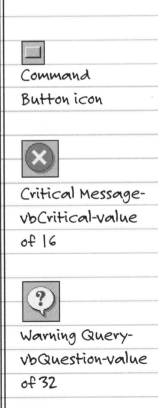

Command
Button icon

Critical Message-
vbCritical-value
of 16

Warning Query-
vbQuestion-value
of 32

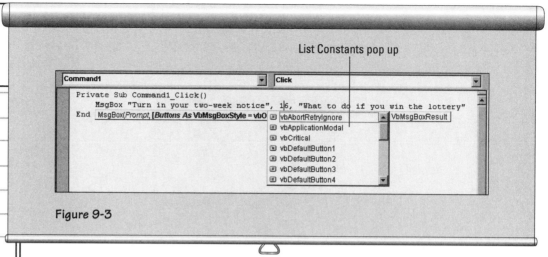

List Constants pop up

Figure 9-3

Progress Check

If you can do the following, you've mastered this lesson:

❑ Create a simple dialog box.

❑ Modify the message, title, and icon in a dialog box.

heads up

Visual Basic also provides something called a *constant.* Programmers found that keeping track of what various numbers meant was difficult, so they started using a piece of text to represent the number. For example, you can use `vbCritical` to represent the number 16. A constant always represents a single unchanging value — usually a number.

Go back to step 3, replace the number 16 with 32, 48, or 64, and run the program again to see a different icon appear. Make sure that you try out the constant values as well. Just right-click on the number you typed, choose List Constants from the context menu, and then select a value from the List Constants pop up.

Lesson 9-2   Getting Results from a Dialog Box

The simplest dialog boxes just display a message from the computer without giving users a chance to respond, other than to click on OK. In most cases, however, a dialog box needs a reply from the user. For example, when you delete a file, most programs display a dialog box verifying if you really want to delete the file; you respond Yes or No.

Displaying different types of command buttons

Visual Basic gives you six different command button combinations to display in a dialog box. You can tell Visual Basic which combination you want by including the appropriate value, shown in Table 9-1, in your dialog box code. Notice that you can use a constant in place of a number to make your code more readable.

use constant values in place of numbers to make code more readable

Figure 9-4

Figure 9-4: A dialog box displaying Yes and No command buttons.

Table 9-1 Command Button Display Values

Command Button	Value to Use	Constant
OK	0	vbOKOnly
OK and Cancel	1	vbOKCancel
Abort, Retry, and Ignore	2	vbAbortRetryIgnore
Yes, No, and Cancel	3	vbYesNoCancel
Yes and No	4	vbYesNo
Retry and Cancel	5	vbRetryCancel

To see how these command button values work and to continue your Visual Basic education, follow these steps to create a dialog box that displays different types of command buttons:

1 **Double-click on the command button you drew in Lesson 9-1.**

The Code window appears.

2 **Modify the event procedure so it looks like the following:**

```
Private Sub Command1_Click()
 MsgBox "Do you want to turn in your two-week
        notice?", vbYesNo, "You just won the
        lottery"
End Sub
```

3 **Press F5.**

4 **Click on the command button.**

Notice that Visual Basic now displays a dialog box with Yes and No command buttons, as shown in Figure 9-4.

5 **Click on Yes.**

six different dialog box command button combinations in Visual Basic

learn more about BASIC code in Part III

Notes:

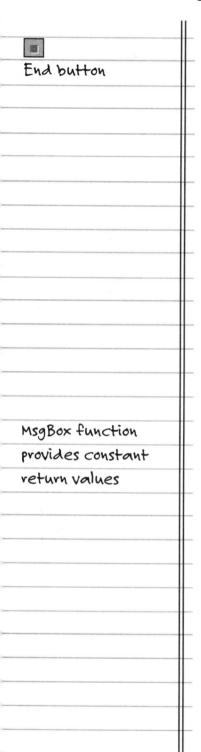

End button

MsgBox function
provides constant
return values

6 **Click on the End button in the Toolbar.**

If you want to include one of the four icons described in Lesson 9-1, you just have to type both numbers in the MsgBox command, such as:

```
MsgBox "Do you want to turn in your two-week notice?",
       vbYesNo Or vbCritical, "You just won the
       lottery"
```

Now that you have asked the user for a specific reply, you need to know how to tell which command button the user chose.

Getting a reply from a dialog box

After you've created a dialog box that gives the user two or more command buttons to choose from, you need to know which command button the user chooses. For example, suppose your program displays a dialog box that asks the user, "Do you really want to turn in your two-week notice?" If the user clicks on the Yes button, then another dialog box can pop up where the user types a resignation to the boss. If the user clicks on the No button, the program does nothing.

Fortunately, when someone chooses a command button in a dialog box, Visual Basic assigns a number telling you which command button was clicked. Then you can write BASIC code to find out what command button the user clicked on so your program can take the appropriate action.

Table 9-2 shows the different values Visual Basic uses to represent different command buttons. Notice that there are constants for return values, just like there are constants for icon and button values.

Table 9-2	Reply Values for Command Buttons	
If User Clicks on This Command Button	*This Is Its Value*	*Constant*
OK	1	vbOK
Cancel	2	vbCancel
Abort	3	vbAbort
Retry	4	vbRetry
Ignore	5	vbIgnore
Yes	6	vbYes
No	7	vbNo

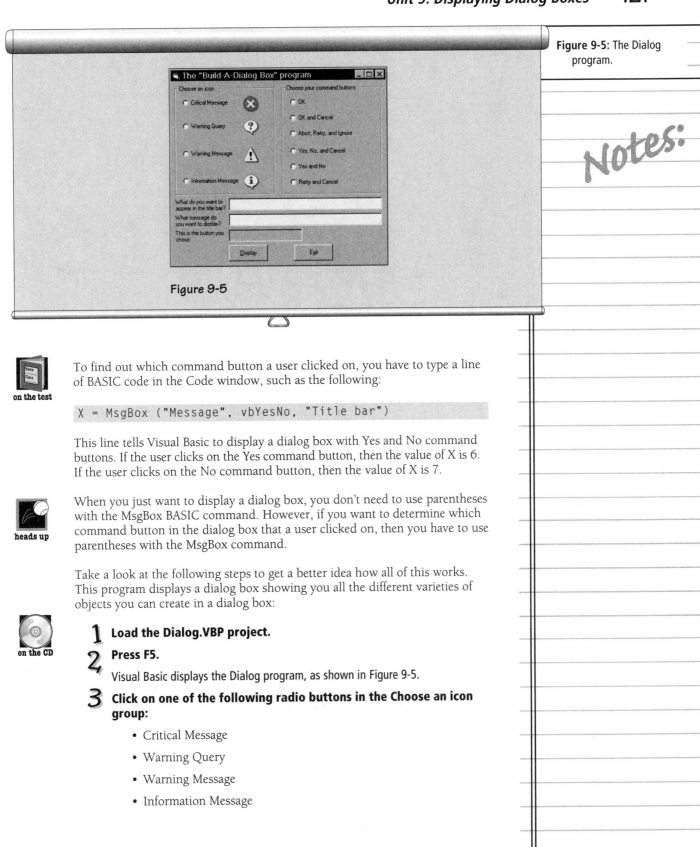

Figure 9-5: The Dialog program.

Figure 9-5

Notes:

on the test

To find out which command button a user clicked on, you have to type a line of BASIC code in the Code window, such as the following:

```
X = MsgBox ("Message", vbYesNo, "Title bar")
```

This line tells Visual Basic to display a dialog box with Yes and No command buttons. If the user clicks on the Yes command button, then the value of X is 6. If the user clicks on the No command button, then the value of X is 7.

heads up

When you just want to display a dialog box, you don't need to use parentheses with the MsgBox BASIC command. However, if you want to determine which command button in the dialog box that a user clicked on, then you have to use parentheses with the MsgBox command.

Take a look at the following steps to get a better idea how all of this works. This program displays a dialog box showing you all the different varieties of objects you can create in a dialog box:

on the CD

1 Load the Dialog.VBP project.

2 Press F5.

Visual Basic displays the Dialog program, as shown in Figure 9-5.

3 Click on one of the following radio buttons in the Choose an icon group:

- Critical Message
- Warning Query
- Warning Message
- Information Message

4 **Click on one of the following radio buttons in the Choose your command buttons group:**

- OK
- OK and Cancel
- Abort, Retry, and Ignore
- Yes, No, and Cancel
- Yes and No
- Retry and Cancel

5 **Type something in the text box that appears next to the What do you want to appear in the title bar? label.**

6 **Type something in the text box that appears next to the What message do you want to display? label.**

7 **Click on Display.**

Visual Basic displays a dialog box custom-built to your specifications.

8 **Click on any button in the dialog box.**

Visual Basic names the button you clicked on in the label that appears next to the This is the button you chose: label.

9 **Click on Exit.**

10 **Press Ctrl+R to display the Project window and click on View Code.**

11 **Click in the Object list box in the Code window and choose cmdDisplay.**

Browse through the cmdDisplay_Click event procedure to see how the BASIC code creates a dialog box based on the radio buttons you choose and the text you type into the txtMessage and the txtTitle text boxes.

Recess

Dialog boxes make it easy for you to display messages or ask additional information from the user without writing much BASIC code. Just remember that displaying a dialog box and making it actually work are two different topics.

☑ **Progress Check**

If you can do the following, you've mastered this lesson:

❑ Write BASIC code to display different types of command buttons on a dialog box.

❑ Write BASIC code to determine which command button the user chose.

Lesson 9-3

Using Common Dialog Boxes

Visual Basic lets you create common dialog boxes to open, save, or print files, making programming even easier. Of course, although creating these dialog boxes is easy, you have to write BASIC code to make them do any real work.

on the test

To create a common dialog box, click on the Common Dialog icon in the Toolbox and draw the Common Dialog icon on a form. Then you use BASIC code to tell Visual Basic which of the following five dialog box types to display:

- ◗ Open
- ◗ Save As
- ◗ Print
- ◗ Color
- ◗ Font

To choose which dialog box you want the Common Dialog icon to display, you have to write BASIC code that identifies the dialog box you want. Table 9-3 shows the values Visual Basic uses to represent different dialog boxes.

Table 9-3   Selecting a Dialog Box with BASIC Code

To Display This Dialog Box	Use This BASIC Code
Open	CommonDialog1.Action = 1
Save As	CommonDialog1.Action = 2
Color	CommonDialog1.Action = 3
Font	CommonDialog1.Action = 4
Print	CommonDialog1.Action = 5

To show how you can use the common dialog box to display an Open dialog box to pick a file, try the following and see what happens:

1 **Choose File⇨New Project and then open a Standard EXE project using the New Project dialog box.**

2 **Look for a Common Dialog icon in your Toolbox. If you have one, skip to step 6.**

3 **Right-click on the Toolbox and then choose Components from the context menu.**

Visual Basic displays the Components dialog box shown in Figure 9-6.

4 **Check the Microsoft Common Dialog Control 5.0 entry highlighted in Figure 9-6.**

5 **Click on OK.**

Congratulations! You've just added a new component to your Toolbox.

6 **Double-click on the Common Dialog icon in the Toolbox.**

Visual Basic automatically draws the Common Dialog icon on your form.

7 **Double-click on the Command Button icon in the Toolbox.**

Visual Basic draws a command button for you.

Notes:

Common Dialog icon

Command Button icon

Figure 9-6: The Components dialog box.

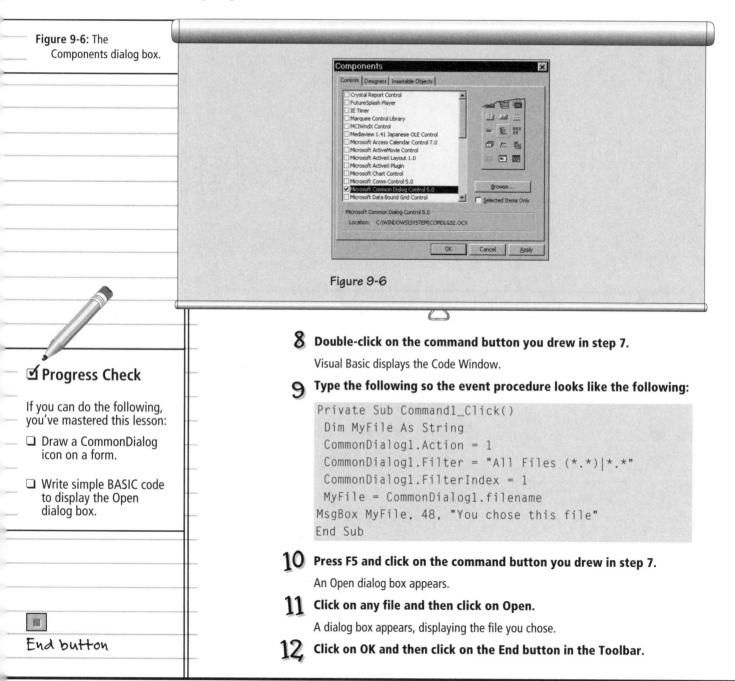

Figure 9-6

End button

8 **Double-click on the command button you drew in step 7.**

Visual Basic displays the Code Window.

9 **Type the following so the event procedure looks like the following:**

```
Private Sub Command1_Click()
 Dim MyFile As String
 CommonDialog1.Action = 1
 CommonDialog1.Filter = "All Files (*.*)|*.*"
 CommonDialog1.FilterIndex = 1
 MyFile = CommonDialog1.filename
MsgBox MyFile, 48, "You chose this file"
End Sub
```

10 **Press F5 and click on the command button you drew in step 7.**

An Open dialog box appears.

11 **Click on any file and then click on Open.**

A dialog box appears, displaying the file you chose.

12 **Click on OK and then click on the End button in the Toolbar.**

Unit 9 Quiz

Circle the letter of the correct answer or answers for each of the following questions. Some of the questions may have more than one correct answer.

1. **What is the purpose of a dialog box?**

    A. A dialog box lets your program carry on a "conversation" with the user, such as asking for additional information or confirmation.

    B. A dialog box lets you talk to your computer and give it verbal commands — not that it will do anything with them.

    C. A dialog box holds all the words you've ever spoken to your computer, so talk nicely to your computer or you may be embarrassed in the future.

    D. A dialog box is supposed to cover up a crucial part of the screen while you use a program.

    E. Dialog boxes have only one purpose in life: to make you completely happy in every way possible. Is it working yet?

2. **What does the MsgBox BASIC command do?**

    A. The MsgBox command lets loose a virus on your hard disk that will wipe out everything you own.

    B. The MsgBox command displays an error message at random on the screen.

    C. The MsgBox command blanks out your screen so your boss can't see that you really play games instead of work on your computer.

    D. The MsgBox command displays a dialog box on the screen.

    E. The MsgBox command lets you store any messages that you don't want to read or reply to right away.

3. **What are the three basic elements that you need to define to create a simple dialog box?**

    A. Color, shape, and texture.

    B. Dialog boxes are highly complex creations that cannot be defined by just three basic elements.

    C. Salt, food coloring, and fat. No wait, those are the three basic elements of a typical hot dog.

    D. A title, a message, and a descriptive icon.

    E. Hydrogen, helium, and copper.

4. **If you create a dialog box with two or more command buttons, how can you tell which command button someone clicked on?**

    A. Display another dialog box and ask the user to type in the name of the command button he or she clicked in the previous dialog box.

    B. Dust each command button for fingerprints.

    C. Use BASIC code to store the result, such as:

    ```
    X = MsgBox ("Message", 4, "Title bar")
    ```

D. Just ignore anything the user tries to do, because your program obviously knows what to do without some person meddling in its affairs.

E. Keep displaying the same dialog box over and over again until the user chooses the command button you want him or her to choose.

5. What does the CommonDialog icon do?

A. The CommonDialog icon lets you create one of the following five dialog boxes: Open, Save As, Print, Color, or Font.

B. The CommonDialog icon prevents other people from modifying your program by throwing useless dialog boxes on the screen at random.

C. Uh, can I go back and look for the answer?

D. The CommonDialog icon helps clutter your user interface with even more cryptic icons to paralyze users with the fear that they'll never be able to learn how to use a computer.

E. The CommonDialog icon looks fairly innocent until you click on it. Then the icon blows up your computer in a spectacular display of pyrotechnics.

Unit 9 Exercise

on the CD

1. Load the Common.VBP Project.

2. Press Ctrl+R to display the Project window.

3. Click on the Common.FRM Form file and click on View Object.

4. Double-click on the Open radio button.

5. Modify the second line in the event procedure so the whole thing looks like the following (the bold is what you type):

```
Private Sub optOpen_Click()
   CommonDialog1.Filter = "Text Files (*.TXT)|*.TXT"
  CommonDialog1.FilterIndex = 1
CommonDialog1.Action = 1
End Sub
```

This BASIC code tells Visual Basic, "Use the common dialog icon on the form to display an Open dialog box. Filter out all file names so only those files with the .TXT file extension appear."

6. Press F5 and click on the Open radio button.

7. Notice that the Open dialog box now only displays files that end with the .TXT file extension.

8. Click on Cancel.

9. Click on Exit.

List Boxes and Combo Boxes

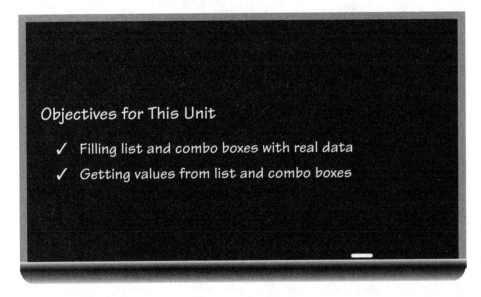

Objectives for This Unit

✓ Filling list and combo boxes with real data

✓ Getting values from list and combo boxes

Prerequisites

▶ Using the Toolbox to draw objects on a form (Lesson 4-1)

▶ Opening the Properties window and changing properties (Lesson 3-1)

▶ Making check boxes and radio buttons colorful (Lesson 6-2)

▶ Refund.VBP

on the CD

Sometimes you may need to provide your program's user with several options. For example, if the user wants to change the appearance of text, your program may ask the user what font, point size, and style to use. Rather than overwhelm the user with endless radio buttons or check boxes, Visual Basic provides two alternatives: list boxes and combo boxes.

A list box displays a list of options the user can choose from, as shown in Figure 10-1. A combo box is a combination (that's where the term *combo* comes from) of the features of a list box and an ordinary text box. Like a list box, the user can choose from a list of options. But like a text box (discussed in Unit 7), you can also type your own answer in the box.

Remember: If you want to force users to choose from a limited number of choices, use a list box. If you want to offer users a list to choose from or give them the option of typing in something themselves, use a combo box.

list boxes give a user a limited number of choices

combo boxes give users a list and the option to type in another choice

Figure 10-1: Typical uses
for list boxes and combo
boxes.

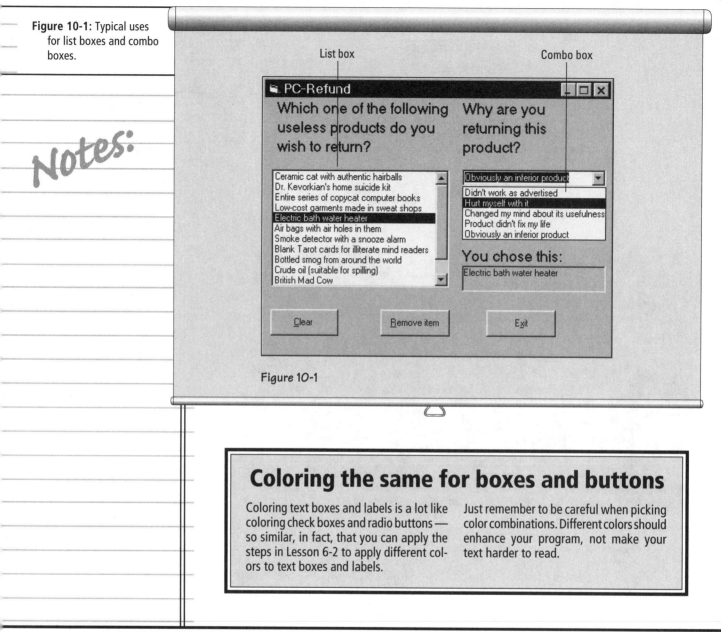

List box

Combo box

Figure 10-1

Coloring the same for boxes and buttons

Coloring text boxes and labels is a lot like coloring check boxes and radio buttons — so similar, in fact, that you can apply the steps in Lesson 6-2 to apply different colors to text boxes and labels.

Just remember to be careful when picking color combinations. Different colors should enhance your program, not make your text harder to read.

Lesson 10-1

Filling List and Combo Boxes with Real Data

When you first create a list or combo box, the box has nothing inside it. Because the whole purpose of list and combo boxes is to provide items for the user to choose from, you need to stuff your list and combo boxes with text.

You can fill your list boxes and combo boxes with text in two ways. The first is to type the entries into the List property that both objects provide. The second is to fill them when you run your program, which requires writing BASIC code. Don't worry — the code is pretty simple.

Stuffing list boxes and combo boxes with data

Using the List property in the Properties window is the easiest way to add data to your list boxes and combo boxes. With this method, you don't have to write any additional code. Look at how easy filling in a list box is by using this method:

1 Start Visual Basic, select a Standard EXE project type, and draw a list box anywhere on the form.

If you need a refresher on how to draw an object on a form, look back at Lesson 4-1.

2 Open the Properties window by pressing F4.

3 Select the Categorized page of the Properties window.

You'll see a categorized list of properties for the combo box as shown in Figure 10-2.

on the test

The Categorized page comes in handy when you want to see which properties go with each other. For example, the IntegralHeight, ListData, and List all belong in the List category. Using categories reduces the time you spend scrolling through the list to change something like the object's height and width. You can also reduce screen clutter by clicking on the minus sign next to a category entry. Doing so hides the properties until you need them.

4 Double-click in the List property.

Visual Basic displays a drop-down list.

5 Type a word, such as it, press Ctrl+Enter, and then type another word, such as works.

Visual Basic places each word on a separate line in the list box.

6 Press Enter to close the drop-down list.

Visual Basic displays the two words you typed in the list box that you drew in step 1.

Using code to stuff your list boxes and combo boxes

The magic BASIC command for adding text to appear in a list box or combo box is AddItem. To use the AddItem command, you need to specify two items:

- The name of the list box or combo box that you want to use, followed by a period, followed by the AddItem command
- The actual text that you want to appear

choose the Alphabetic page of Properties window to see property list in alphabetical order

choose the Categorized page of Properties window to see like properties grouped together

Figure 10-2: The Categorized page of the Properties window allows you to see properties in groups.

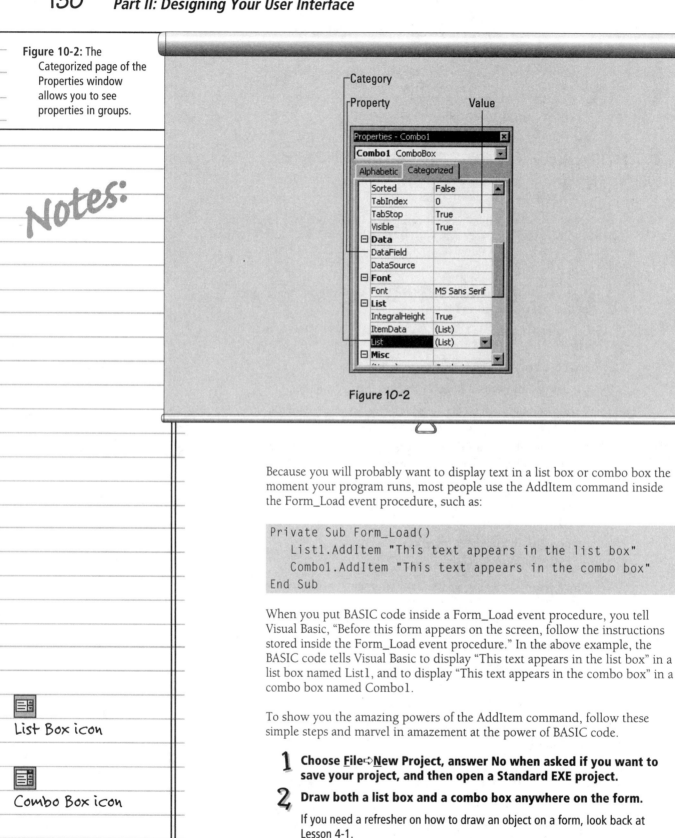

Figure 10-2

Because you will probably want to display text in a list box or combo box the moment your program runs, most people use the AddItem command inside the Form_Load event procedure, such as:

```
Private Sub Form_Load()
   List1.AddItem "This text appears in the list box"
   Combo1.AddItem "This text appears in the combo box"
End Sub
```

When you put BASIC code inside a Form_Load event procedure, you tell Visual Basic, "Before this form appears on the screen, follow the instructions stored inside the Form_Load event procedure." In the above example, the BASIC code tells Visual Basic to display "This text appears in the list box" in a list box named List1, and to display "This text appears in the combo box" in a combo box named Combo1.

To show you the amazing powers of the AddItem command, follow these simple steps and marvel in amazement at the power of BASIC code.

List Box icon

Combo Box icon

1 **Choose File⇨New Project, answer No when asked if you want to save your project, and then open a Standard EXE project.**

2 **Draw both a list box and a combo box anywhere on the form.**

If you need a refresher on how to draw an object on a form, look back at Lesson 4-1.

3 **Select the form and then press F7.**

Visual Basic displays the Code window with a blank event procedure that looks like the following:

```
Private Sub Form_Load()
End Sub
```

4 **Insert the two lines of code given as an example earlier, so the event procedure looks like this listing:**

```
Private Sub Form_Load()
    List1.AddItem "This text appears in the list box"
    Combo1.AddItem "This text appears in the combo
            box"
End Sub
```

5 **Press F5.**

The program runs and displays text in the list box. However, the combo box doesn't display any text until the user clicks on it.

6 **Click on the downward-pointing arrow in the combo box.**

Visual Basic now displays the combo box text in a drop-down list.

7 **Click on the End button in the Toolbar.**

8 **Meditate upon the wonders you have just witnessed.**

Highlighting a default item in a combo box

on the test

Combo boxes exist to display multiple choices for the user. Because users sometimes need help, your combo box can highlight one item that you expect the user will need most of the time, as the combo box shown in Figure 10-1 does.

For example, say your combo box displays a list of different state abbreviations. If you do most of your business in California, you can highlight the CA abbreviation to make it the default item. That way CA is automatically highlighted when your program runs, and the user can select it by simply hitting Enter.

Default items in combo boxes simply make it easier for the user to choose a likely item without having to search for it.

on the CD

1 **Load the Refund project (Refund.VBP).**

2 **Right-click on the Refund.FRM Form file and choose View Object from the context menu.**

3 **Click on the Combo1 combo box and press F4 to display the Properties window.**

4 **Double-click in the Text property in the left-hand column.**

F7 = View Code
window command
key

End button

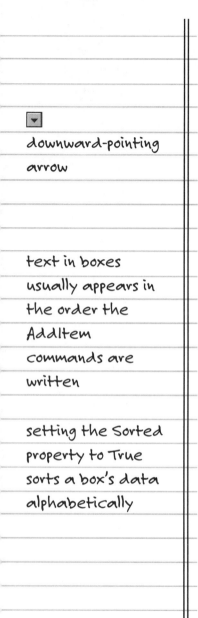

downward-pointing
arrow

text in boxes
usually appears in
the order the
AddItem
commands are
written

setting the Sorted
property to True
sorts a box's data
alphabetically

5 **Type** Obviously an inferior product **and press Enter.**

6 **Press F5 to start the program.**

Notice that the combo box now displays your default item in the combo box.

7 **Click on the downward-pointing arrow in the combo box.**

Notice that Visual Basic highlights the obviously inferior product item.

8 **Click on the End button in the Toolbar.**

Sorting your list boxes and combo boxes

The order that you write your AddItem BASIC commands determines the order that your text appears in a list box or combo box. For example, suppose you use the following BASIC commands:

```
Private Sub Form_Load()
    List1.AddItem "This item appears at the top"
    List1.AddItem "This item appears at the middle"
    List1.AddItem "This item appears at the bottom"
End Sub
```

Your list box displays the data as shown in Figure 10-3.

on the test

You can also let Visual Basic sort your data alphabetically. To sort data in a list box or combo box alphabetically, set the box's Sorted property to True. For example, if the list box in Figure 10-3 had its Sorted property set to True, it would display data as shown in Figure 10-4.

on the CD

1 **Load the Refund project (Refund.VBP).**

2 **Press F5.**

Notice the way the list box sorts the data under the label Which one of the useless products do you want to return?

3 **Click on the Exit button.**

4 **Click on the Refund.FRM Form file and click on View Object.**

5 **Click on the List1 list box and press F4 to display the Properties window.**

6 **Double-click in the Sorted property in the left-hand column (it's in the Behavior category).**

Visual Basic sets the Sorted property to True.

7 **Press F5.**

Notice that now the list box displays the data in the list box alphabetically.

8 **Click on Exit.**

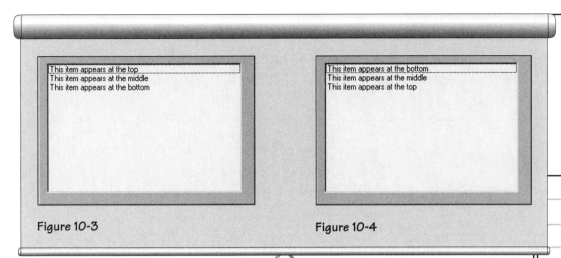

Figure 10-3

Figure 10-4

Figure 10-3: A list box displays data in the order of your AddItem commands.

Figure 10-4: A list box sorting data alphabetically with its Sorted property set to True.

Removing items from list boxes and combo boxes

on the test

You can remove an item from a list box or combo box in two ways: Use the RemoveItem BASIC command or the Clear BASIC command. To use either of these commands, you have to type them in the Code window. The RemoveItem command lets you remove items individually from a list box or combo box. The Clear command simply acts like a madman on a rampage and wipes out everything displayed in a list box or combo box.

When using the RemoveItem command, you have to specify two items:

- ◆ The list or combo box name containing the item you want to remove
- ◆ The number of the item you want to remove

Visual Basic numbers items in a list box or combo box from top to bottom. The very top item is numbered 0 (zero), the next item down is numbered 1, and so on. So if you want to remove the fourth item from the top (remember, the first item is numbered 0), you use this command:

```
List1.RemoveItem 3
```

When using the Clear command, all you have to specify is the list box or combo box name you want to clear, such as:

```
List1.Clear
```

To discover the fun you can have removing items from a list box, follow these steps:

on the CD

1 **Load the Refund project (Refund.VBP).**

2 **Right-click on the Refund.FRM Form file and choose View Object from the context menu.**

3 **Double-click on the <u>C</u>lear command button.**

A Code window appears, showing how to use the Clear command.

Notes:

the top item in a list box or combo box is numbered 0

Figure 10-5: The three
styles in which a list box
can display columns.

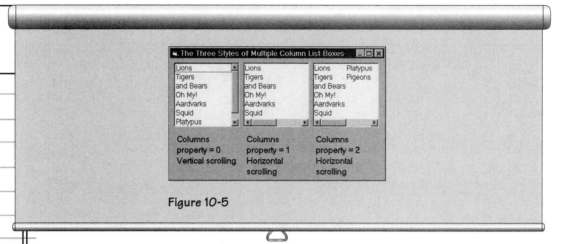

Figure 10-5

☑ Progress Check

If you can do the following,
you've mastered this lesson:

❏ Use the Categorized page
of the Properties window
to find a group of like
properties.

❏ Add items to a list box or
combo box using the List
property of the Properties
window.

❏ Use the AddItem BASIC
command to store text in
a list box or combo box.

❏ Use the RemoveItem or
Clear BASIC commands
to remove text in a list
box or combo box.

❏ Sort items in a list box
and combo box.

❏ Define a default item for
a list box and a combo
box.

❏ Display two columns in a
list box.

4 **Click in the Object list box in the Code window and choose
cmdRemove.**

The Code window shows how to use the RemoveItem command to remove the
fourth item in a list box.

5 **Press F5.**

6 **Click on the Remove item command button.**

Notice that Visual Basic removes the item that appears fourth from the top of
the list box.

7 **Repeat step 7 several more times to watch this wondrous feat in
action.**

8 **Click on the Clear command button.**

Notice that Visual Basic wipes out everything remaining in the list box.

9 **Click on the Exit command button.**

Creating multiple-column list boxes

Normally a list box displays items in a single column. If you want to get fancy,
you can make a list box display items in columns in three different styles as
shown in Figure 10-5.

The Columns property determines the style in which a list box displays its
items. If the Columns property is set to zero, the list box uses vertical scrolling.
If the Columns property is set to one, the list box uses horizontal scrolling. If
the Columns property is set to two or higher, the list box displays multiple
columns and uses horizontal scrolling.

on the CD

1 **Load the Refund project (Refund.VBP).**

2 **Right-click on the Refund.FRM Form file and choose View Object
from the context menu.**

3 **Click on the List1 list box and press F4 to display the Properties
window.**

4 **Double-click on the Columns property in the left-hand column.**

5 **Type** 1 **and press Enter.**

6 **Press F5.**

Notice that the list box now displays a horizontal scroll bar.

7 **Click on the Exit command button.**

Getting Values from List Boxes and Combo Boxes

When a user chooses an item from a list box or combo box, your program has no idea what the user picked. To tell your program which item a user picked, your program needs to check that list box or combo box's Text property.

To retrieve the item a user chose in a list box or combo box, you have to use BASIC code. Depending on the item that the user chose in a list box or combo box, your program may need to make a decision about what to do next.

For example, your program can display a list box containing different products that the user can buy. The moment the user chooses an item, your program needs to determine the price of that item and display that on the screen.

To see how to use the Text property of a list box and a combo box, go through the following steps:

retrieve values
from list or combo
boxes using a
BASIC code

1 **Load the Refund project (Refund.VBP).**

2 **Click on the Refund.FRM Form file and click on View Code.**

Visual Basic displays the Code window.

3 **Click in the Object list box of the Code window and select Combo1.**

The code window displays the following BASIC code:

```
Private Sub Combo1_Click ()
    lblChoice.Caption = Combo1.Text
End Sub
```

This code simply tells Visual Basic, "When the user clicks on the Combo1 combo box, look in the Text property of that combo box to find out what the user chose. Then store this value into the Caption property of a label named lblChoice."

4 **Click in the Object list box of the Code window and choose List1.**

The code window displays the following BASIC code:

```
Private Sub List1_Click ()
    lblChoice.Caption = List1.Text
End Sub
```

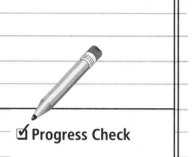

☑ Progress Check

If you can do the following, you've mastered this lesson:

❑ Explain in which property Visual Basic stores the item that a user chooses from a list box or combo box.

❑ Write BASIC code to retrieve information stored in the Text property of a list box or combo box.

This code simply tells Visual Basic, "When the user clicks on the List1 list box, look in the Text property of that list box to find out what the user chose. Then store this value into the Caption property of a label named lblChoice."

5 **Press F5 to run your program.**

6 **Click on any item in the list box that appears underneath the label reading Which one of the useless products do you wish to return?**

Your chosen item appears underneath the label that reads You chose this.

7 **Click on the combo box and choose any item.**

Your chosen item now appears underneath the label that reads You chose this.

8 **Click on Exit.**

Recess

By using a list box, you make sure that the user can't type invalid data into your program, such as typing "Yes" in reference to a question that asks for the user's sex. Likewise, combo boxes provide an additional level of flexibility by letting users either choose an option from the combo box or type in an answer. Use combo boxes when a list box can't offer all possible answers, such as a list of Eastern European countries, a group that seems to change almost daily.

Unit 10 Quiz

For each of the following questions, circle the letter of the correct answer or answers. Remember, some questions may have two correct answers, actually increasing the chance you'll get one right, even if you guess.

1. **What is the difference between a list box and a combo box?**

   A. A list box is something Santa Claus uses to see who's naughty or nice. A combo box is like a blender because it mixes stuff up in any combination you choose, hence the name combo box.

   B. A list box only lets users choose from a limited choice of options. A combo box lets users choose from a list or type in something different altogether.

   C. A list box and a combo box are the same thing. It just depends on how you pronounce their names, that's all.

   D. List boxes can hold a variety of items and shred them at a moment's notice. A combo box requires a secret combination before it will display anything at all.

   E. A list box is the mispronunciation of the term "lisp box."

2. **Why would you use the Categorized page of the Properties window?**

   A. To get all your valuables organized into neat little boxes.

   B. As a means to confuse your boss when he looks over your shoulder to see what you're doing.

   C. To see which properties go with each other or to edit them without scrolling back and forth through the list of properties.

   D. Ours is not to reason why, ours is but to do or die!

   E. As a method for reducing screen clutter by clicking on the minus sign next to a category entry.

3. **What is the purpose of defining a default item to appear in a list box or combo box?**

   A. A default item is the one item that everyone can pin the fault on when your computer crashes, such as "It's not my fault your computer is lousy. It's default of that list box you created."

   B. A default item lets you define the most common item you expect the user to choose. That way the user can choose it just by pressing Enter.

   C. A default item is the item you want to hide from the user, because it's the one item the user will most likely want to choose.

   D. The default item is the item that nobody wants to choose. That's why it's important to make sure that it doesn't appear in your list box or combo box.

   E. Default items are accusations that politicians cleverly avoid by pointing out the flaws of their rivals rather than honestly answering directly any questions they themselves are asked.

4. **How does Visual Basic sort data in a list box or combo box?**

   A. You can sort data by the order in which you type your AddItem BASIC commands, or you can let Visual Basic sort your data alphabetically.

   B. You can sort your data by throwing it all on the floor and picking it back up again.

   C. There is no way to sort data because even Visual Basic doesn't know where it stores your data.

   D. You can sort data from A to Z, or you can sort data by specifying the location of your data in a list or combo box.

   E. Why bother sorting your data? The whole purpose of programming is to make users feel as intimidated as possible.

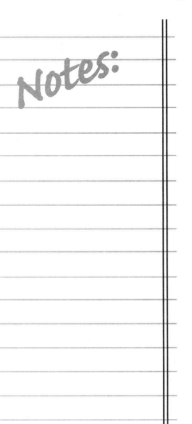

Notes:

5. **Name the two ways to remove an item from a list or combo box.**

   A. Erase your entire hard disk or throw your computer in the garbage can.

   B. Use the RemoveItem BASIC command to remove one item at a time, or use the Clear BASIC command to delete an entire list at once.

   C. Don't put anything in a list or combo box in the first place, and don't use list or combo boxes at all.

   D. Use correction fluid to paint out an item on your screen, or turn off your screen altogether so you can't see anything in a list or combo box.

   E. There is no way to remove anything from a list or combo box. After you've stored text in a box, taking the text out again is impossible.

6. **When a user chooses an item in a list box or combo box, where does Visual Basic store this result?**

   A. As soon as the user chooses an item in a list box or combo box, Visual Basic stores the chosen item in the Text property of the list box or combo box.

   B. The moment the user clicks on an item in a list box or combo box, Visual Basic immediately forgets what the user chose.

   C. The moment the user chooses an item in a list box or combo box, Visual Basic stores the results in a place located far, far away.

   D. Users can't choose anything from a list box or combo box, so this question doesn't make any sense.

   E. The only place that Visual Basic stores anything is on your floppy disk somewhere.

Unit 10 Exercise

on the CD

1. Load the Refund project (Refund.VBP).

2. Click on the Refund.FRM Form file and click on View Object.

3. Change the list box's Columns property to 1 (one).

4. Change the list box's Sorted property to True.

5. Click in the close box of the Properties window to make it go away.

6. Double-click on the Remove item command button.

7. Edit the event procedure so it looks like this:

```
Private Sub cmdRemove_Click ()
    List1.RemoveItem 2
End Sub
```

8. Press F5 to see how the program looks with the changes you've made.

Part II Review

Unit 5 Summary

- **Command button caption:** Displays a descriptive word or phrase on a command button.

- **Hot key:** Allows the user to choose a command button by pressing the Alt key and the hot key simultaneously, such as Alt+X.

- **&&:** Use a double ampersand if you want an ampersand in the button caption.

- **Default button:** The command button that the user can choose by pressing Enter before doing anything else.

- **Cancel button:** The command button that the user can choose by pressing Esc before doing anything else.

- **Event procedure:** A small program telling Visual Basic what to do when a certain event occurs, such as the user clicking on a command button.

Unit 6 Summary

- **Check box:** A box that lets the user choose one or more options.

- **Radio button:** A button that lets the user choose one (and only one) option.

- **Frame:** Lets you group check boxes or radio buttons.

- **Value property:** Indicates which check box or radio button the user picked.

- **Picture property:** Allows you to use pictures instead of text.

- **System/Custom colors:** System colors are standard throughout Windows, while custom colors are specific to your application.

Unit 7 Summary

- **Text box:** A box that can display text or let the user type in text.

- **Label:** Can only display text on a form.

- **Alignment:** The appearance of text in a text box or label. The three choices are left justified, centered, or right justified.

- **Word-wrapping:** The ability to display multiple lines of text in a text box or label.

- **Text property:** Contains the text that appears inside a text box.

- **Caption property:** Contains the text that appears inside a label.

- **ToolTipText property:** Displays a pop-up window for the user that contains a short, helpful hint on how to use an object.

Unit 8 Summary

- **Menu Editor dialog box:** Where you can create pull-down menus.

- **Menu bar:** A list of menu titles that appears at the top of the screen.

- **Menu commands:** A list of commands that appears underneath a menu title.

- **Keystroke shortcut:** A keystroke combination that chooses a menu command, such as Ctrl+S.

- **Separator bar:** A line that divides groups of commands within a pull-down menu.

- **Check mark:** A check that appears next to a chosen menu command.

Part II Review

Unit 9 Summary

▶ **Dialog box:** A small window that displays a message.

▶ **Quick Info pop up:** Provides a list of information Visual Basic needs before it can execute a function.

▶ **List Constants pop up:** Contains a list of constants that you can use for a function argument.

▶ **Constant:** A human readable representation of a number or text required by Visual Basic to execute a function.

▶ **Command button:** Appears on a dialog box, giving the user a choice of commands to choose from.

▶ **MsgBox:** The BASIC code that displays a dialog box on the screen.

Unit 10 Summary

▶ **List box:** A small rectangle that displays one or more items stacked inside.

▶ **Combo box:** A drop-down list that lets you choose an item or type text inside.

▶ **AddItem:** The BASIC code that stores text in a list box or combo box.

▶ **RemoveItem:** The BASIC code that removes text from a list box or combo box.

▶ **Clear:** The BASIC code that completely empties a list box or combo box of text.

▶ **Categorized page of Properties window:** A specialized list that groups object properties by type or function, rather than in alphabetical order.

Part II Test

The questions on this test cover material presented in Part II, Units 5, 6, 7, 8, 9, and 10. The answers are in Appendix A.

True False

T   F   1. A hot key lets you choose a command by pressing Alt and the hot key, such as Alt+X.

T   F   2. Always use a double ampersand (&&) if you want to see an ampersand on the command button.

T   F   3. A command button must always be bigger than the form window it appears on.

T   F   4. The Picture property allows you to use pictures instead of text for a caption.

T   F   5. A user can choose an item or type an answer inside a combo box.

T   F   6. System colors will systematically make the user blind by forcing them to view terrible color schemes.

T   F   7. A user can choose only one radio button in a group at a time.

T   F   8. The Quick Info pop-up menu gives you the number to Microsoft's support line so that they can help you make an even bigger mess of your program.

T   F   9. An event procedure is a small program that tells Visual Basic what to do when a certain event occurs.

T   F   10. A text box can display text or let the user type in text.

Multiple Choice

For each of the following questions, circle the correct answer or answers. Some questions may have more than one right answer, so read all the answers carefully.

11. **What does a separator bar do in a pull-down menu?**

    A. The bar keeps menu commands from fighting with one another.

    B. The bar divides groups of commands in a pull-down menu.

    C. The separator bar keeps commands from escaping from a menu.

    D. Separator bars are places where divorce lawyers hang out.

    E. Separator bars keep your pull-down menus invisible.

12. **What are the two ways to select color in a Visual Basic application?**

    A. All Visual Basic applications are in black and white, so no color selection is required.

    B. Adding color may make your application enjoyable to use and you wouldn't want that.

    C. Use a paint brush to add color to your monitor.

    D. Select a color name from the System page of the color pop-up menu.

    E. Choose one of the custom colors from the Palette page of the color pop-up menu.

Part II Test

13. **What does word-wrapping do?**

    A. Word-wrapping plays rap music on your computer.

    B. Word-wrapping hides the meaning of your words.

    C. Text boxes and labels use word-wrapping to display multiple lines of text.

    D. Word-wrapping is another term for taping a talkative person's mouth shut.

    E. Word-wrapping describes a method of using newspapers as wrapping paper for gifts.

14. **Why would you use a constant?**

    A. Doing so is better than using a fry pan to swat mosquitoes.

    B. To make it easier to remember what a particular value is used for.

    C. You'd never use a constant, because the universe is in a continual state of flux.

    D. To make it easier for other programmers to understand your code.

    E. For about the same purpose as an army ant.

15. **What does the Menu Editor dialog box do?**

    A. The Menu Editor dialog box lets you create pull-down menus for your program.

    B. It lets you rearrange your menu titles and commands.

    C. It forces you to use dialog boxes instead of pull-down menus in your programs.

    D. The Menu Editor dialog box lets you give verbal commands to your computer.

    E. The Menu Editor dialog box is what restaurants use to design their menus.

16. **In a group of five check boxes, how many check boxes can a user select?**

    A. A user can pick any or all of the check boxes.

    B. A user can only pick 3 different check boxes.

    C. The user must pick them all.

    D. You can't pick any check boxes.

    E. A user can only pick six or more check boxes, even if only five are available.

Part II Test

Matching

17. Match the following properties with the object they belong to.

A. Value

B. Caption

C. Text

D. Boardwalk

E. Redmond, WA

1. A text box

2. Microsoft Corporation

3. A check box or radio button

4. A label

5. A Monopoly game

18. Match the following menu names to what they represent.

A. mnuFile

B. mnuFileExit

C. mnuEdit

D. mnuEditCut

E. mnuHelp

1. The Cut command on the Edit menu

2. The Help menu

3. The Exit command on the File menu

4. The Edit menu

5. The File menu

19. Match the following properties with the description of what they do.

A. Caption

B. Text

C. Alignment

D. DisabledPicture

E. Multiline

1. Lets you display multiple lines of text in a text box

2. Contains a word or phrase that appears on the screen

3. Contains text that appears in a text box

4. Left-justifies, centers, or right-justifies text in a text box or label

5. Contains the picture that Visual Basic displays when an object is disabled

20. Match the following foods to the type of restaurant you might find them in.

A. Kung Pao chicken

B. Linguini with clam sauce

C. Sushi

D. Tofu burger

E. Gyros

1. Japanese restaurant

2. Greek restaurant

3. Chinese restaurant

4. Italian restaurant

5. Vegetarian restaurant

Part II Lab Assignment

In this lab assignment, you create a program from scratch. Have fun with it.

Step 1: Start a new project

You may want to save your project under a unique name so you can find it again.

Step 2: Draw two command buttons and one text box

Modify the appearance of your command buttons, and text box with borders, colors, captions, or anything else your heart desires to make your user interface look pleasing to the eye.

Step 3: Write BASIC code to make your program work

Write BASIC code to make one command button exit your program. Write BASIC code for the second command button to make it yank text out of the text box and display it in a dialog box using the MsgBox BASIC command.

Step 4: Run your program to see if it works

Test your program. If it works, try adding pull-down menus to your program with menu commands that perform the same function as your two command buttons.

Writing BASIC Code

Part III

In this part...

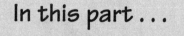

No matter how pretty you make your program look, what ultimately matters is whether or not your program actually does something useful. That's where this part of the book comes in. In Part III, you learn how to write BASIC commands that tell your program how to work and how to save information in a database file.

Writing BASIC code is much like writing a recipe: You have to write step-by-step instructions to make your computer do anything worthwhile. Fortunately, Visual Basic makes writing code easier by providing plenty of helpful hints in the form of pop ups. In this part, you look at how these pop ups work.

Once you get used to writing BASIC commands that tell your program how to work, you'll soon discover a newfound power over your computer. Armed with this power, you can start writing all types of programs for your kids, for your job, or for your own amusement. But first, of course, you have to learn how to write BASIC commands, and that's what this part of the book helps you do.

The Basics of Writing BASIC Code

Prerequisites

▶ Using the Toolbox (Lesson 1-2)

▶ Opening the Code window (Lesson 1-2)

▶ Understanding the purpose of BASIC commands (Lesson 1-2)

▶ Using the Visual Basic Application Wizard (Lesson 2-3)

Objectives for This Unit

✓ Understanding the purpose of BASIC code

✓ Understanding the structure of a typical BASIC procedure

✓ Writing BASIC code

▶ Obvious.VBP

on the CD

After you design your program's user interface by using command buttons, pull-down menus, check boxes, picture boxes, and list boxes and combo boxes, you have nothing but an empty shell of a program. The second step in writing a Visual Basic program is writing BASIC commands that tell your program what to do when someone clicks on a radio button or types something in a text box.

on the test

You can get Visual Basic to do some of the work for you by using the VB Application Wizard instead of selecting the Standard EXE option in the New Project dialog. If you want to look at how the VB Application Wizard works, then go back to Lesson 2-3. Besides creating a basic application shell and some forms for you, the VB Application Wizard will write some of the more mundane code for you. Even with the VB Application Wizard's help, though, you'll still need to add some code to your program before it will do anything beyond the basics.

Lesson 11-1   The Purpose of BASIC Code

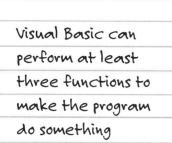

Visual Basic can perform at least three functions to make the program do something

on the test

No matter how much you may enjoy designing your program's user interface, you must eventually write some BASIC code. BASIC code can perform at least three tasks to make your program do something:

- ◗ Respond to the user
- ◗ Calculate a result
- ◗ Display the calculated result (by changing the property of an object)

Responding to the user means that when the user clicks on a command button or menu command, your program does something worthwhile, like saving a file or exiting the program.

Calculating a result lets your program use data to perform an operation such as addition or multiplication. Every program needs to do something with the data it gets. A word processor formats and prints characters, a spreadsheet adds and multiplies numbers, and a game translates your keyboard or joystick movements into a video image of you blasting aliens with your ray gun.

Changing the property of an object lets your program display messages back to the user. For example, a program may ask the user for an annual income and then calculate the income tax based on that amount. Finally, the program has to change the property of an object, such as the Text property of a text box or the Caption property of a Label, to display the result.

Because talk (or writing) is cheap (and easy to forget), try the following to get a better idea of the purpose of writing BASIC code:

on the CD

1 **Load the Obvious.VBP Project.**

2 **Press F5.**

Notice that the Obvious.VBP program consists of one form, one text box, two command buttons, and two labels, as shown in Figure 11-1.

3 **Type the name of your current or previous boss in the text box.**

4 **Click on the Tell me the obvious command button.**

Visual Basic displays a message in the second label.

5 **Click on Exit.**

In the above program, Visual Basic responds to you twice, once when you click on the Tell me the obvious command button (step 4) and again when you click on the Exit command button (step 5).

The moment you click on the Tell me the obvious command button, Visual Basic calculates a result. Although you can't see it just yet, the result Visual Basic calculates is nothing more than taking the name you typed in the text

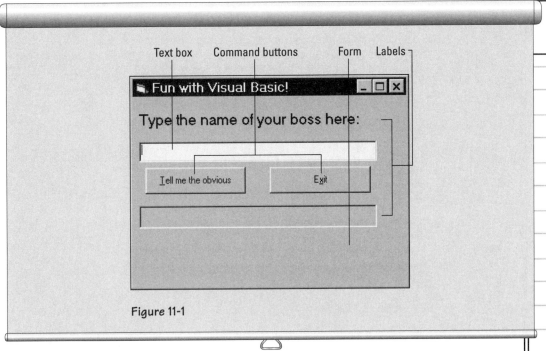

Text box   Command buttons   Form   Labels

Figure 11-1

Figure 11-1: Running the Obvious.VBP program.

box (in step 3) and tacking on the additional string? `That's obviously an unusual name.` So if you type the name **John Doe**, the program creates the string `John Doe? That's obviously an unusual name.`

When you first run this program, the Caption property of the second label (named `lblReply`) is blank. So Visual Basic changes the Caption property to the name plus the string `? That's obviously an unusual name.`

As you can see, this program responds to the user, calculates some result based on the data you give it, and changes the property of an object (in this case the label caption) to show you the final result.

The Structure of a Typical BASIC Procedure

Lesson 11-2

Now that you have a rough idea of what BASIC code can do and how it works, you need to know how to write BASIC code for your own programs.

on the test

Visual Basic lets you write BASIC code inside something called an *event procedure*. An event procedure is a miniature program that tells your program what to do when an event occurs.

So now your next question may be, "What the heck is an event?" In Visual Basic's world, an event occurs anytime the user does something to your program. Clicking the mouse is an event, tapping a key on the keyboard is another event, and moving the mouse is still another event.

event procedure =
miniature program
that tells the
program what to
do when an event
occurs

events happen any
time the user does
something to your
program

an event
procedure won't do
anything until
BASIC instructions
are written inside
an event
procedure

Notes:

When an event occurs, your program needs to determine what the user is trying to do. If a user clicks on a command button, your program must act differently than if a user clicks on a menu command.

So whenever an event occurs, Visual Basic needs to answer two questions:

- What event occurred?
- On what object on the user interface did it occur? (While the user was pointing at a command button, on a pull-down menu, or what?)

The combination of an event occurring on a specific object (command button, check box, and so on) defines a unique event procedure. Every object that you draw on a form automatically has an empty event procedure that looks like the following:

```
Private Sub Command1_Click()

End Sub
```

This event procedure tells Visual Basic, "The moment the user clicks on a command button named Command1, follow the instructions listed here." Until you write BASIC instructions inside an event procedure, the event procedure won't do anything.

See why giving your objects descriptive names is important? In this example, Command1 is a generic name that gives you a clue as to which command button Visual Basic is referring. However, if you name the command button cmdExit, then the event procedure would look like the following, which is easier to find:

```
Private Sub cmdExit_Click()

End Sub
```

To see how real-live Visual Basic uses event procedures, take some time to study the Obvious.VBP program and see how BASIC code can do its programming magic.

on the CD

1 **Load Obvious.VBP (if you haven't already done so in Lesson 11-1).**

2 **Right-click on the Obvious.FRM Form file in the Project window and choose View Object from the context menu.**

Visual Basic displays the Obvious.FRM user interface.

3 **Double-click on the Tell me the obvious command button.**

Visual Basic displays the Code window that contains the following:

```
Private Sub cmdObvious_Click()
    lblReply.Caption = txtName.Text & "? That's
            obviously an unusual name."
End Sub
```

This event procedure tells Visual Basic, "The moment someone clicks on the cmdObvious command button, take the name the user typed in the txtName text box, add it to the string '? That's obviously an unusual name,' and display the whole string in the lblReply label."

 Click on the Object list box in the Code window and choose cmdExit.

Visual Basic displays the following event procedure:

```
Private Sub cmdExit_Click()
  End
End Sub
```

This event procedure tells Visual Basic, "The moment someone clicks on the command button named cmdExit, follow the End instruction." The End instruction just tells Visual Basic to end (or stop running) the program.

☑ **Progress Check**

If you can do the following, you've mastered this lesson:

❑ Understand what an event procedure is and how it works.

❑ Use the Object list box in the Code window to view different event procedures.

Writing BASIC Code
Lesson 11-3

To make your user interface responsive, you have to write BASIC code inside your event procedures. The moment an event occurs on a specific object (such as clicking on a command button), the BASIC code inside that event procedure tells Visual Basic what to do next.

Any time a program doesn't work right, the problem's called a *bug*. When you search for problems to remove them from a program, it's called *debugging*. You can learn more about debugging in Units 16 and 17.

The two most common types of instructions that BASIC code can perform are:

▶ Assigning a value to a property

▶ Running a BASIC command

Assigning a value to a property lets you display information on the screen. For example, the following command displays the message "This is important" in a label named lblMessage:

```
lblMessage.Caption = "This is important."
```

Running a BASIC command lets you use one of Visual Basic's many built-in commands that perform a specific task. For example, the End command tells Visual Basic to stop a program. The following command tells Visual Basic to stop running a program the moment the user clicks on a command button named cmdExit:

```
Private Sub cmdExit_Click()
    End
End Sub
```

debugging means to search for problems and remove them from a program

the End command tells Visual Basic to stop a program

Figure 11-2: The List Properties/Methods pop up appears automatically when you type an object name Visual Basic recognizes.

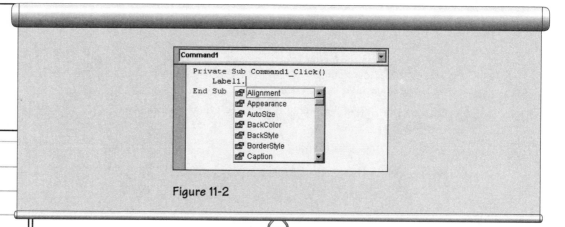

Figure 11-2

The simplest and most common BASIC command you can use inside an event procedure is the End command, which tells your Visual Basic program to stop running.

An event procedure can have zero or more instructions. However, if an event procedure has zero instructions, it won't do anything. Visual Basic automatically creates event procedures with zero instructions in them so that you can fill in the event procedure with actual BASIC code.

If an event procedure has two or more instructions, Visual Basic follows each instruction from top to bottom, one after the other. For example, the following event procedure tells Visual Basic to display the message "You clicked on the right button" in the lblMessage label whenever the user clicks on the cmdExit command button:

```
Private Sub cmdExit_Click()
    lblMessage.Caption = "You clicked on the right button"
    End
End Sub
```

To get beyond this abstract yacking about programming and give yourself some honest-to-goodness experience, try the following:

1 **Choose File➪New Project.**

Visual Basic displays a blank form.

2 **Click on the Label icon in the Toolbox and draw a label anywhere on the form.**

3 **Click on the Command Button icon in the Toolbox and draw one command button anywhere on the form.**

4 **Double-click on the command button on the form.**

The Code window appears.

5 **Type Label1. right below the Private Sub Command1_Click() line (the cursor should position itself here automatically).**

the List Properties/
Methods pop up lets
you choose a
method or property
from a list

Notes:

Visual Basic displays the List Properties/Methods pop up shown in Figure 11-2. This is another way in which Visual Basic tries to help you write code. If Visual Basic recognizes an object name, it'll display a list of properties and methods that you can use with that object.

6 **Double-click on Caption in the List Properties/Methods pop up.**

Visual Basic automatically adds the property to the Code window for you.

7 **Type the following so the entire event procedure looks like this:**

```
Private Sub Command1_Click()
    Label1.Caption = "You clicked the button"
    MsgBox "Here is a message", 48, "Message"
    End
End Sub
```

8 **Press F5.**

Notice that the label displays Label1.

9 **Click on the Command1 command button.**

Notice that the label now displays "You clicked the button". The program also displays a message box.

10 **Click on OK.**

Visual Basic removes the message box and stops your program.

The event procedure in step 5 consists of three separate instructions. The first instruction tells Visual Basic to display the string You clicked the button in the Caption property of the Label1 label. The second instruction tells Visual Basic to display a message box using the MsgBox BASIC command. The third instructions tells Visual Basic to stop the program using the End BASIC command.

You also saw a new coding helper in this lesson. Even though the List Properties/Methods pop up only appears automatically the first time, it is always available for you to use. Just right click after an object name and select List Properties/Methods from the context menu.

The List Properties/Methods pop up displays two different kinds of entries for an object like a command button or label. The first is a *property,* which defines how the object looks. The second is a *method,* which defines how you can interact with the object. For example, the *drag method* allows you to move the object from one place to another. Each of these entries uses a different icon in the pop up, so that they're easy to identify.

Recess

BASIC code is often used to change the property of another object. By doing so, your program can display a message on the screen. Another use for BASIC code is to run a built-in BASIC command, such as End (which stops your program) or MsgBox (which lets you display a message box on the screen).

Writing BASIC code in an event procedure is nothing more complicated than giving your program step-by-step instructions on what to do, much like a recipe.

---

most common BASIC command is the End command, which stops your program from running

Property icon in List Properties/Methods pop up

Method icon in List Properties/Methods pop up

☑ Progress Check

If you can do the following, you've mastered this lesson:

❏ Write a simple BASIC instruction inside an event procedure.

❏ Write a BASIC instruction that changes the property of another object.

❏ Write a BASIC instruction that stops your program.

❏ Use the List Properties/ Methods pop up to make writing code easier.

Unit 11 Quiz

For each of the following questions, circle the letter of the correct answer or answers. Some questions may (or may not) have more than one right answer.

1. **How can you use the VB Application Wizard?**

   A. To zap aliens using the magic wand supplied in the Visual Basic box.

   B. Only professional programmers can use the VB Application Wizard, it's too difficult for a beginner to use.

   C. To help you write some of the more mundane application code.

   D. As a means for world domination through "Very Big" application development.

   E. In an alternate universe where wizards, not programmers, write application code.

2. **What are the three steps that BASIC code must do?**

   A. BASIC code must be complicated, tedious, and repetitious in order to be useful in the computer industry.

   B. Respond to the user, calculate a result, and change the property of an object to display that result on the screen.

   C. Wipe out your important files, erase your hard disk, and crash your computer.

   D. BASIC code must not do anything or else it may threaten the power and authority of your local government officials.

   E. Order out for pizza, return your overdue video, and find the remote control for your TV.

3. **What is an event procedure?**

   A. An event procedure is a miniature BASIC program that is printed in type so small that it requires a magnifying glass to see properly.

   B. Event procedures are step-by-step instructions that tell people how to enjoy an event such as a family reunion or a backyard barbecue.

   C. An event procedure is a program that only runs when a really special and memorable event occurs, like the election of an honest politician or the establishment of a democracy in a Third World country. Because these things never happen, event procedures are worthless.

   D. An event procedure is a BASIC program that every object of a user interface has. Event procedures are always empty until you write BASIC code to make the event procedure do something.

   E. An event procedure is a miniature program that runs whenever a specific event (such as the user clicking the mouse) occurs on an object (such as a command button) on the user interface.

4. **Explain where event procedures come from and why you need to write BASIC code.**

    A. Event procedures are created automatically the moment you draw an object on a form. Because event procedures are initially empty, you need to write BASIC code to make them do something useful.

    B. Event procedures come from the depths of the unknown and are the subject of numerous studies and conspiracy theories.

    C. Some people say that event procedures spring into being the moment you create an object on a form. Other people say that event procedures evolve from a single cell and gradually develop into a fully formed BASIC program.

    D. Event procedures appear spontaneously, like mold on your refrigerator leftovers. You need to write BASIC code to remove the event procedures you don't need.

    E. Every program has only one event procedure that keeps your program from working. This event procedure is called a bug, an insect, or a really ugly creature.

5. **Name one way that your program can display a message on the screen for the user to see.**

    A. The best way to display a message on your screen is to write it on a yellow Post-it Note and paste it directly on your screen.

    B. A program can change the property of another object, such as the Caption property of a label or the Text property of a text box.

    C. If you make sure that your program doesn't do anything useful, then you won't need to worry about displaying any messages on the screen.

    D. Your program can display a message by using the DisplayMessageOnScreen BASIC command. If that doesn't work, just write your message directly on the screen, using a permanent marker.

    E. Your program can't display anything on the screen. Doing so would be a violation of government controls that require computers to be as difficult to use as possible.

6. **Give two examples of typical BASIC commands.**

    A. End (which stops your program) and MsgBox (which displays a message box on the screen).

    B. Sit and Play Dead.

    C. No such thing as a typical BASIC command exists. Every command you write must be different from anything else ever seen before. That way your program will truly be unique.

    D. BASIC only contains one command, so this question is a trick that doesn't make sense after all.

    E. Some basic commands that every teenager needs to know are "Duh!" and "No way, dude!"

Unit 11 Exercise

on the CD

1. Load the Obvious.VBP Project.

2. Click on the Obvious.FRM Form file in the Project window and click on View Code.

3. Click in the Object list box in the Code window and choose cmdObvious.

4. Add to the event procedure so it looks like this:

```
Private Sub cmdObvious_Click()
 Label1.Caption = "You typed " & txtName.Text
 lblReply.Caption = txtName.Text & "? That's obvi-
         ously an unusual name."
End Sub
```

5. Press F5.

6. Type a name in the text box underneath the "Type the name of your boss here" label.

7. Click on the Tell me the obvious command button. Notice that Visual Basic now changes two label captions on the form.

8. Click on Exit.

Playing with Variables

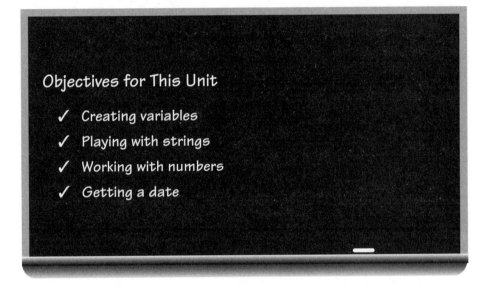

Objectives for This Unit

✓ Creating variables

✓ Playing with strings

✓ Working with numbers

✓ Getting a date

Prerequisites

▶ Drawing objects using the Toolbox (Lesson 4-1)

▶ Using the Code window (Lesson 1-2)

▶ Writing BASIC code (Unit 11)

on the CD

▶ String.VBP

▶ Number.VBP

▶ Date.VBP

If your boss asked you to add 239 to 122, you'd probably reach for a piece of paper so that you could write the numbers down. Then you'd add them together and give your boss the result.

Computers are no different. When you write a program to calculate some sort of result, your computer needs to temporarily store the data you give it. Because computers can't reach for a piece of paper, they have to use something called a *variable*.

A variable temporarily holds data, much like a box. To use a variable, you have to give it a name. When you write a program, you tell the computer, "See that variable called NameStuff? Put the string 'Bo the Cat' in the NameStuff variable."

variables
temporarily hold
data

variables come in
seven categories:
strings, numbers,
boolean, object,
variant, user
defined, and
dates

on the test

Because the type and size of data you may need to store can vary, Visual Basic provides several different kinds and sizes of variables, each of which is designed for a specific purpose. The seven main categories of variables are:

- **Strings.** A string variable holds text such as a person's name or a message like "Stop that!" A string variable can also hold text and numbers, like "San Francisco 49ers."

- **Numbers.** Four kinds of number variables exist: integers, real, decimal, and currency. Integer variables hold numbers like 2, 89, and 1,209. Real variables hold numbers like 2.34, 3.1459, or 890.8. Currency variables hold numbers like $45.90, $1,869.45, or $5.80. Decimal variables hold high accuracy numbers in decimal (human-readable form) rather than binary (0's and 1's like a computer uses) format like 1.23456789.

- **Boolean.** A variable that's either true or false. You can use a Boolean variable to hold the results of a comparison like 4 is greater than 3.

- **Object.** At times, you may want to create an object like a command button at run time rather than during the design phase. For example, you may want to add a button to a form when a special event happens like the boss' anniversary.

- **Variant.** Just to make things complicated, this variable type is for those times when you can't make up your mind. It allows one variable to contain any number of variable types including: string, number, and date.

- **User Defined.** If Microsoft didn't happen to think of the variable type you need to get a certain job done, you can use a user defined type instead.

- **Dates.** Most people look at dates as either strings or numbers, but computers are too stupid to do even that. Instead, they require a special date variable to hold dates such as January 1, 1999.

use only letters
and numbers in
variable names;
letters first, no
punctuation except
the underscore (_)

heads up

Variable names must contain only letters and numbers; begin with a letter; use no punctuation except the underscore character (_); and must not use a Visual Basic reserved word, such as Case or Loop.

Lesson 12-1

Creating Variables

create a variable
in one of three
ways in Visual
Basic

on the test

To create a variable, just give it a unique name. You can create any kind of variable in one of three ways:

- Name the variable and assign a value to it
- Declare a general purpose variable using the Dim statement
- Declare the variable and its data type

Creating variables only when you need them is convenient when you're writing a program, but terribly inconvenient when you want to understand how the program works at a later date. For example, consider the following:

```
Private Sub Command1_Click()
    BadString = "This is no good."
    txtMessage.Text = BadString
End Sub
```

In this example, BadString is a variable that holds the string "This is no good." While the above event procedure is perfectly good BASIC code (because it works), it does have one drawback. Just by looking at this short procedure, you can't easily see how many variables this procedure uses.

If this were a really large procedure written by someone else, you would have to take time to dig through the entire procedure, line-by-line, just to find out how many variables it uses and how it uses them.

As a better solution, declare *general purpose* variables by using the Dim keyword, such as:

```
Private Sub Command1_Click()
    Dim GoodString
    GoodString = "This is better."
    txtMessage.Text = GoodString
End Sub
```

In this example, the first line of the procedure tells exactly how many variables are used. Unfortunately, this method tells how many variables are used, but not *how* they are used.

The best solution of all is to define a variable name and define the type of data it can hold, such as:

```
Private Sub Command1_Click()
    Dim BetterString As String
    BetterString = "This is better."
    txtMessage.Text = BetterString
End Sub
```

In this example, the BetterString variable gets defined right away to contain strings and nothing else.

heads up

Whenever possible, always use the third method for defining variables — doing so makes your BASIC code much easier to understand. Because the majority of programming requires rewriting code that you or someone else wrote, do yourself (and others) a favor and define your variables and the type of data they can hold (strings, numbers, dates, and so on).

Notes:

make a habit of defining your variables and the type of data they can hold

Figure 12-1: The List Properties/Methods pop up displays a list of words you can use after As.

Figure 12-2: If you define a variable as a constant type, Visual Basic displays a list of constant values you can use with it.

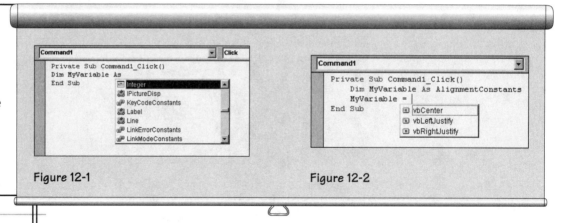

Figure 12-1   Figure 12-2

Standard variable icon

Constant icon

Object icon

☑ **Progress Check**

If you can do the following, you've mastered this lesson:

❑ Explain why variables exist and what they do.

❑ Define a variable using one of three methods.

❑ Use the List Properties/ Methods pop up to help define a variable.

❑ Identify the best way to define a variable.

So whenever you need to define a variable, use the following template as a guideline:

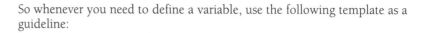

```
Dim VariableName As DataType
```

Just substitute your own variable name in VariableName and your own data type (string, number, and so on) in DataType.

Fortunately, Visual Basic will help you create your variable by using the List Properties/Methods pop up shown in Figure 12-1. As soon as you type **As**, this pop up appears. It lists all the words you can type after As, not just variable types. Fortunately, you can see a standard variable, constant, or object icon next to the variable type to make sure that you've selected the right word.

heads up

If you want Visual Basic to force you to declare all variables in a program, use the Option Explicit command. To use the Option Explicit command, open the Code window, choose (General) in the Object list box, choose (declarations) in the Proc list box, and type **Option Explicit**.

As shown in Figure 12-1, Visual Basic allows you to define a variable that only holds constant values. So, what good is such a variable? You can use it in your code to keep track of object status information like the alignment used by a label.

Whenever you type the name of a variable designed to hold constant values and then an = sign, Visual Basic displays a pop up like the one shown in Figure 12-2. This pop up shows what kinds of constants you can assign to that variable. Using this technique ensures that you always assign the right constant value to a variable, even if Microsoft happens to change the meaning of that constant in a later revision of Visual Basic.

Playing with Strings

Strings are the easiest variables to use because every Visual Basic object (such as a text box or label) stores data in its properties as strings. For example, the Caption property of a label is a string and the Text property of a text box is a string. When you type a number in a text box, guess what? Visual Basic stores that number as a string, not as an actual number.

Visual Basic supports two kinds of strings: fixed-length and variable-length. The only major difference between these two types is the number of characters that they'll hold.

on the test

A fixed-length string variable can hold up to 65,500 characters. That's not enough for *War and Peace,* but it should be enough for most uses. Visual Basic 5.0 users can also use a variable-length string variable that holds up to 2,147,483,648 characters, but you won't normally need one this long. Even the Windows 95 Notepad program can't hold more than 65,500 characters.

To show you how string variables can work, try the following:

on the CD

1 **Load the String.VBP project.**

2 **Click on View Object if necessary to display the form.**

The String1.FRM user interface appears as shown in Figure 12-3. This window has a label, a text box, and two command buttons.

3 **Double-click on the This is String 3 command button.**

Visual Basic displays the Code window as shown in Figure 12-4. Notice that the first line defines MiddleMan as a variable that can only hold strings. The next line stores the value of the Label1 Caption property into the MiddleMan variable.

The very next line replaces the contents of the Label1 Caption property with the text stored in the Text1 Text property. The next line replaces the contents of the Text1 Text property with the string stored in the Command1 Caption property.

The final line of code takes the value stored in MiddleMan and displays it in the Command1 Caption property.

4 **Press F5.**

5 **Click on the This is String 3 command button.**

Notice that each time you click on the command button, its caption changes.

6 **Type** New Value **in the text box.**

7 **Click on the This is String 1 command button.**

The command button caption changes to This is String 2 and New Value moves to the label.

8 **Click on Quit.**

☑ **Progress Check**

If you can do the following, you've mastered this lesson:

❏ Tell someone the longest string you can create.

❏ Understand how to get a string from the Caption property or the Text property of an object.

❏ Define the difference between a fixed-length and a variable-length string.

❏ Assign a string to the Caption property or Text property of an object.

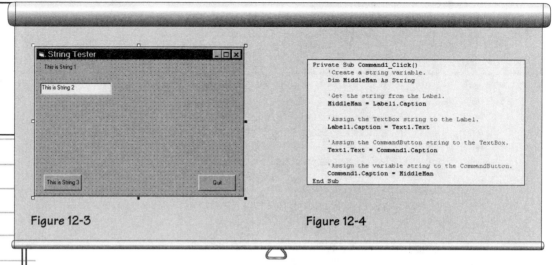

Figure 12-3: The String program allows you to see how to use a String variable.

Figure 12-4: An example of using a String variable in code.

Figure 12-3

Figure 12-4

Lesson 12-3   Working with Numbers

an Integer has a value from –32,768 to 32,767

a Long has a value from –2,147,483,648 to 2,147,483,647

on the test

Most programs need to perform some kind of math calculations. Because numbers are so important, Visual Basic provides several kinds of numerical data types as shown below:

- **Integer.** An Integer is a whole number. You use integers for things like choosing an item from a list or counting the number of times you do something. An Integer has a value from –32,768 to 32,767.

- **Long.** Sometimes you need to hold a number that's larger than an integer variable can hold. You use a Long integer to hold any number from –2,147,483,648 to 2,147,483,647. So why wouldn't you use a Long instead of an Integer all the time? Because a Long uses up more memory than an Integer does.

- **Single.** Scientific calculations require the use of real numbers, those that have both an integer part and a decimal part like 2.5. A Single data type can hold any number between –3.402823E38 to –1.401298E-45 and 1.401298E-45 to 3.402823E38. (The E means that the number is represented in scientific notation.)

- **Double.** A Double data type can hold much larger numbers than a Single can, but requires more memory as well. You can store numbers from –1.79769313486232E308 to –4.94065645841247E-324 and 4.94065645841247E-324 to 1.79769313486232E308.

- **Decimal.** This special number type allows computers to display decimal scientific numbers with 100 percent accuracy. A Decimal variable requires both more memory and more processing cycles to do its work. A Decimal number can store numbers from –79,228,162,514,264,337,593,543,950,335 to

Notes:

79,228,162,514,264,337,593,543,950,335. One oddity of a Decimal number is that it's always 29 places long with one place reserved in front of the decimal point. The smallest nonzero number you can create is: +/–0.0000000000000000000000000001.

♦ **Currency.** This special number type allows computers to display decimal monetary numbers with 100 percent accuracy, but requires more memory to do so. A Currency number can store values from –922337203685477.5808 to 922337203685477.5807.

Visual Basic stores numbers as integers or real data types, but it displays numbers on the screen as text strings. If you want to display a number on the screen (or if you want to retrieve a number that the user typed from the screen), you need to use special BASIC conversion commands.

on the test

These conversion commands convert a number into a string or vice versa. That way Visual Basic can display the number on the screen or yank a number off the screen. Some of the more common BASIC conversion commands are listed in Table 12-1.

Table 12-1   Common BASIC conversion commands

BASIC Command	What Command Does
CInt	Converts a string into an integer data type
CSng	Converts a string into a single data type
CDbl	Converts a string into a double data type
CDec	Converts a string into a decimal number
CCur	Converts a string to a currency number
CStr, Str	Converts a number into a string

Now that you know what all the number types are used for, you're ready to goof around with Visual Basic some more and see how they work.

on the CD

1 **Load the Number.VBP project.**

2 **Click on the Number1.FRM Form file and click on View Object.**

The Number1.FRM user interface appears as shown in Figure 12-5. This window has three different test buttons — one for each of the number types that we'll test.

3 **Double-click on the Test Integer button.**

Visual Basic displays the Code window as shown in Figure 12-6. This window displays only three lines of code. The first line creates an integer variable. The second line asks the List1 list box for the item that the user clicked on (returned as an index number). The third line takes the index number from the list box and converts it into a string before displaying a message box.

4 **Press F5.**

5 **Click on Seven in the Select list box.**

Figure 12-5: The Number Tester window allows you to test the three types of numeric variables.

Figure 12-6: An example of using an Integer variable.

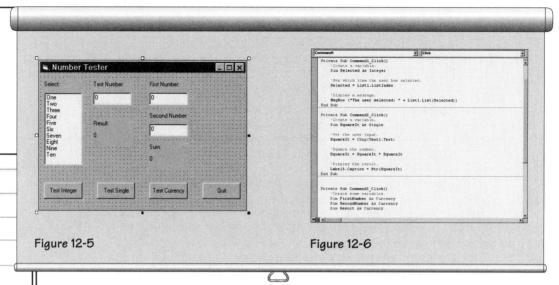

Figure 12-5   Figure 12-6

the Str function converts a string to a single number

☑ **Progress Check**

If you can do the following, you've mastered this lesson:

❏ Understand the different uses for Single, Double, Integer, and Currency variables.

❏ Convert a number to a string.

❏ Convert a string to a number.

6 **Click on the Test Integer command button.**

A message box appears as shown in Figure 12-7. Notice that the message box shows you the user entry Seven as text, not as a number.

7 **Click on Quit.**

8 **Double-click on the Test Single button.**

Visual Basic displays the Code window as shown in Figure 12-8. This procedure takes a number that the user types in the Text1 text box, converts it from a string to a single number, multiples that number by itself, and then converts the number into a string to store in the Caption property of the Label3 label.

The Str() function converts a number to a string, and always reserves a leading space for the string's positive or negative sign (+ or −).

9 **Press F5.**

10 **Type** 1.25 **in the Test Number text box.**

11 **Click on the Test Single command button.**

The number 1.5625 appears in the label underneath the word Result.

12 **Click on Quit.**

13 **Double-click on the Test Currency button.**

Visual Basic displays the Code window as shown in Figure 12-9.

14 **Press F5.**

15 **Type** 12.34 **in the First Number text box and type** 56.78 **in the Second Number text box.**

16 **Click on the Test Currency command button.**

The number 69.12 appears in the label beneath the word Sum.

17 **Click on Quit.**

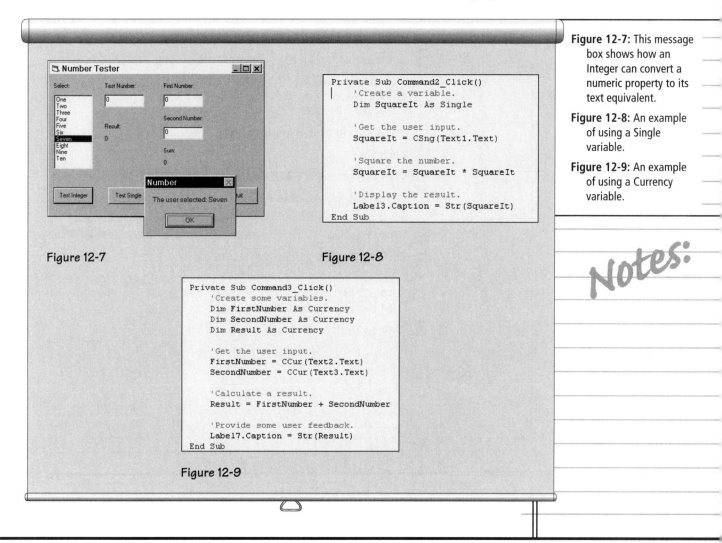

Figure 12-7

Figure 12-8

Figure 12-9

Figure 12-7: This message box shows how an Integer can convert a numeric property to its text equivalent.

Figure 12-8: An example of using a Single variable.

Figure 12-9: An example of using a Currency variable.

Notes:

Getting a Date

Lesson 12-4

Business is very time-oriented, which is probably why so many people feel like they never have enough time. Because time is so precious, Visual Basic even provides a special Date variable type that you can use.

heads up

Visual Basic dates can range from January 1, 100, to December 31, 9999. Some archeologists won't be happy with that time span, but just about everyone else will be.

on the CD

1 **Load the Date.VBP project.**

2 **Click on the Date1.FRM Form file and click on View Object.**

The Date1.FRM user interface appears.

date variables
can range from
1/1/100 to 12/31/9999

CDate() function converts string to date

Cdate() function accepts any legal date format as input

☑ **Progress Check**

If you can do the following, you've mastered this lesson:

❑ Explain how dates work in Visual Basic.

❑ Perform date calculations with Visual Basic.

3 **Double-click on the Add a Week command button.**

Visual Basic displays a Code window. This procedure creates a Date variable, gets the date that the user typed into the Text1 text box, adds a week to it, and then displays the result in the Label3 Caption.

The CDate( ) function converts the string to a date.

4 **Press F5.**

5 **Click on the Add a Week command button.**

The program displays a Result Date value of 1/8/96. Notice that the format of the input date matches the output date in the figure.

6 **Type** 21 January 1997 **in the text box underneath the Test Date label.**

7 **Click on the Add a Week command button.**

The program displays a new date seven days ahead of the one in the Test Date text box. Even though you type the date in a different format, Visual Basic is smart enough to figure out how to use it.

8 **Click on Quit.**

Recess

Take a breather. Get some coffee. Pet the cat. Keep in mind that the best way to declare a variable is to decide beforehand into which category the information best fits: string, number, boolean, object, variant, user defined, or date. Then declare the variable and its data type right at the start. Declaring your variables takes a little more planning than naming variables on the fly, but it pays off with a better organized, more understandable program.

Unit 12 Quiz

For each of the following questions, circle the letter of the correct answer or answers. Each question may have more than one correct answer, so don't get too complacent if you find one right answer first.

1. **Visual Basic supports seven different categories of variables. Which of the following answers tell about Visual Basic variables?**

   A. A String variable that holds text and numerals.

   B. A numerical variable that has three different data types: integers, real numbers, decimal, and currency. (Numbers are the biggest variable category that Visual Basic supports.)

   C. Even though most of us tend to look at dates as strings or numbers, computers can recognize dates only with a special variable type called Date.

D. Visual Basic supports some special variable types, like object, that we don't cover in this chapter because they're normally only used in complex programs.

E. Only evil scientists use variables. Everyone else uses boxes.

2. **How many characters can a string variable hold?**

   A. It depends on the size of your computer's display, because the string variable has to fit on the screen.

   B. It's a variable, so the amount changes just about every day (except on Tuesdays).

   C. A fixed-length string variable can hold up to 65,500 characters.

   D. It can't hold any characters; after all, it's made out of string.

   E. A variable-length string variable can hold up to 2,147,483,648 characters.

3. **What are the three ways you can declare a variable?**

   A. Go to customs and tell them all about your program prior to leaving the country.

   B. You can simply assign a value to the variable.

   C. Set up a podium in your office and make a speech about the variable.

   D. Define a general purpose variable and worry later about the type of data it will hold.

   E. Define a variable and the type of data it can hold.

4. **What are the six standard number types supported by Visual Basic?**

   A. Integers are whole numbers. You use them for things like choosing an item from a list or counting the number of times you do something.

   B. Longs are a larger form of the Integer.

   C. Singles contain an integer and a decimal part. You use them for scientific calculations.

   D. Doubles are a larger form of the Single.

   E. Currency and Decimal are special number types that allows computers to display decimal numbers with 100 percent accuracy, but wastes some memory to do so.

5. **What Visual Basic functions do you use to convert numbers to strings and vice versa?**

   A. Visual Basic doesn't provide any way to convert numbers to strings (or the other way around neither).

   B. Use the CSng( ) function to convert a string to a single number. Use the CDbl( ) function to convert a string to a double number. Use the CCur( ) function to convert a string to a currency number.

Notes:

C. Parts is parts; you take the parts and string them together to get a number or string.

D. Why would you even want to do such a silly thing?

E. Use the Str( ) function to convert a number to a string. The Str( ) function converts a number to a string, and always reserves a leading space for the string's + or – sign.

Unit 12 Exercise

In this exercise you get to modify the Date.VBP program so that it can subtract a week from any given date.

on the CD

1. Load the Date.VBP project.

2. Click on the Date1.FRM Form file and click on View Object.

   The Date1.FRM user interface appears.

3. Double-click on the Command Button icon in the Toolbox.

   Visual Basic adds a Command Button control to Form1.

4. Move the Command2 command button between the Add a Week and the Quit command buttons.

5. Change the Command2 Caption property to Last Week and change the Command 1 Caption property to Next Week.

6. Double-click on the Last Week button. Type the code below into the Command2_Click procedure.

```
Private Sub Command2_Click()
 'Create a date variable.
 Dim NewDate As Date
 'Get the date.
 NewDate = CDate(Text1.Text)
 'Subtract 7 days.
 NewDate = NewDate - 7
 'Store new date.
 Label3.Caption = Str(NewDate)
End Sub
```

7. Press F5.

8. Click on the Last Week button.

   Visual Basic subtracts 7 days from the date in the Test Date text box and then displays it on the screen.

9. Click on Quit.

Notes:

Conditional Code

Prerequisites
- Using the Code window (Lesson 1-2)
- Writing BASIC code (Unit 11)

▶ Decision.VBP
on the CD

Objectives for This Unit

✓ Using If-Then and If-Then-End If Statements

✓ Using If-Then-Else and If-Then-ElseIf Statements

✓ Using Select Case Statements

Making decisions is a part of daily life. You can decide to go to work, or not go to work. Of course, if you decide not to go, then your boss has a decision to make: whether or not to let you keep your job.

Just as people make decisions, you can write a program that makes decisions. For example, a nuclear missile guidance program might need to make a decision such as "If the command post is under attack, then launch the missiles immediately."

Making decisions involves checking whether a certain condition is true or false. In the above example, if the command post is under attack, then the condition is true, and the program launches its missiles. However, if the command post is not under attack, then the condition is false and the program does not launch its missiles.

In programming terms, a *condition* is anything that can be either true or false. A condition can be

▶ A single variable

▶ An expression

condition = anything that can be either true or false

Boolean variable =
one that can only
contain a value of
true or false

If a condition is a single variable, then the variable type must be a Boolean value. A Boolean variable can contain only a value of true or false. For example, you could have the following code:

```
Private Sub Command1_Click()
  Dim Flag As Boolean
  Flag = True
End Sub
```

In this example, the first line of the procedure (Dim Flag As Boolean) defines a variable named Flag and sets it as a Boolean type, which means the variable Flag can only accept a value of True or False. The next line of code sets the value of Flag to True.

Expression conditions, on the other hand, can contain just about anything as long as the end result is either true for false. For example, 2 + 3 is an expression but does not evaluate to either true or false, and so you can't use it as a condition. On the other hand, the expression 5 = 2 + 3 evaluates to true, so you can use it.

heads up

Visual Basic allows you to use the math operators =, >, <, >=, and <= to create expressions. This table lists definitions for math operators and some examples of how they are used in expression conditions:

Situation	Example
A variable is equal to a number	X = 5
A variable is greater than a number	Y > 0
A variable is less than a number	Z < 1
One variable is greater than or equal to another variable	NewValue >= OldValue
A variable is less than or equal to another variable	SomeValue <= AnotherValue

Boolean operators =
words such as and,
or, and not, which
are used to
create
programming
expressions

Besides math operators, you can use *Boolean operators* — words like and, or, and not — to create expressions. These words allow you to combine two ideas together in some way, or modify the result you get. Grouping the expressions using parentheses helps ensure you get the right results. This table lists some examples of Boolean operators.

Situation	Example
Both expressions have to be true	(X = 5) and (Y < 5)
Either or both expressions can be true	(X = 5) or (Y < 5)
The expression must be false	Not (Z < 1)

When you understand how conditions work, include them in your BASIC code to help your program make decisions.

Using If-Then and If-Then-End If Statements

on the test

To make decisions by checking whether certain conditions are true, Visual Basic uses two types of statements:

- If-Then statements
- If-Then-End If statements

The If-Then statement is designed for situations where you only want to take one action, like this:

```
If NumCats < 100 Then  MsgBox ("Not Enough Cats!")
```

This code says, "If the variable NumCats is less than 100, then display a message box." (Notice that the MsgBox( ) function call must appear on the same line as the If-Then statement.)

on the test

The If-Then-End If statement lets you place more than one line of code after the If-Then statement. Here's an example of an If-Then-End If statement:

```
If NumCats < 100 Then
  MsgBox ("Not Enough Cats!")
  lblNumber.Caption = Str(NumCats)
End If
```

In this case, a message box still appears if the variable NumCats is less than 100. In addition to the message box instruction, Visual Basic follows a second instruction, which converts the variable NumCats into a string and displays it in the Caption property of the label named lblNumber.

Unlike the original If-Then statement, the If-Then-End If statement can contain two or more instructions to follow if a certain condition is true.

Tip: If you want to make sure that you're using the right variable in an If statement, right click on the variable and then choose QuickInfo from the context menu. Visual Basic displays a pop up that shows the variable type and its scope (like local or global).

heads up

Notice that in the If-Then-End If statement the MsgBox( ) function appears on the line below the If-Then statement. This order tells Visual Basic to keep following instructions until it runs into an End If.

Now that you're an If-Then statement expert, take a look at an example program:

on the CD

1 **Load the Decision.VBP project.**

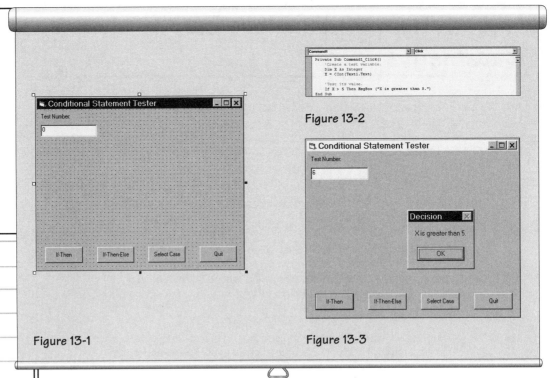

Figure 13-1: The Decision program lets you see how various types of conditional statements work.

Figure 13-2: An example of using an If-Then conditional statement.

Figure 13-3: The If-Then statement code displays a message box when X is greater than 5.

Figure 13-2

Figure 13-1

Figure 13-3

☑ Progress Check

If you can do the following, you've mastered this lesson:

❏ Explain the difference between an If-Then statement and an If-Then-End If statement.

❏ Write a simple If-Then statement.

2 Right-click on the Decision1.FRM file and choose View Object from the context menu.

The Decision1.FRM user interface appears, as shown in Figure 13-1. This program uses one command button for each of the conditional statements discussed in this unit.

3 Right-click on the If-Then button and choose View Code from the context menu.

Visual Basic displays the Code window, as shown in Figure 13-2. The first two lines of code create and initialize X as an integer variable. The If-Then line tests whether the condition is true or false — in this case, whether the value of X is greater than 5. If the condition is true, the program displays a message box.

4 Press F5 to start the program.

5 Click on the If-Then command button.

Nothing happens, because X is not greater than 5.

6 Type 6 in the Test Number text box and then click on the If-Then command button.

A message box appears, as shown in Figure 13-3.

7 Click on OK.

The message box disappears.

8 Click on Quit.

The If-Then statement used by the If-Then command button looks like this:

```
If X > 5 Then MsgBox ("X is greater than 5.")
```

In case you wanted to turn this statement into an If-Then-End If statement, you can rewrite the preceding code as follows:

```
If X > 5 Then
  MsgBox ("X is greater than 5.")
End If
```

This If-Then-End If statement doesn't do anything different — it just shows you how to rewrite an If-Then statement if you really want to.

Using If-Then-Else and If-Then-ElseIf Statements

The biggest limitation of the If-Then statement is that you have to write one If-Then statement to handle a true condition and another If-Then statement to handle a false condition, such as:

```
If Income > 100 Then
  MsgBox ("Get a moose!")
End If

If Income <= 100 Then
  MsgBox ("Get a cat!")
End If
```

Naturally, programming this way can be cumbersome; that's why the If-Then-Else statement exists. The If-Then-Else statement tells Visual Basic, "Follow the first group of instructions if the condition is true. If the condition isn't true, then follow the second group of instructions."

Here's what the above statements would look like using an If-Then-Else statement:

```
If Income > 100 Then
  MsgBox ("Get a moose!")
Else
  MsgBox ("Get a cat!")
End If
```

The preceding If-Then-Else statement tells Visual Basic, "Check the value of the variable called Income. If the value of Income is greater than 100, display a dialog box with the words 'Get a moose!' in it. Otherwise display a dialog box with the words 'Get a cat!' in it."

If-Then-Else statements can choose from two choices

extra credit

Using the IIf() Function

If you have a small If-Then-Else statement, you can also use the IIf() function like this:

```
MsgBox IIf(Income > 100),
  "Get a moose!", "Get a
  cat!")
```

The IIf() function uses three arguments. The first is an expression or variable that evaluates to true or false. The second contains the value you want returned if the first argument is true. The third contains the value you want returned otherwise. The advantage to using the IIf() function is that you can fit it all on one line of code. In the case of our example, you'll display a message box with one of two statements depending on the value of Income.

If-Then-ElseIf statements can choose from three or more choices

You can define two choices with an If-Then-Else statement. If you want to choose among three or more choices, use the If-Then-ElseIf statement, using as many ElseIf clauses as needed to make the decision. Here's what an If-Then-ElseIf statement looks like:

```
If Income > 1000 Then
  MsgBox ("Get a Moose!")
ElseIf Income > 500 Then
  MsgBox ("Get a Cat!")
ElseIf Income > 250 Then
  MsgBox ("Get a Dog!")
Else
  MsgBox ("Get a Mouse!")
End If
```

The If-Then-ElseIf statement tells Visual Basic, "Check the value of the variable called Income." Visual Basic decides what to display based on the value of the variable:

If the Value of Income Is	Then Display a Dialog Box That Says
Greater than 1000	"Get a Moose!"
Less than 1000 but greater than 500	"Get a Cat!"
Less than 500 but greater than 250	"Get a Dog!"
Less than or equal to 250	"Get a Mouse!"

The If-Then-ElseIf statement looks just like the If-Then-Else statement except for the ElseIf clause. Every time you come to an ElseIf, Visual Basic has to make a decision. If the condition is true, then Visual Basic does whatever follows the ElseIf statement.

heads up

The If-Then-ElseIf statement checks conditions from top to bottom, which means that you have to place your conditions in the order you want Visual Basic to check them. As soon as Visual Basic finds a true condition, the program follows the instructions immediately underneath the condition and refuses to check any conditions that may follow later.

In case you don't want to check for every possible condition, use an Else clause at the very end of the code. The Else clause tells Visual Basic that if none of the conditions are true, then do something generic.

Note: You don't have to include an Else clause with an If-Then-ElseIf statement. If you don't include an Else clause and Visual Basic doesn't find any conditions that match, it simply ignores all the instructions stored in the entire If-Then-ElseIf statement.

To see an example of how to use an If-Then-Else statement, follow these steps:

on the CD

1 **Load the Decision.VBP project.**

2 **Right-click on the Decision1.FRM Form file and choose View Object from the context menu.**

3 **Right-click on the If-Then-Else command button and choose View Code from the context menu.**

Visual Basic displays the Code window. The first two lines of code create and initialize an integer variable. Then the If-Then-Else statement checks whether the value of X is greater than 5. If so, Visual Basic displays a message box with the message "X is greater than 5" inside. If not, Visual Basic displays a message box with the message "X is less than or equal to 5."

4 **Press F5.**

5 **Click on the If-Then-Else command button.**

A message box appears. Notice that the message box tells you that X is less than or equal to 5.

6 **Click on OK.**

7 **Type** 6 **in the Test Number text box and then click on the If-Then-Else command button.**

A message box appears, displaying the message "X is greater than 5."

8 **Click on OK.**

9 **Click on Quit.**

Recess

Congratulations on making it this far. As you can see, conditional code can be a powerful addition to your Visual Basic program. Too bad you can't use it in your personal life, like in deciding whether or not to go to work today, whether to drive or take the bus, which video to rent . . .

Else clause = if none of the conditions are true, do something generic

☑ Progress Check

If you can do the following, you've mastered this lesson:

❑ Write one If-Then-ElseIf statement to replace two or more If-Then statements.

❑ Write a simple If-Then-ElseIf statement that uses the Else clause at the end.

❑ Write a simple If-Then-ElseIf statement that does not use the Else clause at the end.

Lesson 13-3   Using Select Case Statements

Select Case
statement lets
program choose
from many choices

The If-Then-ElseIf statement lets you compare a different condition for each ElseIf clause. Unfortunately, typing multiple ElseIf-Then statements over and over again is cumbersome.

on the test

As a simpler solution, use the Select Case statement. Essentially, a Select Case statement lets your program choose from one of many choices. For example:

```
Select Case Dinner
  Case "Chinese"
    MsgBox ("You ordered Chinese")
  Case "Italian"
    MsgBox ("You ordered Italian")
  Case Else
    MsgBox ("You get leftovers.")
End Select
```

In this example, a variable named Dinner contains a string. Visual Basic checks to see whether the string in the Dinner variable matches any of the selections in the list (the *Case* clauses). If you select one of the choices listed, then you get General Tso's chicken or lasagna. If not, you get leftovers.

Note: As with the If-Then-ElseIf statement, you don't have to provide a Case Else clause if you don't want to. To practice using a Select Case Statement, follow these steps:

1 Load the Decision.VBP project.

2 Right-click on the Decision1.FRM file and choose View Object from the context menu.

3 Right-click on the Case Statement command button and choose View Code from the context menu.

Visual Basic displays the Code window. The Select Case statement just compares the value of X to 5 and displays the appropriate message box.

4 Press F5.

5 Type 5 in the Test Number text box and click on the Select Case command button.

A message box appears.

6 Click on OK.

7 Click on Quit.

☑ Progress Check

If you can do the following, you've mastered this lesson:

❑ Explain the advantages of the Select Case statement over the If-Then-ElseIf statement.

❑ Write a simple Select Case statement.

Unit 13 Quiz

Circle the letter of the correct answer or answers for each of the following questions. Each question may have more than one answer, so don't get complacent just because you find the first right answer.

1. **The If-Then-Else statement works in what way?**

   A. Just like politicians: The If-Then-Else statement doesn't do any work at all, but it looks complicated and useful.

   B. With an If-Then-Else statement, if some condition is true, then Visual Basic takes some kind of action. If the condition is false, Visual Basic does something else.

   C. You use If-Then-Else statements when you want your computer to make up your mind for you.

   D. Nobody really knows because only subjective testing can fully realize the true potential of this programming statement.

   E. If some condition isn't true, the If-Then-Else statement works by questioning the wisdom of the programmer who wrote the code in the first place.

2. **A Select Case statement works in a completely different way than a simple If-Then statement. How do the two differ?**

   A. Gee, I don't know. Microsoft didn't document this feature.

   B. The If-Then statement is mundane, but really strange things happen when you use the Select Case statement.

   C. Lawyers use the Select Case statement to determine which cases they should decide to take.

   D. The Select Case statement checks to see whether multiple conditions are true. A simple If-Then statement only checks to see whether one condition is true.

   E. The If-Then statement allows a program to make decisions, but the Select Case statement gets on everyone's case about them.

3. **What special features does an If-Then-End If Statement provide?**

   A. It adds the words End If to the end of the statement.

   B. No special features are provided, but you do get to type more by using this format.

   C. People who have trouble finishing conversations use this format so that they know when the If-Then statement ends.

   D. The If-Then-End If statement is no different from the If-Then statement, except that the If-Then-End If statement is more formal.

   E. The If-Then-End If statement lets you place more than one line of code after the If-Then statement.

4. **The If-Then-ElseIf statement allows you to:**

   A. Select between at least two different items.

   B. Avoid making decisions by obfuscating the facts.

   C. Select between many different items.

   D. Create complex code that no one can possibly understand.

   E. Leave other programmers looking in the online Help for information.

5. **How do If-Then-ElseIf and Select Case statements differ?**

   A. The Select Case statement is designed to work with a single variable.

   B. They don't. Microsoft just created both to fool programmers.

   C. Huh?

   D. The If-Then-ElseIf statement is more flexible because you can check different conditions within each ElseIf clause.

   E. The Select Case statement is less error-prone and faster to use because it requires less typing on the part of the programmer.

Unit 13 Exercise

In this exercise, you get a chance to write real BASIC code to make an If-Then-ElseIf statement work just like a Case Select statement.

on the CD

1. Load the Decision.VBP project.

2. Right-click on the Decision1.FRM form file and choose View Object from the context menu.

3. Right-click on the If-Then-Else button and choose View Code from the context menu.

   Visual Basic displays the Code window (refer to Figure 13-4).

4. Modify the If-Then-Else statement as shown in bold below. Make sure that you modify the last message box caption as shown by removing "less than or."

```
'Test its value.
If X > 5 Then
    MsgBox ("X is greater than 5.")
ElseIf X < 5 Then
    MsgBox ("X is less than 5.")
Else
    MsgBox ("X is equal to 5.")
End If
```

5. Press F5 to start the program.

6. Type 5 in the Test Number text box; click on the If-Then-Else command button.

   A message box appears. Now the If-Then-Else command button works just like the Select Case command button.

7. Click on OK and then click on Quit.

Learning to Loop

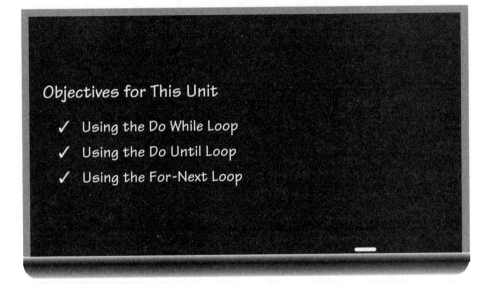

Objectives for This Unit

✓ Using the Do While Loop

✓ Using the Do Until Loop

✓ Using the For-Next Loop

Prerequisites

▶ Opening the Code window (Lesson 1-2)

▶ Writing BASIC code (Lesson 11-3)

▶ Writing If-Then statements (Lesson 13-1)

▶ Doloop.VBP
on the CD

When you write a program, you have to tell the computer what to do step by step. But what happens if you need to tell the computer to perform one or more instructions over and over again?

You can take the time to write each step repeatedly, but this is tedious, not to mention inefficient and downright boring. As a simpler solution, use *loops* instead.

on the test

Loops tell Visual Basic, "See those instructions? I'm only going to write them once, but I want you to repeat them a certain number of times before stopping." By using loops in your program, you can write shorter programs that are easier to write and understand.

Visual Basic provides three kinds of loops. Each type of loop tells your program to keep doing something over and over again. The difference between the three kinds of loops is the way they keep the loop going. The following list defines each loop type:

▶ **Do While.** The Do While loop keeps repeating itself as long as a condition is true. For example, you may want to keep subtracting 1 from a number while the number is greater than 0. As soon as the number is less than or equal to 0, the loop stops.

- ◆ **Do Until.** The Do Until loop keeps repeating itself until a condition becomes true. For example, you can have a loop that keeps adding $1 to your bank account until you're a millionaire.

- ◆ **For Next.** The For Next loop repeats itself a specific number of times. For example, you may have a game program that tells animated androids to fire a missile at you three times before stopping, regardless of whether the missile hits its target or not.

extra credit

Using the With statement

The With statement doesn't actually fit into the category of a looping statement, but it can help you reduce the amount of code you need to type and make your code easier to read. You use it when you need to change two or more properties for one object. Say that you wanted to change the properties for a label. You could use the following With statement to do it:

```
With lblSample

    .Caption = "Hello"

    .BorderStyle =
vbFixedSingle

    .Alignment =
vbRightJustify

End With
```

The sample code would change the Caption, BorderStyle, and Alignment property values for the lblSample object. You always end a With statement with End With. When Visual Basic sees End With, it knows that you are no longer talking about a specific object.

Not only does the With statement make your code easier to read, but it helps you organize your code better. Using a With statement keeps all of the code for a particular object together (as much as possible at least), making it easier for someone to see everything you've done with it.

Lesson 14-1   Using the Do While Loop

Do While loop checks whether the condition is true before running the instructions

on the test

Do While loops have a special feature that the other two types of loops don't. Do While loops check to see whether a condition is true before running the instructions contained inside the loop. Therefore, a loop may not run at all if the condition is not true the first time that Visual Basic checks it.

Consider a Do While loop that looks like this:

```
Do While X > 0
  X = X - 1
Loop
```

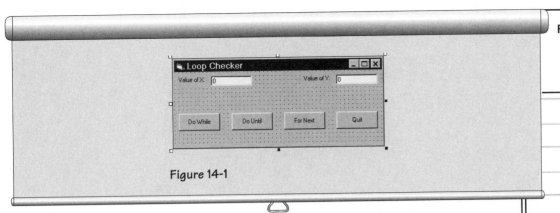

Figure 14-1

Figure 14-1: The Doloop program allows you to see how various types of loops work.

Notes:

This Do While loop tells Visual Basic, "Follow all the instructions sandwiched between the Do While line (which marks the start of the loop) and the Loop line (which marks the end of the loop)." In this case, only one instruction is present, and it tells Visual Basic to subtract one (1) from the value of X as long as the value of X is greater than zero (0).

But what if X is equal to 0? Well, then the loop won't run at all, because the expression X > 0 is not true. X must be greater than 0 before the loop can run even once.

Here's another variation of the Do While loop called (surprise!) the Do-Loop While loop.

```
Do
  X = X - 1
Loop While X > 0
```

It may look like the same loop, but this version always runs at least once. In addition, this variation of the loop checks the condition only after it runs the code inside.

So, now what if X is equal to 0? The loop runs once. Even if X is a negative number, the loop still runs at least once.

Now that you know how this kind of loop works, take a look at a practical example. In this example, you type a number that the program stores in a variable called X. This X variable tells the Do While loop to display a dialog box X number of times, so if you type the number 3 into the program, the Do While loop displays a dialog box three times.

Do While loops always run at least once

on the CD

1 Load the Doloop.VBP project.

2 Right-click on Form1 and then choose View Object from the context menu.

The user interface appears as shown in Figure 14-1. This window has one command button for each of the loops described in this unit.

Figure 14-2: The Do While loop code displays a message box and changes a text box value.

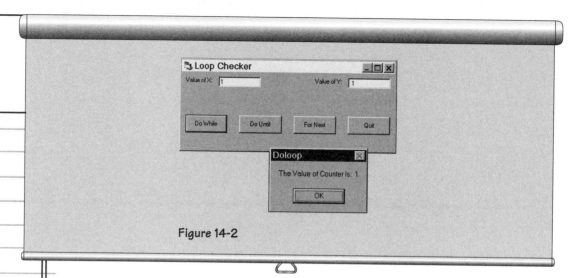

Figure 14-2

Notes:

3 **Right-click on the Do While command button and then choose View Code from the context menu.**

Visual Basic displays the Code window. The first two lines of code create and initialize Counter as an integer variable. The next line (X = CInt(Text1.Text)) gets the number from the Text1 text box (the one labeled Value of X in Figure 14-1) and stores the number in variable X.

The Do While loop checks to see if the value of Counter is less than X. If the value of Counter is less than the value of X, the loop adds 1 to the value of Counter and displays this value in the Text2 text box.

4 **Press F5 to run the program.**

5 **Click on the Do While command button.**

Nothing happens because Counter is equal to X.

6 **Type 1 in the Value of X text box and click on the Do While command button.**

A message box appears, as shown in Figure 14-2. Notice that the Value of Y text box contains a value of 1.

7 **Click on OK.**

The message box disappears, and the loop stops. The Value of Y text box still contains a value of 1.

8 **Click on Quit.**

The Do While loop and its cousin the Do-Loop While loop are just two ways that Visual Basic lets you repeat one or more instructions over and over until a value or an expression becomes true. Lessons 14-2 and 14-3 show you the other ways that Visual Basic can repeat one or more instructions.

☑ **Progress Check**

You've mastered this lesson if you can do the following:

❑ Explain the differences between the Do While loop and Do-Loop While loop.

❑ Write a simple Do While loop and a Do-Loop While loop.

Using the Do Until Loop

A Do Until loop keeps running the same instructions over and over until a certain condition becomes true. This means that a loop may not run at all if the condition is true the first time that Visual Basic checks it.

For example, study this typical Do Until loop:

```
Do Until X <= 0
    X = X - 1
Loop
```

This Do Until loop tells Visual Basic, "Follow all the instructions sandwiched between the Do Until line (which marks the start of the loop) and the Loop line (which marks the end of the loop)." In this case, there's only one instruction, and that tells Visual Basic to subtract one from the value of X until the value of X is less than zero.

What if X is equal to 0? Then the loop won't run at all, because the expression X <= 0 is already true. X must be greater than 0 before the loop can run even once.

heads up

If you're not careful about your conditions, you may create an endless loop by mistake. For example, consider this Do Until loop:

```
Do Until X > 0
    X = X - 1
Loop
```

If the value of X is 0 to begin with, this loop will never end, because X will just get more and more negative.

on the test

An endless loop is a common problem that occurs when a loop starts and never stops. If you ever write a program that seems to freeze, it may be stuck in an endless loop. If your program ever gets stuck in an endless loop, you can often break out of it by pressing Ctrl+Break and clicking on the End button in the Toolbar, pressing Ctrl+Alt+Delete and ending the program using the Task Manager, or (as a last resort) turning your computer off and then turning it back on again.

To give you some real-life, hands-on, hyphenated terminology in seeing how a Do-Until loop works, try the following steps:

on the CD

1 Load the Doloop.VBP project.

2 Press F5 to start the program.

3 Click on the Do Until command button.

The Value of Y text box displays the number 1, and a message box appears (see Figure 14-2).

---

break out of an endless loop by pressing Ctrl+Break and then clicking on the End button

Break key shares the same position as the Pause key on most keyboards

Notes:

☑ Progress Check

You've mastered this lesson if you can do the following:

❑ Understand how to avoid writing an endless loop.

❑ Write a simple Do Until loop.

4 **Click on OK.**

Another message dialog box appears. The value of Counter will increase by one. You can keep clicking on OK all day long — the code is stuck in an endless loop. Now you can start to appreciate the problem of getting caught in an endless loop in a program.

5 **Press Ctrl+Break and then click on the End button on the Toolbar.**

6 **In the Code window, change the Do Until Counter < X line in the Do Until loop so it looks like the following line of code:**

```
Do Until Counter >= X
```

7 **Press F5.**

8 **Type 1 in the Value of X text box and click on the Do Until button.**

The Value of Y text box changes and displays a message box, as in Figure 14-2.

9 **Click on OK.**

The message box disappears and the loop stops. The Value of Y text box still displays the value of 1.

10 **Type 0 (zero) in the Value of X text box and click on the Do Until command button.**

Nothing happens. The Do Until button works just like the Do While button now.

11 **Click on Quit.**

So now you know how to make a Do Until loop behave like a Do While loop — just change the test condition. It may not always be easy to change the condition (conditions are covered in Unit 12), so make sure you know how to use both kinds of loops.

There's another version of the Do Until loop called the Do-Loop Until loop. The Do-Loop Until loop always runs at least once, because it doesn't check if a condition is true until the end of the loop.

Lesson 14-3

Using the For-Next Loop

Both the Do While and the Do Until loops may loop zero or more times, depending on their condition. But what if you want to repeat certain instructions a fixed number of times? That's when you have to use a For-Next loop.

For-Next loops are unique because they can count. The following For-Next loop loops exactly four times:

```
For Counter = 1 to 4
    MsgBox ("The value of Counter is: " + CStr(Counter))
Next Counter
```

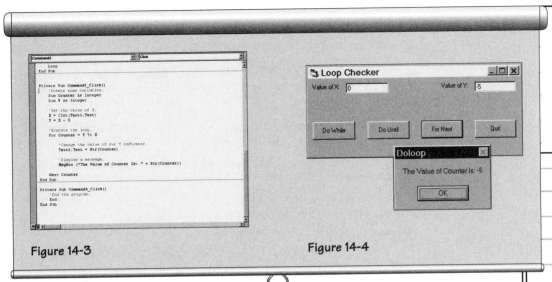

Figure 14-3
Figure 14-4

Figure 14-3: An example of using a For-Next loop.

Figure 14-4: The For-Next loop code displays a message box and changes a text box value.

Besides counting, For-Next loops can also count by specific increments, such as counting by 5 or 3 using the Step clause (which is an optional part of the loop command). The same Step clause lets the loop count backwards. The following examples show how these two forms of the For Next loop work.

```
'Count by five.
For Counter = 0 to 100 Step 5
   MsgBox ("The Value of Counter Is: " + CStr(Counter))
Next Counter
```

```
'Count backwards by five.
For Counter = 100 to 0 Step -5
   MsgBox ("The Value of Counter Is: " + CStr(Counter))
Next Counter
```

Both examples display a message box 21 times. The first example counts up by 5 from 0 to 100. The second example counts down by 5 from 100 to 0.

To see how a For-Next loop works in an actual program, try the following steps:

on the CD

1 Load the Doloop.VBP project.

2 Right-click on the For Next command button and then choose View Code from the context menu.

Visual Basic displays the Code window, as shown in Figure 14-3. The first four lines of code create and initialize two integer variables named Counter and Y. Notice that this code makes Y equal to X – 5. Pay attention to this very important line of code; you'll see why in a few moments.

The For Next line (For Counter = Y To X) is where all the loop action takes place. Counter starts at the value of Y. Because we didn't specify the Step clause, Visual Basic will add one to the Counter variable every time it completes a loop. When Counter equals X, the loop stops.

3 Press F5 to run the program.

use the Step clause in the For Next loop to increase or decrease a variable by a specific amount

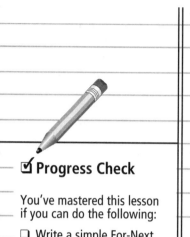

☑ Progress Check

You've mastered this lesson if you can do the following:

❑ Write a simple For-Next loop.

❑ Write a For-Next loop that can count up by five.

❑ Write a For-Next loop that can count backwards by five.

 Click on the For Next command button.

The Value of Y text box changes and displays a message box, as shown in Figure 14-4.

5 Click on OK.

The message box reappears with a new value. In fact, you have to click on OK a total of six times before the loop ends.

6 Type any number into the Value of X text box and click on the For Next command button.

You get the same results as before. Visual Basic asks you to press OK six times before the loop ends. Only the counter value changes.

7 Click on Quit.

on the test

The preceding example program shows how to define the starting and ending point for the Counter variable. The For-Next loop doesn't care what the starting and ending values are. Visual Basic always places the starting value into the counter variable, runs the code in the loop, and then increments the counter. The loop continues these steps until the counter reaches the end value.

Recess

Knowing how to create loops can make programming a lot easier. Instead of writing every possible step that your program must follow, you can use a loop to make your code repeat certain steps over and over. Just make sure your loops eventually end, or you'll find your programs stuck in an endless loop that will keep the program from working right.

Unit 14 Quiz

Circle the letter of the correct answer or answers for each of the following questions. You could find more than one correct answer for each question, so don't get complacent if you find one answer that looks good.

1. **Why would you want to use the With statement in your code?**

   A. As a means for confusing the issue.

   B. To show someone that you're with them in spirit as they read your code.

   C. To reduce the amount of code you need to type and make it easier for someone else to read.

   D. There is no such thing as a With statement.

   E. As a method for organizing all of the code for an object into one place.

2. **Choose the three types of loops that are provided in Visual Basic.**

   A. Fruit Loops, because Bill Gates really likes that toucan.

   B. Do While loops, which you use to keep repeating something until a condition is no longer true.

   C. Do Until loops, which repeat something until a condition becomes true, the opposite of Do While loops.

   D. You have to use the C programming language if you want to create loops.

   E. For Next loops, which allow you to repeat something a specific number of times.

3. **The special feature of Do While loops is that they**

   A. Run around in circles and scream things in Latin.

   B. Can leap tall buildings in a single bound.

   C. Muffle the noise of jets passing overhead.

   D. Check to see whether a condition is still true before they run the instructions contained within the loop.

   E. Change the space/time continuum.

4. **The special variation of the Do Until loop is the Do-Loop Until loop. What makes this variation so special?**

   A. The loop always executes at least once.

   B. This type of loop doesn't even exist.

   C. The Do-Loop Until loop allows you to show up your boss at programmers' conventions.

   D. You can use the Do-Loop Until loop to check the speed of your new computer.

   E. The condition doesn't get checked by the Do-Loop Until loop until the end of the loop.

5. **What does the Step clause of the For-Next loop do?**

   A. The Step clause allows you to build programs by taking one step at a time.

   B. You can use the Step clause to count by a specific increment.

   C. You can use the Step clause to count backwards.

   D. Actually, it is called the Steep clause — so named for the price of Visual Basic and other related Microsoft products.

   E. You can use the Step clause while power walking to increase your speed — the clause doesn't help your computer at all.

Notes:

6. **How do the start and end values for a For-Next loop affect the counter variable?**

   A. Visual Basic loads the start value into the counter variable at the start of the loop.

   B. There aren't any start or end values; Visual Basic actually refers to them as go and stop.

   C. The counter variable gets the Step value (or 1) added to it for each loop until it is equal or greater than the end value.

   D. You should never provide a start or end value because it causes your screen to turn green, which means you have to get a new monitor.

   E. The start and end values determine what time the loop starts and ends.

Unit 14 Exercise

This exercise lets you try some new For-Next loop effects.

on the CD

1. Load the Doloop.VBP project.

2. Right-click Form1 in the Project window and then choose View Object from the context menu.

3. Right-click on the For Next command button.

   Visual Basic displays the Code window (refer to Figure 14-3).

4. Change the For-Next loop code as highlighted below.

```
Y = X + 20


'Execute the loop.
For Counter = Y To X Step -5
```

5. Press F5.

6. Click on the For Next command button.

   The Value of Y text box changes and displays a message box.

7. Click on OK.

   The message box reappears with a new value. In fact, you have to click OK a total of five times before the loop ends. Did you notice that the loop stopped early this time? What about the values in the Value of Y text box? Notice that they counted backward by 5 instead of forward by one. Using a negative Step value allows you to count backward.

8. Click on Quit.

Using Database Files, Using ActiveX Controls, and Creating EXEs

Prerequisites

▶ Using the Toolbox (Lesson 1-2)

▶ Opening the Code window (Lesson 1-2)

▶ Writing BASIC code (Lesson 11-3)

on the CD ▶ Mydata.MDB

Objectives for This Unit

✓ Connecting a database to Visual Basic

✓ Displaying, adding, and deleting information from a database

✓ Using ActiveX controls in Visual Basic

✓ Creating an EXE

Databases enable you to store on a computer a great deal of information that you think may be important in the future, such as phone numbers, addresses, or names of people. Of course, the real value of databases isn't just in storing information but in making it easy to find that information later.

Think of a database as you think of a closet. Like a closet, you could just dump stuff into a database without regard to order or organization. The trouble is that trying to find something in that closet again is nearly impossible (as any parent with a teenager can testify).

To make finding information that you've stored in a database easy, databases organize information in several different ways. The first way is to place the information into something called a *table*. A database can contain one or more tables where each table contains one type of information.

One table is typically related to another table. For example, one table may contain employee names, and another table may contain salary information for each employee. Because tables can be related, the computer industry came up with the term *relational database*.

Every table is divided into two additional parts that are known as *fields* and *records*. A field contains specific information, such as a first name, a last name, an employee number, or a phone number.

Each record contains one or more fields. For example, storing a bunch of first names is fairly useless. However, a record enables you to store someone's first name, last name, address, phone number, and employee number together so that the information is much more useful to you.

extra credit

The handy-dandy index

To help you find information buried in a database, many databases use something called an *index*. An index is nothing more than an ordered list that points to different pieces of information that are stored in a table. Using an index is like looking for a telephone number in a telephone book or a definition in a dictionary. Without an index, you would have to search a database from start to finish to find what you're looking for. With an index, you can quickly jump to the type of information that you want.

To summarize, here are the major parts of a database:

- A *field* stores specific information, such as a person's name, address, or phone number.
- A *record* contains one or more fields that are related.
- A *table* contains one type of information that is organized into records.
- A *database* can contain any type of information. To organize information easily, a database may store information in *tables*.

Now that you have a rough idea of the different parts of a database, you can better understand how Visual Basic can use a database to store information. Databases can be much more complicated — many publishers even print big, fat books that try to explain databases in three easy steps — but the preceding points should help you understand how the example programs in this unit work.

There are two other things that apply to programming in Visual Basic as a whole. Most database programmers use third-party tools (program parts written by other people) to make database programming as easy as possible. ActiveX controls are an example of these third-party tools. You learn more about ActiveX controls in Lesson 15-3.

fields store specific information

records contain fields

tables organize records

databases may store information as tables

Most database programs are also compiled, which we talk about in Lesson 15-4. There are a lot of reasons to compile a program, but the two most common reasons are:

▶ Compiling makes the database application run faster. A database program has to handle a lot of data, which slows it down. Anything you can do to make the program run faster makes your boss very happy.

▶ Not everyone has a copy of Visual Basic installed on their machine. If you want to give your application to someone else, you have to put it in a form he can use by compiling it to an EXE. A database program always runs on a lot of machines, so database programmers always create EXE files.

Connecting a Database to Visual Basic

Lesson 15-1

Most programs need to store data on disk where the program can retrieve it again at a later time. For example, a word processor needs to store documents, a spreadsheet needs to store worksheets, and games may need to store a list of scores.

When you write a Visual Basic program, you may need to store data on a disk. To make information storage easy, Visual Basic can store and retrieve data in a special database format. Even though you can use the VB Application Wizard to make it easy to add a database to your program (see Lesson 2-3) or the VB Data Form Wizard to create a form when you've already made the connection to a database, it's handy to know how to do it by hand as well.

Tip: Visual Basic can store data in the same file format used by the Microsoft Access database program.

Of course, you can't just plop a database file on a disk and expect your Visual Basic program to magically connect to that file. Instead, you have to use something from the Toolbox called a data control. The data control provides the crucial link between Visual Basic and a database file. To use a data control, follow these steps:

1 Choose **File**⇨**New Project** and then double-click on the Standard EXE icon in the New Project dialog box.

2 Click on the Data icon in the Toolbox and draw the data control on the form, as shown in Figure 15-1.

Depending on your version of Visual Basic, your toolbox may include additional objects called DBGrid, DBList, and DBCombo. These objects let you display information from database files in different ways. You may not always see the additional database objects in your toolbox. If not, just right-click on the toolbox and then choose Components from the context menu (see Lesson 15-3 for details on adding components to your toolbox).

Notes:

Data icon

Figure 15-1: The data
control enables you to
make a connection to
a database.

Figure 15-2: Visual Basic
can connect to many
different database
types.

Notes:

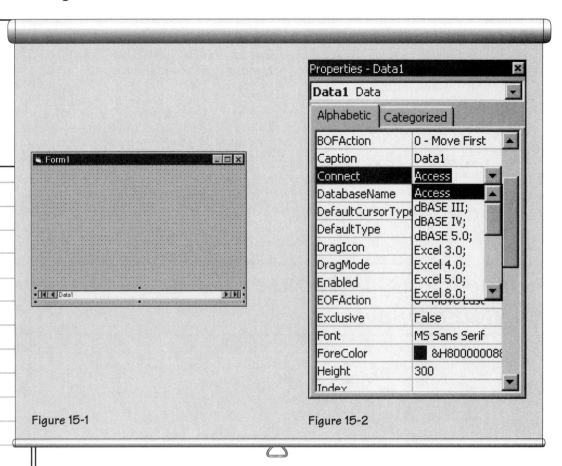

Figure 15-1   Figure 15-2

on the CD

3 **Click on the Connect property in the left-hand column.**

A gray downward-pointing arrow appears in the right-hand column.

4 **Click on the gray downward-pointing arrow in the right-hand column.**

A list like the one shown in Figure 15-2 appears, displaying all the types of
database file formats that Visual Basic can use. In this exercise, select Access
from the Connect property drop-down list.

5 **Double-click in the DatabaseName property in the left-hand column.**

The DatabaseName dialog box appears, as shown in Figure 15-3. You may have
to change drives or directories to find the MyData.MDB database file that you
installed from your Dummies 101 companion CD.

6 **Select the MyData database (see Figure 15-3) and click on Open.**

Visual Basic connects your program to the MyData database. The database
filename and path appear in the DatabaseName property.

7 **Click in the RecordSource property in the left-hand column.**

A gray downward-pointing arrow appears in the right-hand column.

8 **Click on the gray downward-pointing arrow in the right-hand
column.**

After a few seconds, Visual Basic displays a list of available tables within the
database, as shown in Figure 15-4.

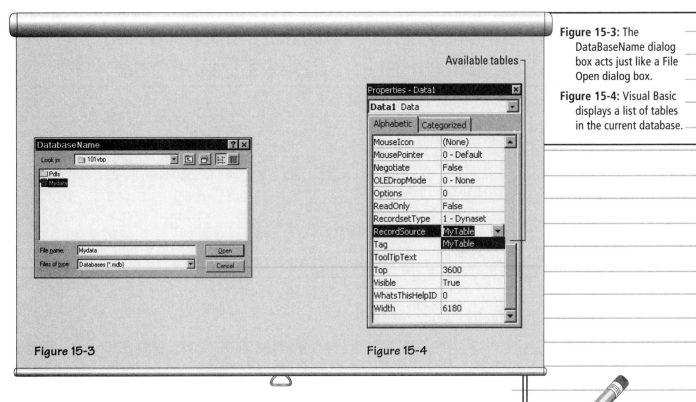

Available tables

Figure 15-3: The DataBaseName dialog box acts just like a File Open dialog box.

Figure 15-4: Visual Basic displays a list of tables in the current database.

Figure 15-3   Figure 15-4

9 **Select the MyTable table.**

Congratulations! By assigning a database name (steps 5 through 6) and a table (steps 7 through 9), you've just connected a database to the data control in your Visual Basic program. At this point, you won't be able to see any of the data in the database file — for that you need to continue to the next lesson.

In summary, to connect a Visual Basic program to a database file, you need to do just the following:

▶ Draw the data control on a form

▶ Set the data control's DatabaseName property to the name of the database file

▶ Set the RecordSource property to a table in the database file

heads up

You may want to save this database connection to use in the next three lessons and the exercise at the end of this unit.

☑ **Progress Check**

If you can do the following, you've mastered this lesson:

❑ Draw the data control on a form.

❑ Change the DatabaseName property to choose a database file.

❑ Change the RecordSource property to choose a table.

Lesson 15-2

Displaying, Adding, and Deleting Information from a Database

After you connect your Visual Basic program to a database file, the next step is to display the database information within your program so you can add, delete, edit, or just plain stare at the information trapped within the database file.

The following objects enable you to view data stored in a database file:

- Check box
- Combo box
- Image box
- Label
- List box
- Picture box
- Text box

Depending on the version of Visual Basic that you have, your Toolbox may include additional objects called DBGrid, DBList, and DBCombo. These additional objects let you display information from database files in different ways.

To get a text box or list box to display information in a database file, you have to set the following two properties:

- DataSource
- DataField

The DataSource property must be set to the name of the data control that you drew on the form. The DataField property can be set to a field. To learn how to display database information within your program, try the following example.

heads up

The following steps assume that you've already drawn a data control on a form as explained in Lesson 15-1. In this exercise you draw a text box to display the contents of a database field.

1 **Click on the TextBox icon in the Visual Basic Toolbox and draw the TextBox control on the form.**

2 **Click in the DataSource property in the left-hand column.**

A gray downward-pointing arrow appears in the right-hand column.

3 **Click on the gray downward-pointing arrow in the right-hand column.**

A list like the one in Figure 15-5 appears, showing all the names of all the data controls that you've drawn on the form. (If you've only drawn one data control, you only see one name on the list.)

4 **Select Data1.**

TextBox icon

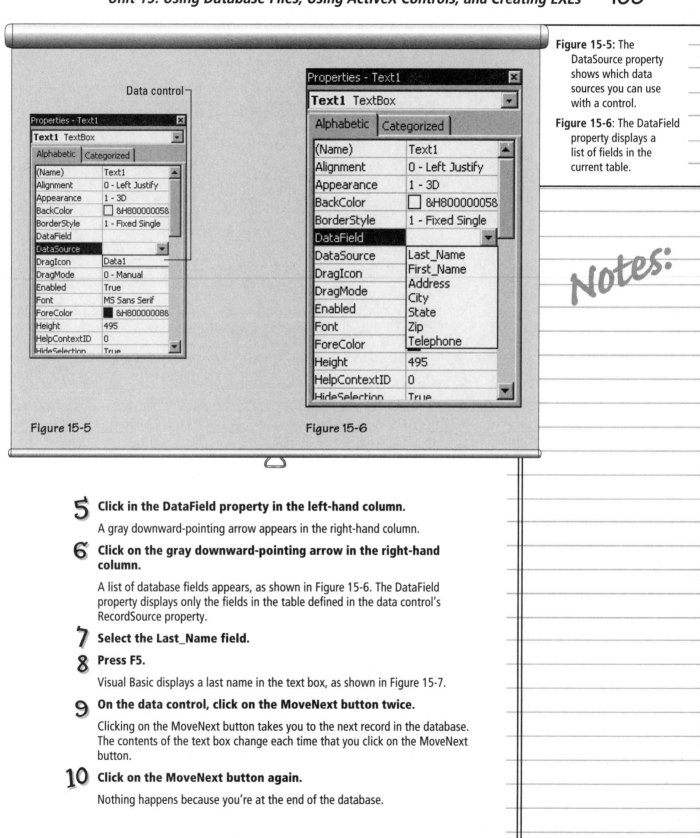

Data control

Figure 15-5: The DataSource property shows which data sources you can use with a control.

Figure 15-6: The DataField property displays a list of fields in the current table.

Figure 15-5   Figure 15-6

Notes:

5 **Click in the DataField property in the left-hand column.**

A gray downward-pointing arrow appears in the right-hand column.

6 **Click on the gray downward-pointing arrow in the right-hand column.**

A list of database fields appears, as shown in Figure 15-6. The DataField property displays only the fields in the table defined in the data control's RecordSource property.

7 **Select the Last_Name field.**

8 **Press F5.**

Visual Basic displays a last name in the text box, as shown in Figure 15-7.

9 **On the data control, click on the MoveNext button twice.**

Clicking on the MoveNext button takes you to the next record in the database. The contents of the text box change each time that you click on the MoveNext button.

10 **Click on the MoveNext button again.**

Nothing happens because you're at the end of the database.

Figure 15-7: Visual Basic replaces the default text in the text box with the current last name in the MyData table.

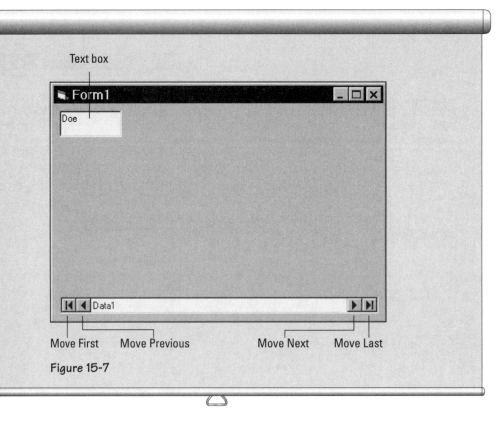

Text box

Move First   Move Previous   Move Next   Move Last

Figure 15-7

☑ **Progress Check**

If you can do the following, you've mastered this lesson:

❏ Make an object (such as a text box or label) display data stored in a database file.

❏ Set the DataSource and DataField properties of an object.

❏ Use the data control to scroll through a database.

11 **Click on the MovePrevious button twice.**

Clicking on the MovePrevious button takes you to the previous record in the database. Again, the contents of the text box change each time that you click the MovePrevious button, but the names appear in the opposite order from step 10.

12 **Click on the End button on the Toolbar.**

You may want to save this simple database application to use in the next two lessons and the exercise at the end of this unit.

Recess

In the old days of programming, it was extremely difficult to write a program that could share data with a database file. When Microsoft introduced this cooperative feature in Visual Basic, programmers all over the world heralded this obvious advantage as a new revolution in programming. It was like General Motors introducing a car with four wheels and everyone wondering why no one thought of the idea before.

While you take a break, think of all the programs you can write that will store information in a database file. With these possibilities racing through your mind, sip another cup of a caffeinated beverage and relax until you feel like moving on to the next lesson.

Using ActiveX Controls
Lesson 15-3

After you write programs for a while, you'll find that Visual Basic doesn't always provide every component you might ever needed to write an application. Even if it does provide a component that you could use, you might be able to find a third-party component that works better or requires less code.

There are a lot of third-party vendors, like Crescent, who write components specifically designed for Visual Basic. Microsoft usually provides a catalog containing a few of these vendors right in the Visual Basic package.

on the test

ActiveX controls are just another kind of component that you can use to make Visual Basic work better. They're actually a "lighter" version of the controls you get in the Visual Basic package because they're designed to work on the Internet. (No one wants to visit a Web site that takes 20 minutes to download.) An ActiveX control file will have the same OCX file extension that the components shipped with Visual Basic do.

Using ActiveX controls means that your applications will be smaller and run somewhat faster. Unfortunately, using ActiveX controls also means that you can't be quite sure where you got a control unless you actually verify the source, which could mean a few extra legal problems if you decide to sell or give your application to others. You'll get ActiveX controls installed on your machine by four different sources: Visual Basic, Web sites on the Internet, other application programs, and ActiveX controls that you write yourself.

ActiveX controls are light versions of the components that come with Visual Basic

Notes:

extra credit

ActiveX controls and your machine

You may eventually get so many ActiveX controls installed on your machine that you feel the need to remove some of them. Every Web site you visit could add some ActiveX controls to your machine. Unlike the applications you install on your machine, these Web sites probably won't remove the ActiveX controls from your machine. That way you won't need to download the ActiveX control again the next time you visit.

Windows 95 comes with a special application in the SYSTEM folder (it's in the main Windows 95 folder on your machine) named RegSvr32. This program is responsible for registering all of the ActiveX controls on your machine. You must register an ActiveX control before you can use it.

Registering a control is easy. Just type RegSvr32 <Name of OCX File> at the DOS command prompt. For example, if you wanted to register an ActiveX control named AControl, you would type: RegSvr32 AControl at the DOS command prompt. RegSvr32 will display a success dialog when it registers your ActiveX control.

You have to "unregister" an ActiveX control before you can remove it from your machine. That way, Windows knows that it's no longer available. To unregister an ActiveX control, just type RegSvr32 -U <Name of OCX File> at the DOS command prompt. RegSvr32 will display a success dialog after it unregisters the ActiveX control.

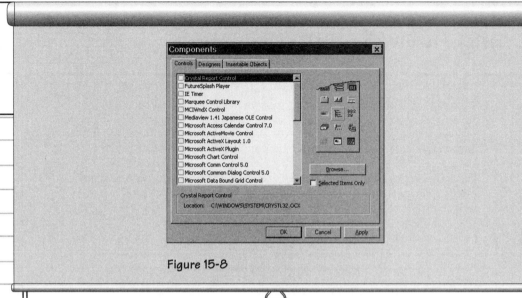

Figure 15-8

Adding and removing ActiveX controls

Just having an ActiveX control installed on your machine won't add it to your program. You have manually add the control so that Visual Basic knows that you want to use it. Likewise, you'll want to remove the ActiveX control if you no longer need it. That way you won't clutter your Toolbox up with unneeded components.

In this exercise you'll add and remove an ActiveX control from your Toolbox.

1 **Right-click on the Toolbox and select Components from the context menu.**

You'll see a Components dialog box as shown in Figure 15-8. There are three different pages in this dialog. The one you're looking at now is the Control page. It contains a list of all the ActiveX controls installed on your machine, even if they didn't come with Visual Basic.

One way that you can begin to figure out whether you should use a control or not is to look at where it's stored. You'll always see a storage location for the currently highlighted control at the bottom of the Components dialog box. If the control is in the SYSTEM folder like the Crystal Report Control is, then you at least know that it's a permanent Windows control. If the control appears anywhere else, you'll want to make sure that it's safe to use. Any controls you find in the OCCACHE folder are Internet specific.

2 **Check the Microsoft ActiveMovie Control entry.**

3 **Click on Apply.**

Visual Basic adds the Microsoft ActiveMovie Control to your Toolbox.

4 **Uncheck the Microsoft ActiveMovie Control entry.**

all ActiveX controls stored in the SYSTEM folder are permanent

all ActiveX controls stored in the OCCACHE folder were downloaded from the Internet

Microsoft ActiveMovie Control icon

5 **Click on Apply.**

Visual Basic removes the Microsoft ActiveMovie Control from your Toolbox.

6 **Click on Cancel.**

The Components dialog box disappears.

See how easy it is to add ActiveX controls to your Toolbox? Once you add the ActiveX control, you can use it just like any other component in your Toolbox.

There were two other pages of ActiveX controls in the Components dialog box shown in Figure 15-8. The Designers page will contain ActiveX controls that help you design something like an entire form. The Insertable Objects page will contain a list of ActiveDocument objects like a Microsoft Word Document or a Corel Draw Graphic that you can insert into your program.

Using an ActiveX control in your program

ActiveX controls get used in your program just like any other component. The big difference is that an ActiveX control could be just about anything. You don't necessarily have to restrict yourself to components like labels or text boxes. Just to show you how easy it is to use an ActiveX control in your application, follow this procedure. (This procedure assumes that you saved the database example from Lesson 15-2.)

1 **Right-click on the Toolbox and then choose Components from the context menu.**

Visual Basic displays the Components dialog box shown in Figure 15-8.

2 **Check the Microsoft Data Bound Grid Control.**

3 **Click on OK.**

Visual Basic adds the Microsoft Data Bound Grid Control to the Toolbar. Even though Microsoft gave this ActiveX control such a long name in the Components dialog box, moving your mouse over the control shows that its short name is DBGrid.

4 **Click on the text box you added previously and then press Delete to remove it.**

5 **Click on the DBGrid component and draw the control on the form as shown in Figure 15-9.**

6 **Click in the DataSource property in the left-hand column.**

A gray downward-pointing arrow appears in the right-hand column.

7 **Click on the gray downward-pointing arrow in the right-hand column.**

A list of data sources appears.

Notes:

Microsoft Data Bound Grid Control (DBGrid) icon

Figure 15-9: The DBGrid component.

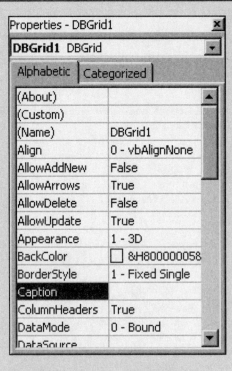

Figure 15-9

☑ Progress Check

If you can do the following, you've mastered this lesson:

❑ Add ActiveX controls to your Toolbox.

❑ Remove ActiveX controls from your Toolbox.

❑ Identify the purpose for each page in the Components dialog.

❑ Use an ActiveX control to make your programming job easier.

8 **Select Data1.**

9 **Press F5.**

Visual Basic displays some records from the database as shown in Figure 15-10.

10 **On the data control, click on the MoveNext button twice.**

Clicking on the MoveNext button moves the DBGrid record pointer down.

11 **Click on the MovePrevious button twice.**

Clicking on the MovePrevious button moves the DBGrid record pointer up.

12 **Click on the End button on the Toolbar.**

As you can see, using ActiveX controls can make your programming job a lot simpler. Make sure you save this project in a separate file for use in the next lesson. The exercise at the end of the Unit uses the project you saved in Lesson 15-2.

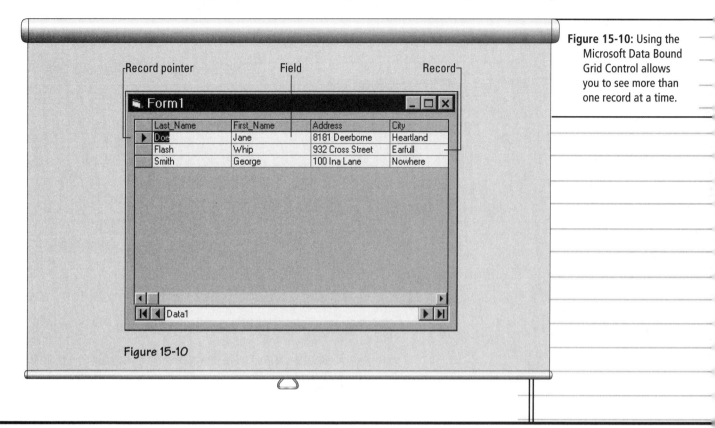

Figure 15-10

Creating EXEs

Lesson 15-4

Somewhere along the way you'll want to give your application to someone else. Unless that person has Visual Basic, you'll need to save your program in a way that they can actually use. In most cases that means creating an EXE file.

There are two kinds of EXE files you can create with Visual Basic. The default type is the P-Code EXE that Visual Basic has always created in the past. A P-Code EXE uses special "tokens" that represent actions that the program is supposed to perform. A run-time interpreter takes the tokens and translates them into something that your machine can understand. The advantage of using a P-Code EXE is that it doesn't take nearly as long to produce. P-Code EXEs are what you should use as you write your program and test it.

on the test

Visual Basic 5.0 can also use something known as a *native code compiler* to create EXE files. A native code EXE file contains instructions that your machine can use directly. It provides the fastest method for executing code and usually results in a smaller program file as well. You pay for these extra features by waiting longer for Visual Basic to produce the EXE file.

Creating a native code EXE file doesn't have to be hard — it's actually pretty simple. Let's take a look at how easy it can be. (This exercise assumes you saved the database programming example from Lesson 15-3.)

Figure 15-11: The Make Project dialog box.

Figure 15-12: The Compile page of the Project1 - Project Properties dialog box allows you to choose a native code EXE.

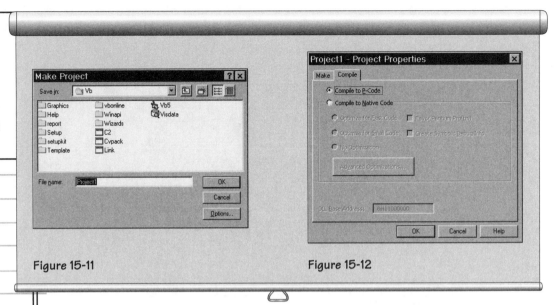

Figure 15-11   Figure 15-12

1 Choose File⇨Make Project1.exe.

Visual Basic displays the Make Project dialog box shown in Figure 15-11. Visual Basic assumes that you want to use the P-Code version of the EXE file because it's faster to create. You need to do some special setups to get the benefits of the native code EXE file.

2 Click on Options.

Visual Basic displays the Project 1 - Project Properties dialog box.

3 Select the Compile page.

You'll see the Compile page shown in Figure 15-12. This is where you'll tell Visual Basic to create a native code EXE in place of a P-Code EXE.

4 Click on the Compile to Native Code option button.

Notice that you can choose the kind of EXE optimization to use. You can choose to make the file smaller or to make the EXE faster. You also get an option for not using any form of optimization, but you won't use this feature very often.

The two check boxes allow you to further optimize how Visual Basic creates the native code EXE file. You can choose to favor Pentium Pro processors, which means that older processors may not execute your program as fast as possible. The Create Symbolic Debug Info check box is for advanced programmers who need to have this information available when using Visual Basic to create something like an ActiveX control.

5 Click on OK.

6 Click on OK again to close the Make Project dialog box.

Visual Basic compiles the EXE file and then places it on disk. You can give the EXE to someone else now so they can benefit from your program as well.

Unit 15 Quiz

For each of the following questions, circle the letter of the correct answer or answers. Be careful! There may be more than one correct answer for each question.

1. **How can you find information in a database?**

    A. To find information in a database, you need the help of a teenager or a small child to show you how to turn on your computer first.

    B. After you've stored information in a database, you have absolutely no hope of ever finding it again.

    C. You need to know the filename of the database, the table, the record, and the field that contains the information you want, such as Last Name.

    D. Ask one or more CIA agents who have top-secret clearance.

    E. You must buy at least a dozen more computer books, which will teach you the answer in 20 days, 3 hours, or 159 simple steps (in your spare time, of course).

2. **What does the data control do?**

    A. Not a whole lot.

    B. It enables you to connect your Visual Basic program to a database file, and it enables you to scroll through a database one record at a time.

    C. The data control just gets in the way, so you can ignore it.

    D. The data control has funny buttons on it that look like the buttons on a VCR. So that means no one knows how to program it.

    E. The data control controls your data. Without it, your data may go out of control and cause serious legal problems for you later.

3. **If you want to display data in a text box or label, what two properties of the text box or label must you change?**

    A. You must change every property of the text box or label and set everything to False.

    B. You don't have to change anything if you don't want to.

    C. Before you can change any properties, you have to see a real estate broker.

    D. You must change the DataSource property and the DataField property.

    E. Don't change anything that you may regret later.

Notes:

4. **Visual Basic can use the same database files as Microsoft Access. Explain why this fact may be important to you.**

   A. This feature enables you to create Visual Basic programs that can modify information in an Access database. Then you can use existing data rather than typing it in all over again.

   B. This isn't important to me because I don't use a computer. In fact, I don't even know why I'm reading this right now.

   C. Many people have used Microsoft Access to store vast amounts of important data. You can write a Visual Basic program that can retrieve that data in a much simpler way, and will not force a novice to learn how to use Access to do the same task.

   D. This feature is important because it forces you to buy yet another Microsoft product, increasing profits for Microsoft and all its stockholders.

   E. It's never important to share data with another program. Whatever gave you that idea in the first place?

5. **How do ActiveX controls compare to standard Visual Basic components?**

   A. ActiveX controls actually work!

   B. ActiveX controls are lighter forms of the standard Visual Basic components, meaning that they work just the same.

   C. Microsoft devised ActiveX controls as a means to steal the Internet browser market.

   D. Only devious programmers can figure out the differences.

   E. There aren't any differences, vendors are just trying to get you to buy new components.

6. **What are the advantages of using a native code compiler?**

   A. Faster program execution speed.

   B. You can create natives faster.

   C. It's sort of like using Morse code, only different.

   D. There aren't any advantages, just a lot of extra work.

   E. You may see a smaller program size.

Unit 15 Exercise

Lesson 15-2 showed how to display database information in a text box. For this exercise, you get to display database information in a label and a text box. The main reason to display information in a label is so users can view the contents of a database file without the ability to edit that data. (Maybe you want them to view, but not change, that particular information.) If you want users to view and edit the contents of a database file, use a text box.

heads up

This exercise assumes that you have drawn a data control on a form as explained in Lesson 15-1.

1. Draw a text box anywhere on a form.

2. Click on the DataSource property in the left-hand column. A gray downward-pointing arrow appears in the right-hand column.

3. Click on the gray downward-pointing arrow in the right-hand column and choose Data1.

4. Click on the DataField property in the left-hand column. A gray downward-pointing arrow appears in the right-hand column.

5. Click on the gray downward-pointing arrow in the right-hand column and choose First_Name.

   This step tells Visual Basic to display the information stored in the First_Name field in the text box you drew in step 1.

6. Draw a label anywhere on the form.

7. Click on the DataSource property in the left-hand column. A gray downward-pointing arrow appears in the right-hand column.

8. Click on the gray downward-pointing arrow in the right-hand column and choose Data1.

9. Click on the DataField property in the left-hand column. A gray downward-pointing arrow appears in the right-hand column.

10. Click on the gray downward-pointing arrow in the right-hand column and choose Last_Name.

    This step tells Visual Basic to display the information stored in the Last_Name field in the label you drew in step 7.

11. Press F5 to run the program. Notice that the text box displays first names and the label displays last names.

12. Click in the text box and type a new name.

13. Click on the MoveNext button on the data control.

14. Click on the MovePrevious button on the data control. Notice that the text box displays the name you typed in step 14. The name you entered is now permanently stored in the MyData.MDB database file, and you didn't have to write a single line of BASIC code to do it. Now aren't you glad you're learning Visual Basic instead of a cryptic language like C++?

Notes:

Part III Review

Unit 11 Summary

- **BASIC code:** Instructions, written in the BASIC programming language, that tell your program what to do next.

- **Event:** When the user does something, such as click the mouse or press a key.

- **Event procedure:** A miniature program that runs whenever the user performs an event.

- **List Properties/Methods pop-up menu:** A Visual Basic helper that tells you about the properties and methods associated with an object as you type its name.

- **VB Application Wizard:** Helps you design the program shell and some of the standard code to support it.

Unit 12 Summary

- **Variable:** A name that can temporarily hold a value, such as a number or a string.

- **String:** Text consisting of letters and numbers, such as "Hello" or "I own 5 cats."

- **Number:** An integer (such as 4 or 78) or a decimal number (such as 3.14 or –43.091).

- **Boolean:** Values that are either true or false.

- **Object:** Anything like a command button or form that you can interact with by using properties, methods, and events.

- **Variant:** A special kind of variable that can hold numbers, strings, or dates.

- **User Defined:** Variables that hold special kinds of data that don't fit into the predefined Visual Basic data types.

- **Date:** A variable used to hold dates like 1 January 1997.

- **Data type:** Used to define what information a variable can hold, such as a number, a string, or a Boolean (true or false) value.

- **List Properties/Methods pop-up menu:** A Visual Basic helper that lists the kinds of variables you can create.

Unit 13 Summary

- **Condition:** A variable or expression that is either true or false.

- **If-Then statement:** A BASIC statement that makes Visual Basic follow a set of instructions only if a condition is true.

- **If-Then-Else statement:** A BASIC statement that provides two sets of instructions for Visual Basic to follow. If a condition is true, then Visual Basic follows one set of instructions. If a condition is false, then Visual Basic follows a second set of instructions.

- **If-Then-ElseIf statement:** A BASIC statement that provides two or more sets of instructions for Visual Basic to follow based on a condition.

- **Select-Case statement:** A BASIC statement that provides two or more sets of instructions for Visual Basic to follow based on a condition.

- **QuickInfo pop-up menu:** Tells you all about the variable used as a condition.

- **IIf() function:** Replaces a simple If-Then-Else statement with a single line of code.

Part III Review

Unit 14 Summary

▶ **Do-While loop:** A BASIC statement that repeats a set of instructions until a condition is no longer true.

▶ **Do-Until loop:** A BASIC statement that repeats a set of instructions until a condition becomes true.

▶ **For-Next loop:** A BASIC statement that repeats a set of instructions a fixed number of times.

▶ **Endless loop:** A loop that never stops running a set of instructions.

▶ **With statement:** Allows you to group all of the statements for a single object together and reduce the amount of code you write at the same time.

Unit 15 Summary

▶ **Database file:** A file that contains information created by a database program such as dBASE, Access, or Paradox.

▶ **Table:** Part of a database file that organizes related information together.

▶ **Field:** A specific chunk of information, such as someone's name or address.

▶ **Record:** A related group of fields, such as a name, address, or phone number.

▶ **Data control:** An object that you can draw on a form that lets you connect a Visual Basic program to a database file.

▶ **ActiveX controls:** A lightweight form of the components normally used by Visual Basic.

▶ **P-Code EXE:** An executable that relies on tokens that are translated by an interpreter into machine code. The main advantage of using P-Code is faster compiles.

▶ **Native Code EXE:** An executable that contains only machine code. The main advantages of using native code are faster execution speed and smaller EXE file size.

Part III Test

The questions on this test cover all the material presented in Units 11, 12, 13, 14, and 15. The answers are in Appendix A.

True False

T   F   1. BASIC codes are instructions that you can write to make your program work.

T   F   2. The List Properties/Methods pop-up menu displays a list of methods you can use with an object like drag for a command button.

T   F   3. When an event occurs, your program doesn't have to do a thing about it.

T   F   4. You use a Boolean variable to hold values that are true or false.

T   F   5. RegSvr32 is a totally useless utility program that no one ever uses.

T   F   6. The IIf( ) function can replace a simple If-Then-Else statement provided there is only one action for each alternative.

T   F   7. A condition is what happens when the user clicks a mouse.

T   F   8. The For-Next loop runs forever without stopping.

T   F   9. Always use a P-Code version of your EXE when high execution speed and small EXE file size are important.

T   F   10. When you create a variable, you can declare it to hold only specific types of data, such as strings.

Multiple Choice

For each of the following questions, circle the correct answer or answers. Some questions may have more than one right answer, so read all the answers carefully.

11. **What is the advantage of a For-Next loop over a Do-While loop?**

    A. A For-Next loop is genetically superior to a Do-While loop.

    B. The Do-While loop runs faster and less efficiently than a For-Next loop.

    C. A For-Next loop can run a specific number of times. A Do-While loop keeps running until a condition is no longer true.

    D. Neither one holds an advantage over the other. They are equal but different.

    E. A For-Next loop is grammatically correct compared to a Do-While loop.

12. **Where will you normally find ActiveX control files on your hard drive?**

    A. Permanent ActiveX control files will normally appear in the SYSTEM folder.

    B. ActiveX controls hide out in the most devious places, you really need to scout around to find them.

    C. ActiveX controls that you download from the Internet normally appear in a temporary storage folder like OCCACHE.

    D. There aren't any ActiveX controls anywhere, they're just Microsoft hype.

    E. Only the CIA knows the location of the ActiveX controls on your machine — the X stands for spy.

Part III Test

13. Why would you want to connect a database file to a Visual Basic program?

A. Just to prove that you can do it.

B. So you can save information in a file.

C. Connecting your Visual Basic program to a database file can be fun. After you do it, you may want to connect a spreadsheet file to a word processor.

D. So you can turn Visual Basic into a database program and throw out your copy of other database programs, like Access, dBASE, or Paradox.

E. Connecting a database file to Visual Basic lets you view and edit the database information.

14. How can you break out of an endless loop?

A. Cry.

B. An endless loop runs forever. That's why it's called an endless loop.

C. Hit the computer with the palm of your hand.

D. Press Ctrl+Break and then click the End button on the Toolbar.

E. Don't write loops in your programs and you won't have to worry about breaking out of an endless loop.

15. What is the relationship between a field and a record?

A. They are first cousins and married, which makes inbreeding a likely possibility.

B. Fields were once married to records, until they broke up.

C. A record contains multiple fields.

D. A record is black vinyl disk used to store music back in the days before compact discs. A field is a grassy area usually reserved for ball playing.

E. Fields have no relationship with records; the two come from two different family backgrounds.

16. What kinds of data can a variant variable hold?

A. Strings, which are text like "Hello world."

B. Population statistics for the entire world, but only if you write them on the head of a pin.

C. Numbers like integers (1 or -23) and decimals (0.1995 or -18000.005).

D. Very large drums of corn flakes that have been pounded into statistically insignificant dust.

E. Dates like 01/15/97 and 23 November 1996.

Part III Test

Matching

17. **Match the database terms with their correct definitions.**

    A. Field
    B. Record
    C. Table
    D. Database file
    E. Data control

    1. Consists of one or more fields
    2. Contains information stored as a file on a disk
    3. Contains a specific chunk of data, such as a name or age
    4. An object that lets you connect a database file to a Visual Basic program
    5. A related group of information in a database file

18. **Match the following values with their data type definitions.**

    A. 4.56E12
    B. 45
    C. 2,147,483,647
    D. January 1, 1999
    E. "Bo the Cat"

    1. A string
    2. An integer
    3. A date
    4. A single
    5. A long

19. **Match the following statements with their proper name.**

    A.
    ```
    Do Until X > 0
    X = X - 1
    Loop
    ```
    1. Do-While loop

    B.
    ```
    For X = 1 to 5
    Print X
    Next X
    ```
    2. For-Next loop

    C.
    ```
    Do
    X = X - 1
    Loop While X > 0
    ```
    3. If-Then-Else statement

    D.
    ```
    If X > 0
    Then
    X = X - 1
    Else
    X = X + 4
    End If
    ```
    4. Select-Case statement

    E.
    ```
    Select Case X
    Case 1
    Print "X = 1"
    Case 2
    Print "X = 2"
    Case Else
    Print "X is 3"
    End Select
    ```
    5. Do-Until loop

20. **Match the animals with where they are most likely to be found in a typical household.**

    A. Cat
    B. Dog
    C. Goldfish
    D. Hamster
    E. Cow

    1. Floating in an aquarium
    2. In a metal cage with a squeaky wheel
    3. Doghouse
    4. Represented by milk and cheese in the refrigerator
    5. Sleeping across your face

Part III Lab Assignment

In this lab assignment, you create a program that uses a database file.

Step 1: Start a new project

You may want to save your project under a unique name so you can find it again.

Step 2: Draw a data control on the form

Modify the DatabaseName and RecordSource properties to connect the data control to an existing Access (MDB) database file, such as the Mydata.MDB file from the companion CD.

Step 3: Draw text boxes and labels

Modify the DataSource and DataField properties of your text boxes and labels so they display information stored in specific fields of your Access database file.

Step 4: Run the program

Use the data control to view different records. Use the text boxes to modify data.

Step 5: Create an EXE

Save your program first as a P-Code EXE. Write down the size of the EXE file and then run it to see how fast it loads. Next, save your program as a native code EXE. Write down the size of the EXE file and then run it again to see if it runs faster.

Polishing Your Program

Part IV

In this part...

"Programming is an art, not a science" is the computer industry's polite way of saying that 99 percent of the programs ever written will never work 100 percent correctly. You may have already experienced the headaches and frustration of trying to run a program, following its instructions perfectly — and having the darn thing not work at all.

To avoid writing programs that don't work or work incorrectly, you need to test your program and uncover problems before you release the program to an unsuspecting public. The better your program works, the happier your users will be, which could mean either a fat pay raise, a flood of checks coming from happy customers who want to buy your program, or the simple satisfaction of knowing that you wrote a complex program that looks good and works with near-perfection.

You also need to know how to distribute your programs so someone else can use them. Of course, the first thing you need to do is create an EXE file. After that, you need to package your application using the Application Setup Wizard. Then you just stick your program files on a disk or CD and send them to a friend. It's that simple!

Tracing and Watching

Objectives for This Unit

✓ Using the Intermediate window

✓ Adding Debug.Print and Debug.Assert commands

✓ Creating a quick watch

✓ Tracing line by line

Prerequisites

▶ Opening the Code window (Lesson 1-2)

▶ Writing BASIC code (Lesson 11-3)

 ▶ Debug.VBP

on the CD ▶ Buggy.VBP

No matter how well you plan your program, you'll still find errors (known as *bugs*) in it. Finding bugs is just another part of programming. To help you find and ruthlessly destroy any bugs in your program, Visual Basic provides several debugging tools, including the Intermediate window (older versions of Visual Basic call the Intermediate window the Debug window), watches, and tracing.

on the test

Bugs normally hide in one of three ways:

▶ **Syntax Errors.** You misspelled a variable name or command by mistake.

▶ **Logic Errors.** You typed commands that work much differently than what you intended. Logic errors are the main cause of endless loops.

▶ **Math Errors.** Your program calculates the wrong answer, either because it's getting incorrect data or because it's just not calculating a result the way that it's supposed to.

Bugs can completely stop your program from working. Or they can be more subtle and let your program work right 99 percent of the time — and then cause a major problem for that 1 percent of the time that someone else tries to use your program.

heads up

Almost every large program has bugs that may prevent it from working 100 percent correctly. (Won't that be comforting to know the next time you fly in a computer-controlled airplane?)

Before you begin the lessons that will tell you all about debugging your program, you may want to display the Debug toolbar. Just right click on the current toolbar and then select Debug from the context menu. The Debug toolbar appears detached from the Standard Visual Basic toolbar. To attach the Debug toolbar in its normal spot, move the toolbar to the left of the Standard toolbar.

Lesson 16-1   Using the Intermediate Window

on the test

The Intermediate window enables you to peek into the guts of your program while it's running. In the Intermediate window, you can use the following types of commands to see how your program is working:

- ▶ **Print.** This command can display the contents of any variable or expression used by your program.

- ▶ **Call.** This command lets you give different data to a procedure just to see how your program works with this new data.

- ▶ **Query Variable or Property Values.** The Intermediate window allows you to ask Visual Basic about a variable or property value.

- ▶ **Change Variable or Property Values.** This command lets you change the value of a variable or property to see how this change may affect your program.

Try using the Intermediate window in the Debug.VBP project. This program takes two numbers and adds them together. Just to make the program a little exciting, you have a choice of multiplying the first number by 1, 10, or 100 before adding it to the second number.

on the CD

1   **Load the Debug.VBP project.**

2   **Press F5 to run the program.**

The Debug program appears, as shown in Figure 16-1. This program is deliberately loaded with bugs. The first command button contains the buggy code. The second command button contains the corrected, debugged code.

3   **Type 1 in the 1st Number text box and type 2 in the 2nd Number text box.**

4   **Click on the Does it Wrong command button.**

The Result text box displays 12, as shown in Figure 16-2. Because 1 + 2 does not equal 12, something is definitely wrong.

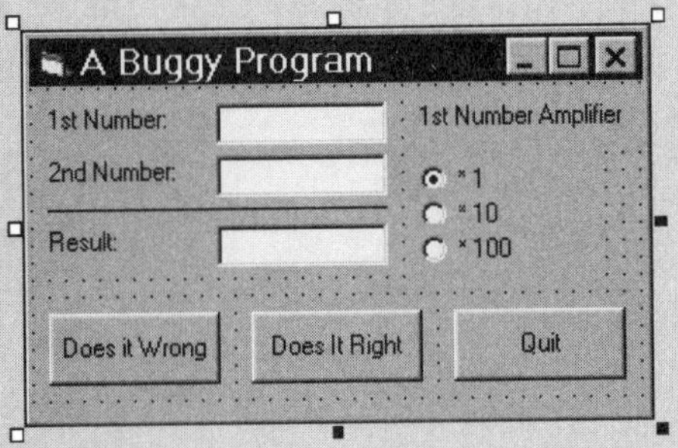

Figure 16-1

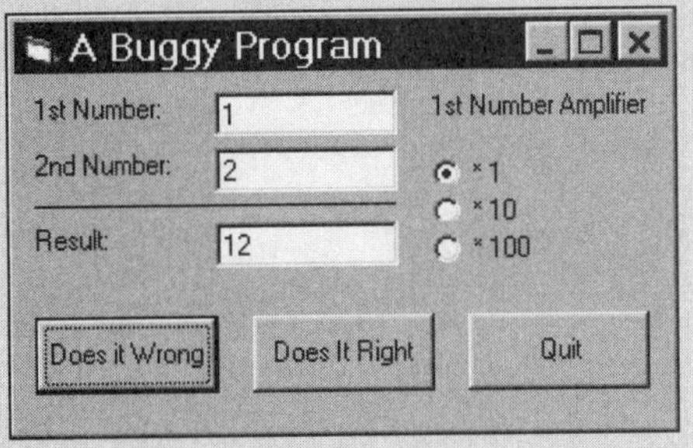

Figure 16-2

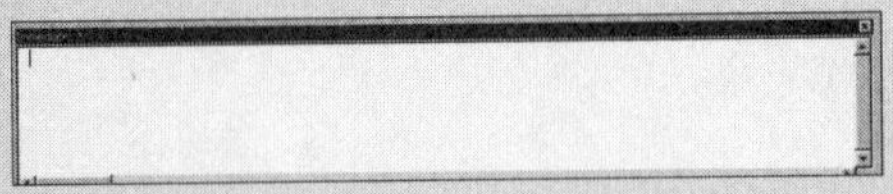

Figure 16-3

Figure 16-4

Figure 16-1: Running the Debug program gives you a screen full of options.

Figure 16-2: A bug that is causing a problem leads to a result like this.

Figure 16-3: The Intermediate window can be used to track down bugs in your program.

Figure 16-4: Using the Call and Print commands in the Intermediate window.

5 **Click on the Does It Right command button.**

The Result text box displays 3, which is the correct answer.

6 **Click on the Break button in the Toolbar to freeze the program so you can examine its guts.**

The Intermediate window appears, as shown in Figure 16-3. (If the Intermediate window doesn't appear, press Ctrl+G or click the Intermediate button on the Debug toolbar.)

7 **Type** call buggyamplify(5, x) **and then press Enter.**

This command gives the BuggyAmplify function a value of 5. If this function works correctly, it should multiply 5 by 1 (because the x1 radio button is checked) and then store the results in the variable X.

8 **Type** print x **and then press Enter.**

The number 50 appears in the Intermediate window, as shown in Figure 16-4. If the BuggyAmplify function is working correctly, it should return a value of 5. Based on the result of 50, you can conclude that the BuggyAmplify function is multiplying incorrectly. In this case, the function is multiplying numbers by 10 when it should be multiplying numbers by 1.

9 **Click on the End button on the Toolbar to stop the program so you can fix the problem.**

10 **Press F7 to display the Code window.**

11 **Click in the Object list box, choose (General) and then click in the Procedure list box and choose Buggy Amplify.**

Break button

Intermediate button

End button

Visual Basic displays the BASIC code belonging to the BuggyAmplify procedure shown here.

```
Public Function BuggyAmplify(OldNumber As Integer,
          NewNumber)
   'Decide which option is selected, then return a
       value.
   If Option1 Then BuggyAmplify = OldNumber * 10
   If Option2 Then BuggyAmplify = OldNumber * 100
   If Option3 Then BuggyAmplify = OldNumber * 1000
End Function
```

12 **Modify the BuggyAmplify function as follows:**

```
Public Function BuggyAmplify(OldNumber As Integer,
          NewNumber)
   'Decide which option is selected, then return a
       value.
   If Option1 Then BuggyAmplify = OldNumber
   If Option2 Then BuggyAmplify = OldNumber * 10
   If Option3 Then BuggyAmplify = OldNumber * 100
End Function
```

What you've just done is correct the buggy code stored in the Does it Wrong command button.

13 **Press F5 to run the program.**

14 **Type 1 in the 1st Number text box, type 2 in the 2nd Number text box, and then click on the Does it Wrong command button.**

This time, you get the correct result of 3. When you're done, click on Quit.

Congratulations, you just debugged a Visual Basic program! After you discovered that the BuggyAmplify procedure was multiplying numbers by 10 by mistake, you corrected the BASIC code so the Does it Wrong command button works correctly (even though the caption still reads "Does it Wrong").

Note: Do not save the Debug.VBP file as modified. You need to use the original Debug.VBP file to complete the remaining lessons in this unit.

Progress Check

If you can do the following, you've mastered this lesson:

❑ Open the Intermediate window.

❑ Type commands in the Intermediate window.

❑ Use the Call command to give test data to a procedure.

❑ Use the Print command to display test data.

Lesson 16-2

Adding Debug.Print and Debug.Assert Commands

As another alternative to typing commands into the Intermediate window, you can use another command called Debug.Print. This command automatically displays the results of specific events in the Intermediate window.

on the test

To use the Debug.Print command, you just have to type **Debug.Print** anywhere in your BASIC code followed by the variable or expression you want to print. For example, if you want to print a variable called FirstNumber, you would use the following code:

```
Debug.Print FirstNumber
```

If this line were inserted in your BASIC code, Visual Basic would find the value of FirstNumber and print it in the Intermediate window for you automatically.

You can also test the value of a variable at certain points in the program and tell Visual Basic to stop, if the variable doesn't contain the value that you expect it to, by using the Debug.Assert command. This command works sort of like pressing the Break button, except the task is done for you automatically.

To use the Debug.Assert command, you just type **Debug.Assert** anywhere in your Basic code, followed by the variable or expression you want to check. For example, if you want to make sure that a variable named Amplified contains the value of 1, you would type:

```
Debug.Assert Amplified = 1
```

To see how these two commands work, try the following experiment:

on the CD

1 Load the Debug.VBP project.

2 Click on View Object to view the user interface of the Debug.VBP program.

3 Double-click on the Does it Wrong command button.

Visual Basic displays the Code window.

4 Type the four Debug.Print and one Debug.Assert commands shown in bold below to make the errors easy to see. (Remember not to save these changes when the lesson is done.)

```
'Get the first two numbers.
FirstNumber = Int(CInt(Text1))
SecondNumber = Int(CInt(Text2))

'Make sure the first number was converted properly.
Debug.Print "First Number:"
Debug.Print FirstNumber

'Amplify the 1st number.
Call BuggyAmplify(FirstNumber, Amplified)

'Check the results.
Debug.Print "Results:"
```

(continued)

Figure 16-5: Debug.Print command prints results in the Intermediate window.

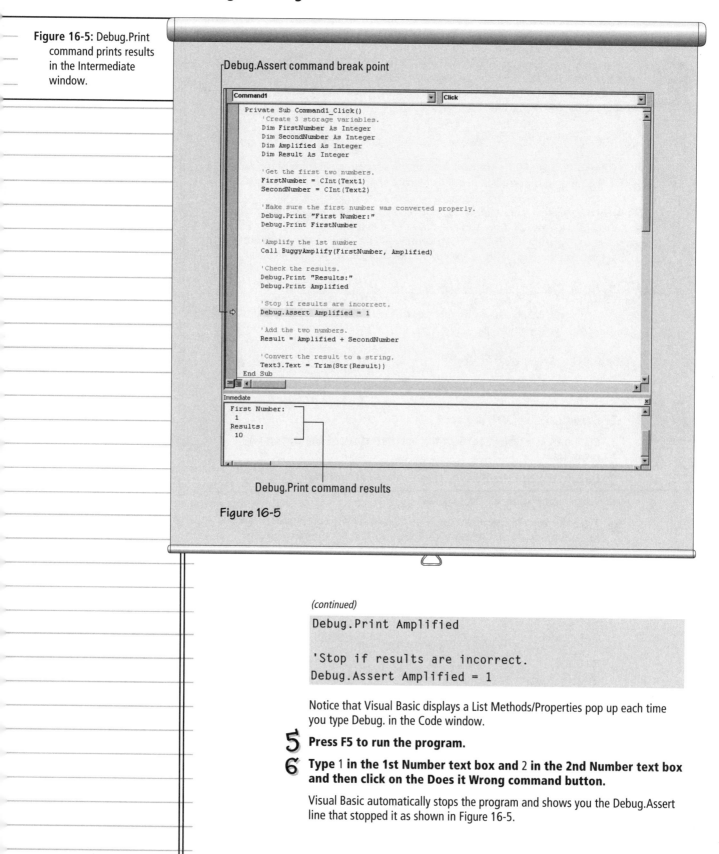

Debug.Assert command break point

```
Command1                                        ▼   Click                                    ▼
Private Sub Command1_Click()
    'Create 3 storage variables.
    Dim FirstNumber As Integer
    Dim SecondNumber As Integer
    Dim Amplified As Integer
    Dim Result As Integer

    'Get the first two numbers.
    FirstNumber = CInt(Text1)
    SecondNumber = CInt(Text2)

    'Make sure the first number was converted properly.
    Debug.Print "First Number:"
    Debug.Print FirstNumber

    'Amplify the 1st number
    Call BuggyAmplify(FirstNumber, Amplified)

    'Check the results.
    Debug.Print "Results:"
    Debug.Print Amplified

    'Stop if results are incorrect.
⇨   Debug.Assert Amplified = 1

    'Add the two numbers.
    Result = Amplified + SecondNumber

    'Convert the result to a string.
    Text3.Text = Trim(Str(Result))
End Sub
```

```
Immediate
First Number:
    1
Results:
    10
```

Debug.Print command results

Figure 16-5

(continued)

```
Debug.Print Amplified

'Stop if results are incorrect.
Debug.Assert Amplified = 1
```

Notice that Visual Basic displays a List Methods/Properties pop up each time you type Debug. in the Code window.

5 **Press F5 to run the program.**

6 **Type** 1 **in the 1st Number text box and** 2 **in the 2nd Number text box and then click on the Does it Wrong command button.**

Visual Basic automatically stops the program and shows you the Debug.Assert line that stopped it as shown in Figure 16-5.

Notice that the program doesn't display any results because you stopped the program before you displayed the information in Text3. However, this time the Intermediate window contains the results of the Debug.Print command (see Figure 16-5). You can see that the first number is incorrectly being multiplied by 10.

7 **Click on Quit.**

Remember: Do not save the changes made in this lesson.

Tip: Whenever you think you know where a bug might be hiding, insert a Debug.Print or Debug.Assert command in that portion of your code.

heads up

Adding comments to your Debug.Print and Debug.Assert commands (like you did in step 5) is a good idea. This additional text helps you identify the location of the Debug.Print and Debug.Assert commands. In small programs, this isn't a big deal, but in large programs, knowing the location of your Debug.Print and Debug.Assert commands can help you identify the exact location where your program is messing up.

In addition, the Debug.Print or Debug.Assert line also helps you locate all the debugging code in your program, so you can remove the debugging code before shipping your program to the market.

☑ Progress Check

If you can do the following, you've mastered this lesson:

❑ Type the Debug.Print command in the Code window.

❑ Type the Debug.Assert command in the Code window.

❑ Determine where the Debug.Assert command stopped the program.

❑ View the results of the Debug.Print command in the Intermediate window.

Creating a Quick Watch

Lesson 16-3

The Debug.Print and Debug.Assert commands can help you pinpoint where your program may be messing up, but what if you don't know the approximate location where a bug may be hiding? For those situations, you can use a quick watch.

A *quick watch* tells Visual Basic, "See that variable? Every time its value changes, print its value in the Intermediate window for me automatically." To discover the wonders of quick watches, try the following:

on the CD

1 **Load the Debug.VBP project.**

2 **Press F5 to start the program.**

3 **Click on the Break button on the Toolbar to temporarily pause the program.**

4 **Press F7 to display the Code window.**

5 **Click in the Object list box of the Code window and choose Command1.**

Visual Basic displays actual BASIC source code that makes the Command1 button work, as shown in Figure 16-6.

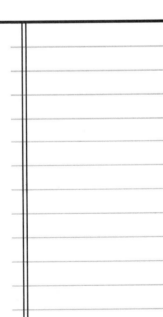

Figure 16-6: Choosing a variable as a quick watch.

Figure 16-7: Viewing a variable in the Quick Watch dialog box.

Figure 16-8: Adding a quick watch results in this type of window.

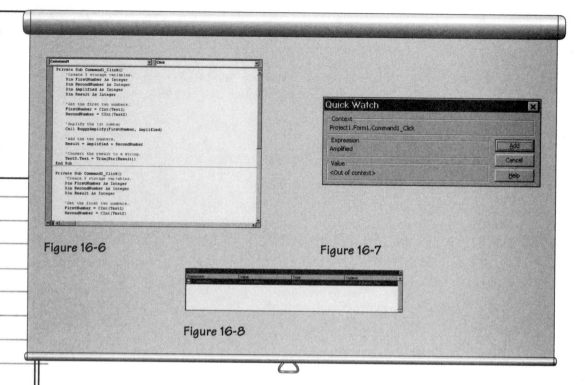

Figure 16-6

Figure 16-7

Figure 16-8

Quick Watch button

Toggle Breakpoint button

End button

6 **Double-click on the word** *Amplified* **in the** Result = Amplified + SecondNumber **source code line.**

Visual Basic highlights the word you selected.

7 **Click on the Quick Watch button on the Toolbar.**

The Quick Watch dialog box appears, as shown in Figure 16-7. The dialog box says that the Value is Out of context.

8 **Click on Add.**

Visual Basic adds the quick watch to the Watches window, as shown in Figure 16-8. Notice that the variable's value is still Out of context. To get the variable into context, we have to stop the program at some point while this procedure is executing.

9 **Click on the** Result = Amplified + SecondNumber **source code line and click on the Toggle Breakpoint button on the Toolbar.**

Visual Basic highlights the line, as shown in Figure 16-9. A *breakpoint* tells Visual Basic to pause the program when it reaches this point. Notice that Visual Basic adds a breakpoint indicator to the left side of the line so that you know the program will stop there.

10 **Press F5 to start the program. Then type** 1 **in the 1st Number text box and** 2 **in the 2nd Number text box.**

11 **Click on the Does it Wrong command button.**

Visual Basic starts the program and then stops it at the breakpoint you set.

Notice that the Watches window now displays the Amplified variable with a value, as shown in Figure 16-10.

12 **Click on the End button on the Toolbar to exit the program.**

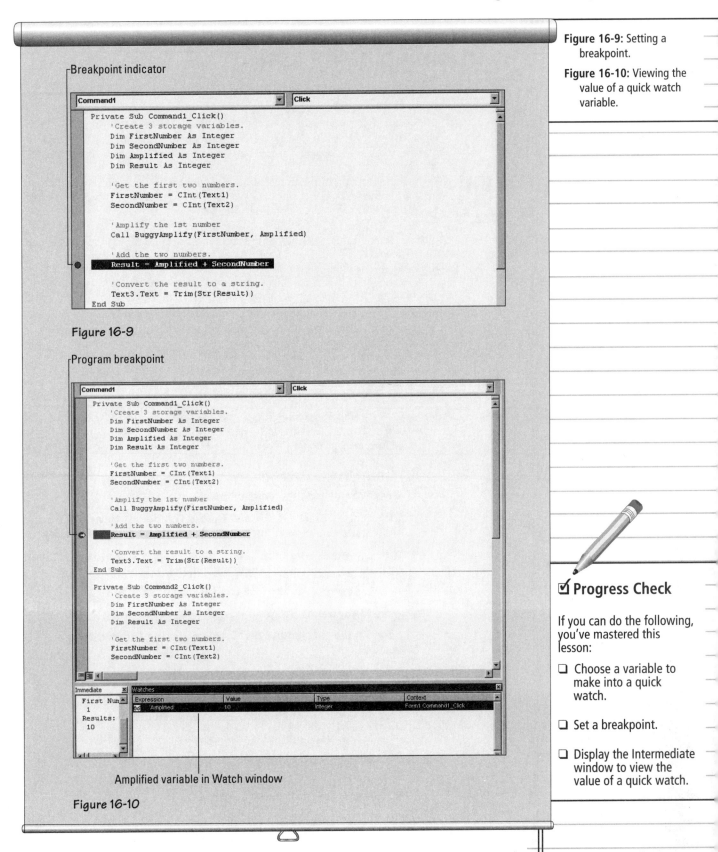

Figure 16-9

Figure 16-10

Figure 16-9: Setting a breakpoint.

Figure 16-10: Viewing the value of a quick watch variable.

☑ **Progress Check**

If you can do the following, you've mastered this lesson:

❑ Choose a variable to make into a quick watch.

❑ Set a breakpoint.

❑ Display the Intermediate window to view the value of a quick watch.

Lesson 16-4

Tracing Line by Line

Instant watches enable you to view a variable as it changes in a program. If the change is good, you can move on to the next step of program execution. An unexpected change usually means that your program has some kind of bug.

on the test

To help you identify the exact location of a bug, Visual Basic gives you the option of tracing through your program line by line. While this procedure can be tedious, it's a sure way of finding a bug.

You can trace through a program in three ways: Step Into, Step Over, and Step Out. The Step Into command enables you to trace through your entire program line by line.

The Step Over command also enables you to trace through your entire program; however, the moment that the command runs across a procedure or function call, the command runs the procedure or function, rather than forcing you to go through the procedure or function one step at a time. If you're absolutely sure that a particular procedure or function works correctly, tracing through that procedure or function's source code is pointless, so step over it instead.

The Step Out command allows you to move up one level if you've stepped into a procedure. You can use this button if you only want to check part of a subprocedure instead of checking every step.

on the CD

1. **Load the Debug.VBP project.**

2. **Press F7 to display the Code window.**

3. **Click on the Object list box and choose Command1 to view the BASIC code that makes the Does it Wrong command button work.**

4. **Click anywhere inside the line** `FirstNumber = CInt(Text1)`; **then click on the Breakpoint Toggle button on the Toolbar.**

   Visual Basic places a breakpoint on the line that you selected.

5. **Press F5 to run the program.**

6. **Type 1 in the 1st Number text box and 2 in the 2nd Number text box.**

7. **Click on the Does it Wrong command button.**

   Visual Basic stops the program at the breakpoint that you set in step 4.

8. **Click on the Step Into button, as shown in Figure 16-11.**

   Visual Basic highlights the next line of code.

9. **Click on the Step Into button twice.**

   Visual Basic steps into the BuggyAmplify function and displays the BuggyAmplify function in the Code window.

Notes:

procedures and functions act like miniature programs that perform specific tasks

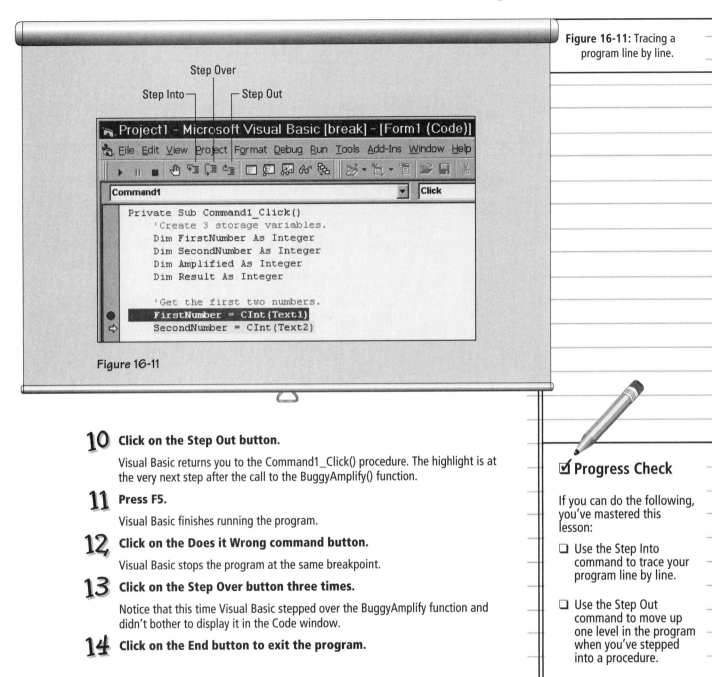

Figure 16-11: Tracing a program line by line.

Figure 16-11

10 **Click on the Step Out button.**

Visual Basic returns you to the Command1_Click() procedure. The highlight is at the very next step after the call to the BuggyAmplify() function.

11 **Press F5.**

Visual Basic finishes running the program.

12 **Click on the Does it Wrong command button.**

Visual Basic stops the program at the same breakpoint.

13 **Click on the Step Over button three times.**

Notice that this time Visual Basic stepped over the BuggyAmplify function and didn't bother to display it in the Code window.

14 **Click on the End button to exit the program.**

Recess

Pat yourself on the back for making it through this unit and seeing the guts of an actual Visual Basic program running. Think of the Intermediate window as an x-ray into the internal working of your programs. By using the Intermediate window along with watches, you can find almost any type of problem that may be keeping your program from working properly.

Now that you know how to fix problems related to your programs, think how much time you might save if you made every effort to write problem-free programs. When writing a program, take your time and do it right. It always

☑ **Progress Check**

If you can do the following, you've mastered this lesson:

❑ Use the Step Into command to trace your program line by line.

❑ Use the Step Out command to move up one level in the program when you've stepped into a procedure.

❑ Use the Step Over command to skip over procedure or function calls.

takes more time to fix a problem than it does to avoid the problem in the first place.

So now that you know this, take a walk and contemplate the wonders of nature, the universe, and Visual Basic programming.

Unit 16 Quiz

For each of the following questions, circle the letter of the correct answer or answers. Because each question may have more than one correct answer, make sure that you circle all the correct answers.

1. **Where are the most common types of bugs that may cause problems in your program?**

   A. In syntax errors, when you make a typing error of some kind.

   B. In logic errors that occur when a command works much differently than you intended.

   C. The most common bugs are cockroaches, ants, and silverfish.

   D. Math errors occur when your program calculates an unexpected result. For example, it may add two numbers instead of subtracting one from the other.

   E. The cause of many errors is the fault of your boss for not doing all of your work for you.

2. **The Intermediate window provides three methods for finding bugs without doing anything special to your code — what are they?**

   A. You can use the Print command to view the contents of any variable or expression that is currently accessible from the Intermediate window.

   B. The Intermediate window doesn't actually exist. It's only the figment of some programmer's imagination.

   C. Always leave debugging for someone else to do. After all, why should you waste your time with perfectly good code that doesn't happen to work in the current situation?

   D. The Call command enables you to check and see if a function is working correctly.

   E. Changing variable values enables you to change the value of any variable in your program.

3. **Why would you want to type the Debug.Print command in your programs?**

   A. The Debug.Print command enables you to display errors in your program automatically, eliminating the need to type commands in the Intermediate window yourself.

B. Typing the Debug.Print commands over and over again is good typing exercise for your fingers.

C. You'd use the Debug.Print command to print the word Debug all over the form.

D. Using the Debug.Print command enables you to create a photograph of your program, which you can then pick up at your local food store.

E. The Debug.Print command is only used in the time of national emergency — any other use is strictly prohibited by law.

4. **How is a quick watch superior to a Debug.Print command?**

A. Your boss won't allow you the luxury of using a quick watch, so why bother to learn how they're superior?

B. A quick watch saves time by moving your clock ahead eight hours when you arrive at work. That way you can go home before you even have to start working.

C. A quick watch is another name for the Windows Clock.

D. A quick watch enables you to see whenever your program changes the value of a variable in your program.

E. Instant watches can tell you the exact time in a split second.

5. **What does tracing line by line enable you to do?**

A. Tracing line by line enables you to draw lines from one line of code to the next to show the direction of program flow.

B. Tracing line by line helps you find all of those hidden messages that the FBI planted in your source code to brainwash the public.

C. It enables you to extend your lunch hour by claiming that the computer's still drawing lines for you.

D. It enables you to remove all doubt as to the location of a flaw in a book.

E. You can use this technique to move one line at a time, looking for bugs in your program.

Unit 16 Exercise

Just to see how much you learned, here's a program loaded with one bug that you can hunt down. This program's supposed to calculate the square of a number, which means that you type in any number (such as 5) and the program displays the result of that number multiplied by itself (such as 5 x 5, or 25). Unfortunately, this program doesn't calculate the square of a number correctly. See if you can find the bug. Good luck.

on the CD

1. Open the Buggy.VBP project.

2. Press F5.

3. Type **4** in the Type a number here text box.

4. Click on the SquareMe command button. Notice that the program doesn't multiply the number 4 times 4 correctly. Instead, the program displays a 0 (zero).

5. Click on Exit.

6. Okay, you're on your own from here. Use the Step Into command to trace through this program line by line to see where the bug may be hiding.

Unit 17

Breakpoints and Watches

Objectives for This Unit

✓ Setting and removing breakpoints

✓ Adding watches manually

✓ Using a value change watch

✓ Using a value true watch

▶ Break.VBP
on the CD

breakpoint tells
program to stop

A *breakpoint* enables you to tell Visual Basic, "Run the program, but pause when you reach a line in the program that I've designated as a breakpoint." After pausing at a specific line in your program, you can then start tracing through your program line by line, or you can watch one or more variables.

Breakpoints make debugging easier because you don't have to trace an entire program from start to finish. Instead, you can skip over 99 percent of your program and just start bug hunting from the location of your breakpoints.

Breakpoints enable you to tell Visual Basic, "I think there may be a bug in this part of my program. Run the program and pause at the breakpoint so I can check for bugs myself."

Setting and Removing Breakpoints
Lesson 17-1

To set a breakpoint, you have to open the Code window of your program, find a line that contains BASIC code, and then set your breakpoint. Visual Basic gives you four ways to set a breakpoint:

- ▶ Press F9.

- ▶ Click on the Toggle Breakpoint button in the Toolbar (the Toggle Breakpoint button appears on both the Edit and Debug toolbars).

- ▶ Right-click the line of code where you want to add the breakpoint and then choose Toggle⇨Breakpoint from the context menu.

- ▶ Choose Debug⇨Toggle Breakpoint.

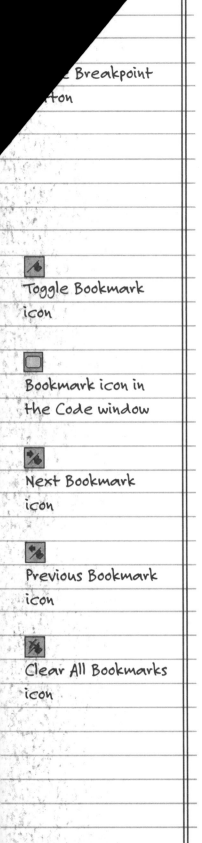

Breakpoint
ton

Toggle Bookmark icon

Bookmark icon in the Code window

Next Bookmark icon

Previous Bookmark icon

Clear All Bookmarks icon

extra credit

Using bookmarks

At times, you may want to simply mark a place in the code without having the program do anything when it reaches that point. For example, you may want to mark the place you were just editing before going home at night so you can find it easily the next day. The bookmark feature fulfills this need.

You can add a bookmark to your code in three ways: choose the Edit⇨Bookmarks⇨ Toggle Bookmark command, right-click the line where you want to add or remove a bookmark, and choose the Toggle⇨ Bookmark command from the context menu, or simply click the Toggle Bookmark button on the Edit Toolbar. (You add the Edit Toolbar to the Visual Basic environment by using the same method as the Debug Toolbar. See the Introduction for Unit 16 if you've forgotten how to do this.)

Every time you add a bookmark to your code, Visual Basic displays a special bookmark symbol on the far left side of the Code window, just like it does when you set a breakpoint. Finding a bookmark that you've set is easy. Just choose Edit⇨Bookmarks⇨Next Bookmark or click the Next Bookmark button on the Edit Toolbar to find the next book mark. You find a previous bookmark by choosing Edit⇨Bookmarks⇨Previous Bookmark or clicking the Previous Bookmark button on the Edit Toolbar.

Eventually you'll want to get rid of all the bookmarks in your program. Choose Edit⇨Bookmarks⇨Clear All Bookmarks or click the Clear All Bookmarks button on the Edit Toolbar to accomplish this task.

Breakpoints exist solely for your convenience in debugging your program. After you've debugged your program completely (or debugged as much as you can before you have to ship the program out to market), you should remove your breakpoints. Visual Basic provides four ways to remove a breakpoint:

- ▶ Move the cursor to or click on an existing breakpoint and press F9.

- ▶ Press Ctrl+Shift+F9.

- ▶ Right click the line of code where you want to remove the breakpoint and then choose Toggle⇨Breakpoint from the context menu.

- ▶ Choose Debug⇨Clear All Breakpoints.

If you want to remove breakpoints one at a time, click on an existing breakpoint and press F9. If you want to remove every single breakpoint in your program, press Ctrl+Shift+F9 or Choose Debug⇨Clear All Breakpoints.

heads up

on the CD

Visual Basic doesn't allow you to place a breakpoint on a blank line or comment line, so don't bother trying or you'll get a dialog box scolding you for disobeying orders.

1 **Load the Break.VBP project.**

2 **Click on View Code to open the Code window.**

3 **Click on three different lines and press F9 to insert your breakpoints.**

4 **Click on any of the existing breakpoints and press F9.**

Notice that the breakpoint now disappears.

5 **Press Ctrl+Shift+F9.**

Notice that all the remaining breakpoints disappear as well.

☑ Progress Check

You've mastered this lesson if you can do the following:

❑ Place a breakpoint in the Code window.

❑ Remove one breakpoint at a time.

❑ Remove all breakpoints from a program at once.

Adding Watches Manually

Lesson 17-2

Breakpoints tell your program to pause while it's running. After your program has paused, you can check the values of your variables to see if they're getting the right data. If your variables aren't getting the right data, then you can look for where the variable is getting the wrong data so you can stomp out the bug that's preventing your program from working correctly.

Here's how to manually have Visual Basic watch for places where variables get incorrect data:

on the CD

1 **Load the Break.VBP project.**

2 **Highlight Form1 in the Project window and then click on View Object.**

The program appears, as shown in Figure 17-1.

3 **Double-click on the Does it Wrong command button.**

The Code window appears, as shown in Figure 17-2.

4 **Double-click on the Amplified variable to highlight it.**

5 **Choose <u>D</u>ebug⇨<u>A</u>dd Watch.**

The Add Watch dialog box appears, as shown in Figure 17-3. This dialog box tells you the name of the variable to watch and the module and procedure that the variable appears in.

Notes:

right-click on a
variable and
choose Add Watch
from Context menu
to display the Add
Watch dialog box

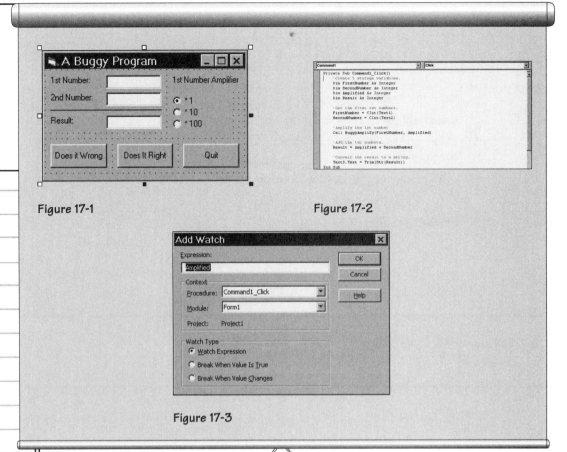

Figure 17-1

Figure 17-2

Figure 17-3

6 **Click on OK.**

Visual Basic displays the Watches window, as shown in Figure 17-4. Notice that the window already contains the watch you set on the Amplified variable.

7 **Press F8 to start stepping through the program line by line.**

8 **Type 1 in the text box that appears to the right of the 1st Number: label, type 2 in the text box that appears to the right of the 2nd Number: label, and click on the Does it Wrong command button.**

Visual Basic highlights the first line of the Command1_Click event procedure in the Code window.

9 **Press Shift+F8 three times to step through the code line by line.**

Notice that the Watches window shows the value of the Amplified variable as 0. The window also shows that Amplified is an integer data type.

10 **Press Shift+F8 once to step past the Call BuggyAmplify procedure.**

Notice that now the Watches window shows the value of the Amplified variable as 10.

11 **Click on the End button in the Toolbar.**

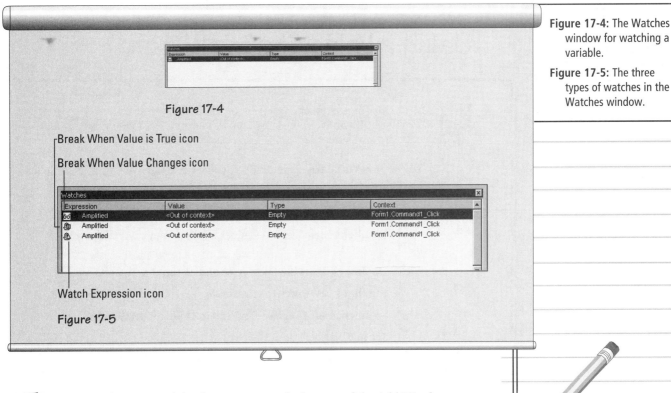

Figure 17-4: The Watches window for watching a variable.

Figure 17-5: The three types of watches in the Watches window.

Break When Value is True icon

Break When Value Changes icon

Watch Expression icon

Figure 17-5

You may have noticed the three options at the bottom of the Add Watch dialog box (see Figure 17-3). Each one of these options creates a different kind of watch:

 ◆ **Watch Expression:** This option enables you to view the value of a variable.

 ◆ **Break When Value Is True:** This kind of watch checks to see if the result of a function or condition is true or false.

 ◆ **Break When Value Changes:** This watch pauses the program whenever the value of the variable changes.

To tell the difference between these three watches in the Watches window, Visual Basic offers some helpful icons to tell them apart, as shown in Figure 17-5.

Recess

Take a break and look for bugs around your computer, because you've already spent enough time looking for bugs inside a Visual Basic program. Just remember that every program in the world has bugs. The larger and more complicated the program, the more likely it will have bugs in it.

Most bugs (fortunately) are harmless or just plain annoying. However, some bugs can be downright dangerous. Rumor has it that NASA had to blow up a multimillion-dollar satellite once because a single bug in a program caused the launching rocket to go out of control. So even though bugs are a fact of life in programs (and apartments), try to stomp out as many of those crunchy little pests as possible — in your programs, and in real life as well.

☑ Progress Check

If you can do the following, you've mastered this lesson:

❑ Highlight a variable name and display the Add Watch dialog box.

❑ Use the Watches window to see how a variable changes its value.

Lesson 17-3

Using a Value Change Watch

on the test

Watching for a value or expression to change is great if you know when to look for it. If you have absolutely no idea when a variable is changing its value, you can have Visual Basic notify you automatically.

To see how Visual Basic can notify you when a variable changes its value, try the following:

on the CD

1 Load the Break.VBP project.

2 Highlight Form1 in the Project window and then click on View Object.

3 Double-click on the Does it Wrong command button.

4 Highlight the Text3.Text variable.

5 Right click on Text3.Text and then choose Add Watch.

The Add Watch dialog box appears.

6 Click on the Break When Value Changes radio button and click on OK.

The Break When Value Changes option tells Visual Basic, "When the Text3.Text variable is assigned a value, notify me right away."

7 Press F5 to start the program.

8 Type 1 in the text box that appears to the right of the 1st Number: label, type 2 in the text box that appears to the right of the 2nd Number: label, and click on the Does it Wrong command button.

The Watches window appears, as shown in Figure 17-6. A box appears around the line of code right after the line that paused the program. Just remember that the line before the line with the box around it is the line that you want to look at.

9 Press F5 to continue running the program.

10 Click on the Does it Wrong command button.

This time the program doesn't pause because the Text3.Text value didn't change. If you had changed either the 1st Number or the 2nd Number fields, then Visual Basic would have paused the program at the same place that it paused the last time.

11 Click on the Quit command button.

☑ Progress check

If you can do the following, you've mastered this lesson:

❑ Highlight a variable name and display the Add Watch dialog box.

❑ Define the variable to break when its value changes.

❑ Run a program to see the Watches window pop up the moment that the variable changes.

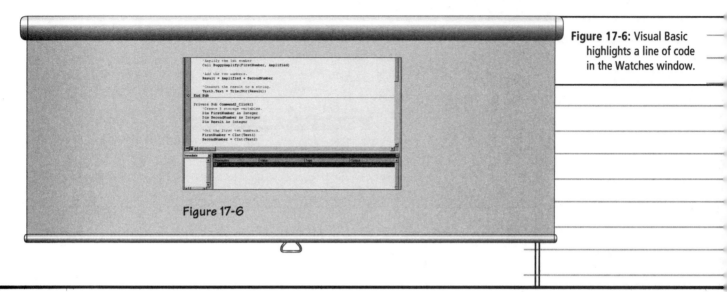

Figure 17-6: Visual Basic highlights a line of code in the Watches window.

Figure 17-6

Using a Value True Watch

Lesson 17-4

on the test

Rather than check to see when a value changes, you may be more interested in knowing when a variable or expression changes from false to true (but not vice versa). As its name implies, a value true watch only pauses a program when its value becomes true. Value true watches can be used to monitor Boolean variables — those whose values are either true or false — or expressions that equate to the value of true or false.

heads up

Sometimes you may have to use what seems like backwards logic to test if an expression becomes true. For example, to check if one variable equals another, you may have to type the expression by using the Not operator, such as Not(Text3 = Text2 + Text1). This tells Visual Basic to break when the entire expression Not(Text3 = Text2 + Text1) becomes true.

on the CD

1 **Load the Break.VBP project.**

2 **Choose Debug⇨Add Watch.**

3 **Type the following in the Expression box: Not(Text3 = Text2 + Text1).**

4 **Click in the Module list box and choose Form1.**

This tells Visual Basic to check the value of the expression (that you typed in step 3) only when the program is using BASIC code stored in the Form1 Form file.

5 **Click in the Procedure list box and choose Command2_Click.**

This tells Visual Basic to check the value of the expression that you typed in step 3 only when the program is using BASIC code stored in the Command2_Click event procedure.

6 **Click on the Break When Value Is True radio button.**

This tells Visual Basic that when the expression Not(Text3=Text2 + Text1) becomes true, it should notify you right away.

Figure 17-7: Breaking automatically when an expression becomes true.

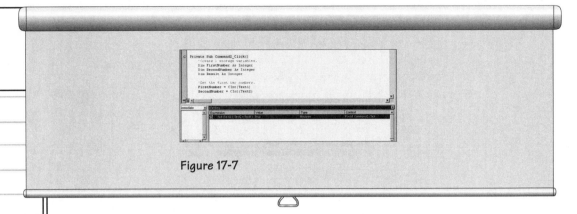

Figure 17-7

☑ Progress Check

If you can do the following, you've mastered this lesson:

❑ Type an expression into the Add Watch dialog box.

❑ Instruct Visual Basic to break when an expression becomes true.

❑ Run the program to see the Watches window pop up the moment the expression becomes true.

7 Click on OK.

8 Press F5 to run the program.

9 Type 1 in the text box that appears to the right of the 1st Number: label, type 2 in the text box that appears to the right of the 2nd Number: label, and click on the Does it Right command button.

Visual Basic displays the Watches window and pauses at the beginning of the Command2_Click procedure, as shown in Figure 17-7.

10 Press F5 to continue running the program.

11 Click on the Does it Right command button.

This time, the application continues running because the expression value didn't change. If you had changed the numbers in either the 1st Number or 2nd Number text boxes, then Visual Basic would have paused the program at the same place that it did the last time.

Unit 17 Quiz

For each of the following questions, circle the letter of the correct answer or answers. Some questions have two or more right answers, so don't give up too soon.

1. **Why should you consider using a breakpoint in your program?**

   A. A breakpoint lets you run your program and pause at a specific location in your BASIC code.

   B. You really want to show off to the boss, and breakpoints are something that sounds cool.

   C. Because it's there.

   D. Because it's a full moon when all the really crazy bugs come out to play.

   E. You know that a specific variable is getting incorrect data, but you really don't know where that value gets placed into the variable.

Notes:

2. **How can you remove all the breakpoints in your program at once?**

   A. Don't put any breakpoints in your program in the first place. That way you won't have to worry about removing them later.

   B. Press Ctrl+Shift+F9 or choose <u>D</u>ebug➪Clear <u>A</u>ll Breakpoints.

   C. After you put a breakpoint in a program, getting it out again is impossible.

   D. Use a pick and shovel.

   E. Aim carefully and use small-caliber ammunition.

3. **What are the three kinds of watches that you can set under Visual Basic?**

   A. Timex, Armitron, and Seiko.

   B. Visual Basic has three kinds of watches?

   C. The three types of ways you can watch anything in Visual Basic are called the Mickey Mouse watch, the Secret Agent watch, and the Bored-Out-of-Your-Mind-in-a-Meeting-So-You're-Staring-at-Your-Watch-to-Pass-the-Time watch.

   D. Obviously, more than three kinds of watches exist. The most common are whale, military, and night.

   E. Watch Expression, Break When Value Is True, or Break When Value Changes.

4. **How can you use a value change watch to detect errors in your program?**

   A. To find the exact place in your program where a variable is getting incorrect data.

   B. You can use a value change watch to check whether two variables remain in sync. One variable may have to increase in proportion to a decrease in another variable.

   C. If you ever buy a watch in an alley from a guy in an overcoat, the value of that watch will decrease dramatically the moment that you pay for it and try to use it.

   D. Monitoring default configuration values in your software application's functionality allows inverse proportional calculations that may allow additional expressiveness in your variables.

   E. You shouldn't be writing programs with errors in them in the first place. Clean out your desk and the guards will escort you out the door.

Notes:

5. **You can use the value true watch in only two ways. What are they?**

    A. Value true watches aren't really all that useful; most programmers just ignore them.

    B. A value true watch is actually a covert expression that refers to a hall monitor who watches out for the boss. When this hall monitor signals true, it's time to get back to work.

    C. The value true watch is really handy for cleaning old medicine bottles and scrubbing walls.

    D. You can use a value true watch to monitor Boolean variables — those whose value is either true or false.

    E. The value true watch can also be used to monitor expressions that equate to a value of true or false.

Unit 17 Exercise

To give you experience debugging a program, try the following steps and see what happens. Feel free to experiment, because the Break.VBP project isn't anything important. And you'll always have a copy of the Break.VBP file on the CD that came with this book, so go wild!

on the CD

1. Load the Break.VBP project.

2. Choose Debug➪Add Watch to display the Add Watch dialog box.

3. Type **CInt(Text1.Text) > 0** in the Expression box.

4. Click in the Module list box and choose Form1.

5. Click in the Procedure list box and choose Command2_Click.

6. Click on Break When Value is True and click on OK.

7. Press F5.

8. Type **1** in the text box that appears to the right of the 1st Number: label, type **2** in the text box that appears to the right of the 2nd Number: label, and click on the Does It Right command button.

    The Watches window appears and the program stops at the beginning of the Command2_Click event procedure.

9. Click on the End button in the Toolbar to exit the program.

. . . .

Compiling Your Program

Objectives for This Unit

✓ Choosing an icon for your program

✓ Compiling and naming your program

✓ Creating a native code EXE

✓ Using the Application Setup Wizard

▶ Shoot.VBP

After you've finished designing your program's user interface, writing BASIC code, and testing the program to make sure that it actually works, you still have one more step to complete before you can start selling your program to others: You need to compile your Visual Basic program.

Choosing an Icon for Your Program

Lesson 18-1

Look on your computer and notice that every program has a pretty icon to go along with it. So before you compile your program, take some time to give your program a descriptive icon.

If you're artistically inclined, you can use a fancy drawing program, such as CorelDRAW or Adobe PhotoShop, and create your own icons. For the rest of us, whose finest drawings consist of stick figures, using one of the many existing icons that Visual Basic provides for free is much easier. To assign an icon to your program, you must first assign the icon to a Form (FRM) file used in your program. After you've assigned an icon to a form, then you can tell Visual Basic to use that icon to represent your entire program as well.

Notes:

extra credit

Technical stuff about compiling

Compiling a program means converting your Visual Basic program into a special file format that the computer can understand, often called an executable file (or just abbreviated with the file extension EXE).

As you may have noticed in earlier units, you can run a Visual Basic program from within Visual Basic itself, so why bother compiling your program? Good question, so here are two answers:

▶ If you compile a Visual Basic program under Windows 95, a user must have Windows 95 or Windows NT to run your program. If you don't compile your program, only people who own Visual Basic can run your program.

▶ When you compile your program, you convert your BASIC code into an executable file. This conversion keeps others from viewing and possibly stealing your precious BASIC code.

on the CD

To see how easily you can assign an icon to a program, try the following:

1   **Load the Shoot.VBP project.**

2   **Highlight Form1 in the Project window and then click on View Object.**

3   **Click in the Icon property in the left-hand column.**

A gray ellipsis (three dots) button appears in the right-hand column.

4   **Click on the gray ellipsis button.**

A Load Icon dialog box appears.

5   **Click in the Look in list box and choose the drive and directory that contains the icon file you want to use. (To use one of the Visual Basic icons, choose the** Program Files\DevStudio\VB\Graphics\Icons **directory.)**

to assign an icon to a program, first assign it to a Form file in the program

☑ **Progress Check**

If you can do the following, you've mastered this lesson:

❑ Understand how Visual Basic chooses a name for your program based on the name of your Visual Basic project name.

❑ Select an icon to represent your Visual Basic program.

extra credit

How the Shoot.VBP program works

In case you're wondering, this program shows an animated butterfly that flaps its wings as it moves across the screen. The butterfly at the bottom left-hand corner is the only image that appears when the program runs. The two butterflies in the top left-hand corner provide the animation by rapidly appearing and disappearing in the image box in the bottom left-hand corner. The two timer controls (the ones that look like a pocket watch) make the butterfly move across the screen at a specific time interval. To shoot the butterfly, move the mouse pointer over the butterfly and then click with the left mouse button.

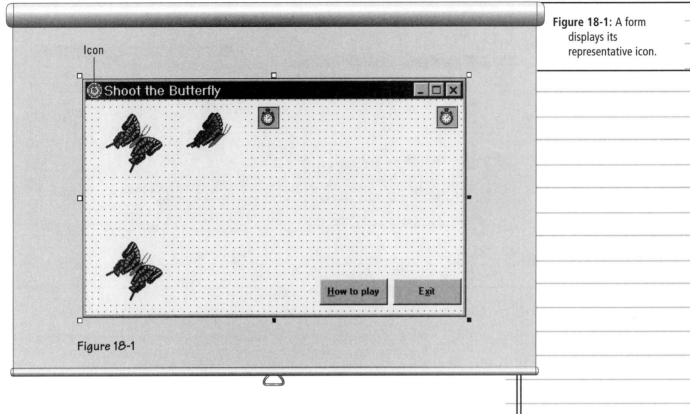

Icon

Figure 18-1

Figure 18-1: A form displays its representative icon.

6 **Click on the icon you want to represent your program and click on Open.**

Visual Basic displays your chosen icon in the upper-left corner of the form, as shown in Figure 18-1.

heads up

The preceding steps assign an icon to the only form in the Shoot.VBP program. At this point, you still haven't defined an icon for your program; Lesson 18-2 shows you how to finish the task.

Compiling and Naming Your Program

Lesson 18-2

on the test

Normally, the name of your program is the name of your Visual Basic project. If you name your program Lousy.VBP, then Visual Basic compiles it into the executable file called Lousy.EXE. So choose your project names as wisely as you would choose names for your own children. After all, most people have heard of Catherine the Great, but would anyone remember someone named Tippi the Great?

heads up

When you actually compile your program, however, Visual Basic gives you a chance to choose a name that's different from your VBP project name.

Figure 18-2: The Make Project dialog box creates an executable file.

Figure 18-3: The EXE Options dialog box stores information about your program.

Notes:

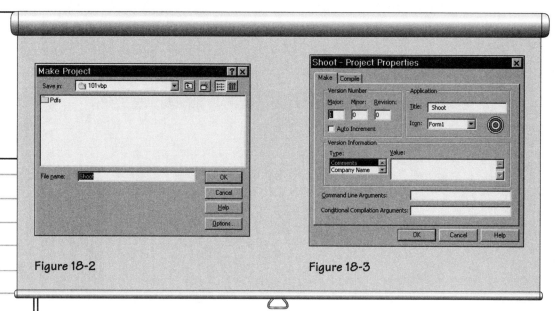

Figure 18-2

Figure 18-3

After choosing a name and an icon for your program, you're ready to compile your program. Compiling your program converts it from a collection of FRM Form files and BAS Module files into a single EXE executable file.

Because writing a program usually means writing it once and then continually updating it, Visual Basic enables you to keep track of the following information:

- Program version number
- Comments
- Company name
- File description
- Legal copyright
- Product name

Visual Basic buries all of this stuff in your program solely for your information. Anyone using your program can view this same information if they view the properties. To view the properties of a file in the Windows 95 Explorer, just click the right mouse button on the file and select Properties.

After you complete your Visual Basic masterpiece and want to distribute it to the world, you first need to compile it. The following steps show you how to compile your work of art:

on the CD

1 **Load the Shoot.VBP project.**

2 **Choose File➪Make Shoot.exe File.**

The Make Project dialog box appears, as shown in Figure 18-2.

3 **Type a new name for your program in the File name text box.**

Giving your program a new name is optional, of course. Select something memorable, why don't you?

4 **Click on Options.**

The EXE Options dialog box appears, as shown in Figure 18-3.

5 **Type** 1 **in the Major version box and type** 0 **in the Minor and Revision boxes.**

The first time you compile your program, the version number will probably be something like Version 1.0.0. Each subsequent time you make changes to your program (and recompile it), enter a new number in these version boxes. For example, if you make two minor changes and one revision to Version 1, your version number would be Version 1.2.1. On the other hand, if you rewrite major portions of your program, you may want to go ahead and give your program a new major version number, such as Version 2.0.0.

6 **Click on Comments, Company Name, File Description, Legal Copyright, Legal Trademarks, or Product Name in the Type list box and type the corresponding information in the Value box (see Figure 18-3).**

For example, Comments can contain the names of all the programmers who worked on the program (so everyone knows who to blame if the program fails dramatically). Company Name can contain (what else?) your company name.

Note: You don't have to type anything in these fields if you don't want to. Keeping track of this information is for your convenience only.

7 **Click in the Icon list box and select the Form file name that contains the icon you designated in Lesson 18-1.**

8 **Click on OK.**

The Make EXE File dialog box appears again.

9 **Click on OK.**

Congratulations! You've just compiled a real Visual Basic VBP project into an honest-to-goodness EXE file, ready for distribution to the rest of the world.

☑ Progress Check

If you can do the following, you've mastered this lesson:

❑ Define the version number of your program.

❑ Compile a VBP Project file into an EXE executable file.

Creating a Native Code EXE

Lesson 18-3

You can create two kinds of EXE files with Visual Basic. The default type is the P-Code EXE that Visual Basic has always created in the past. A P-Code EXE uses special *tokens* that represent actions that the program is supposed to perform. A *run-time interpreter* takes the tokens and translates them into something that your machine can understand. The advantage of using a P-Code EXE is that it doesn't take nearly as long to produce. P-Code EXEs are what you should use as you write your program and test it.

on the test

Visual Basic 5.0 can also use something known as a *native code compiler* to create EXE files. A native code EXE file contains instructions that your machine can use directly. It provides the fastest method for executing code and usually results in a smaller program file as well. You pay for these extra features by waiting longer for Visual Basic to produce the EXE file.

Figure 18-4: The
Compile page of the
Shoot - Project
Properties dialog box
allows you to choose
a native code EXE.

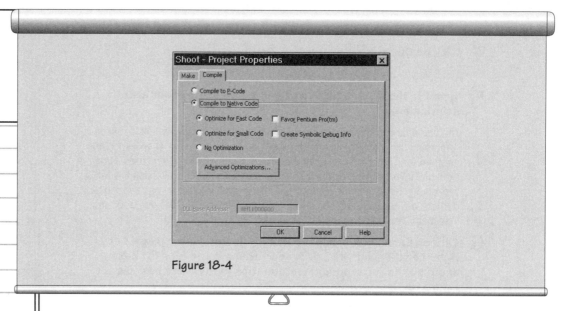

Figure 18-4

Notes:

☑ Progress Check

If you can do the following,
you've mastered this lesson:

❑ Define the difference
between a native code
and a P-Code EXE.

❑ Compile a VBP Project
file into a native code
EXE executable file.

Creating a native code EXE file doesn't have to be hard — it's actually pretty
simple. Take a look at how easy this process can be.

on the CD

1 Load the Shoot.VBP project.

2 Choose File➪Make Shoot.exe.

Visual Basic displays the Make Project dialog shown in Figure 18-2. Visual Basic
assumes that you want to use the P-Code version of the EXE file because this
version is faster to create. You need to do some special setups to get the
benefits of the native code EXE file.

3 Click on Options.

Visual Basic displays the Project 1 - Project Properties dialog box.

4 Select the Compile page.

You'll see the Compile page shown in Figure 18-4. Here is where you tell Visual
Basic to create a native code EXE in place of a P-Code EXE.

5 Click on the Compile to Native Code option button.

Notice that you can choose the kind of EXE optimization to use. You can choose
to make the file smaller or to make the EXE faster. An option for not using any
form of optimization is also available, but you won't use this feature very often.

The two check boxes allow you to further optimize how Visual Basic creates the
native code EXE file. You can choose to favor Pentium Pro processors, which
means that older processors may not execute your program as fast as possible.
The Create Symbolic Debug Info check box is for advanced programmers who
need to have this information available when using Visual Basic to create
something like an ActiveX control.

6 Click on OK.

7 Click on OK again to close the Make Project dialog box.

Visual Basic compiles the EXE file and then places the file on disk. You can give
the EXE to someone else now so he can benefit from your program as well.

Using the Application Setup Wizard   Lesson 18-4

After compiling your VBP Project into an EXE executable file, you can copy, sell, or give away your program to anyone who wants to use it. You can even place your program on the Internet and allow someone to download it from there. Be careful, though — your EXE file may not run without some additional files.

heads up

An additional file a Visual Basic program may need is MSVBVM50.DLL. If someone's computer doesn't have all the files that your program needs to run, your program (guess what?) won't work at all. What does DLL stand for? DLL means *Dynamic Link Library*. A DLL file contains commonly used procedures that you can share among different programs.

DLL = Dynamic
Link Library

extra credit

All about the Visual Basic run-time files

When you compile a Visual Basic program into an EXE file, no computer in the world knows how to use it. That's why you need to include a copy of the VB40032.DLL or VB40016.DLL file along with your Visual Basic EXE file. These run-time files tell another computer how to run your Visual Basic EXE file. If the VB40032.DLL or VB40016.DLL files are missing, the other computer won't know how to use your Visual Basic EXE file.

To make sure that you give users all the files that they need to run your Visual Basic program, Microsoft kindly supplies the Setup Wizard. The Setup Wizard examines your Visual Basic program, determines all the files your program needs to run, and then packages all of those files onto one or more floppy disks that you can give to the lucky user of your Visual Basic program.

Follow these steps to start the Application Setup Wizard application:

1 **Click on the Start button in the left-hand corner of the screen.**

A menu pops up on the screen.

2 **Click on Programs.**

Another menu pops up to the right.

3 **Click on the Visual Basic 5.0 folder.**

Another menu pops up to the right.

4 **Click on Application Setup Wizard application.**

The Application Setup Wizard application appears.

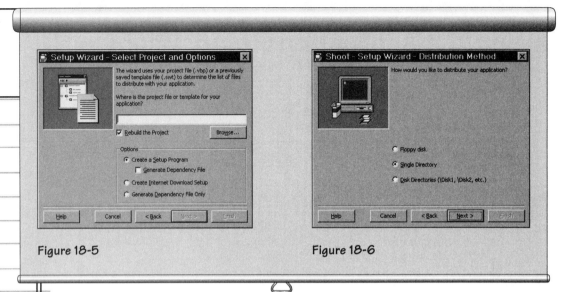

Figure 18-5   Figure 18-6

5 **Click on Next to get past the Introduction page.**

You'll see a Setup Project and Options page, as shown in Figure 18-5. Notice that this page contains options for creating a standard setup or an Internet setup program. You can also create a *dependency file,* which contains a list of the files that your program uses. You only need a dependency file if you plan to use this program along with other programs you create. The dependency file helps to ensure that a big project contains all of the files it needs to run every program.

6 **Click on the Browse button.**

A Locate VB application's VBP file dialog box appears.

7 **Click in the Look in list box (located at the top of the Locate VB application's VBP file dialog box) and choose the drive and directory that contains the Shoot.VBP file.**

8 **Choose the Shoot.VBP file and click on Open.**

9 **Click on Next.**

The Distribution Method page shown in Figure 18-6 appears. Here is where you decide how to distribute your program. In most cases, you'll choose a floppy disk for small programs, single directory for programs you plan to distribute on a LAN or a CD, and disk directories for larger programs.

10 **Click on Next.**

The Setup Wizard - Single Directory page appears, asking for a location to store your setup files, as shown in Figure 18-7.

11 **Click on the Disk Drive radio button or the Directory radio button and choose a drive or directory.**

12 **Click on Next.**

The Application Setup Wizard refuses to go away and informs you that no ActiveX components (OLE servers) are used by your program, as shown in Figure 18-8.

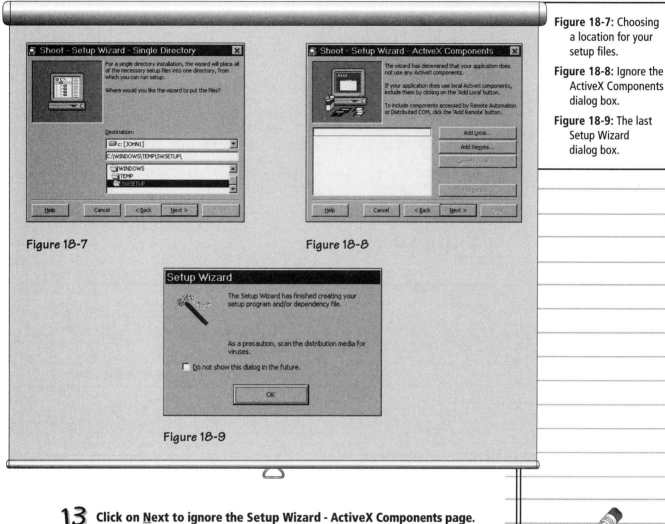

Figure 18-7

Figure 18-8

Figure 18-9

13 **Click on <u>N</u>ext to ignore the Setup Wizard - ActiveX Components page.**

Trust me on this one; OLE servers are not important at this point.

The Setup Wizard - File Summary page appears, listing all the files that Visual Basic thinks you need to run the simple Shoot.VBP project.

14 **Click on <u>N</u>ext.**

You see the Setup Wizard - Finished page.

15 **Click on <u>F</u>inish.**

Visual Basic displays a dialog box, showing how much longer you must stare at your screen until the Setup Wizard is done. Then the last Setup Wizard dialog box appears and advises you that your distribution disks are ready for your future users, as shown in Figure 18-9.

16 **Click on OK.**

And you're done!

☑ Progress Check

If you can do the following, you've mastered this lesson:

❏ Load the Setup Wizard application.

❏ Create setup files for a Visual Basic VBP Project.

Notes:

Recess

Compiling is the final step to shipping your program out the door. Just remember that if your program is popular, you'll have to worry about fixing minor (or major) bugs that keep your program from working. You'll also have to update your program to add even more features (that 99 percent of the population will probably never use anyway).

Now go ahead and congratulate yourself for making it through this entire book and becoming a whiz with Visual Basic.

Unit 18 Quiz

For each of the following questions, circle the letter of the correct answer or answers. Some questions may have more than one right answer, so stay on your toes!

1. **What is the purpose of naming your program and assigning it an icon?**

   A. Busy work. It's just an excuse to make you look like you're doing something important when you'd rather be doing something else.

   B. The name and icon you choose for your program determines how that program appears on a user's computer.

   C. By naming your program, you can get creative and possibly be threatened with legal action if you choose the wrong name.

   D. An icon gives you a chance to pretend you're artistic. Naming a program gives you a chance to choose a unique name that you think sounds useful and highly important.

   E. What's in a name? Ignore it and maybe it will go away.

2. **What is an EXE executable file?**

   A. An EXE executable file is a file that Visual Basic creates from your FRM Form and BAS Module files. If you want to give copies of your program away to other users, you need to convert your Visual Basic VBP Projects into an EXE executable file.

   B. An executable file is a file that has been given the death penalty and is waiting to be executed.

   C. Executable files are files that deserve to be wiped out from your hard disk, such as computer viruses.

   D. Any file that calls itself executable is probably not a file you would want to meet by yourself in a dark alley.

   E. An EXE executable file is a misspelling that looked like a really good idea at the time it was created.

3. **What is your favorite color?**

   A. Red

   B. Orange

   C. Blue

   D. Green

   E. Yellow

4. **What are the advantages of using a native code compiler?**

   A. Faster program execution speed.

   B. You can create natives faster.

   C. It's sort of like using Morse code, only different.

   D. There aren't any advantages, just a lot of extra work.

   E. You may see a smaller program size.

5. **What happens if you give your EXE executable file to another computer but that computer does not have either the VB40032.DLL or VB40016.DLL file?**

   A. Nothing happens.

   B. Your hard disk will emit high doses of radiation in your direction.

   C. If a computer doesn't have the VB40032.DLL or VB40016.DLL file, it won't be able to run your Visual Basic EXE executable file.

   D. If another computer doesn't have either the VB40032.DLL or VB40016.DLL file, then that computer doesn't deserve the privilege of using your Visual Basic program anyway.

   E. Without the VB40032.DLL or VB40016.DLL files, no one can run your Visual Basic EXE executable file, no matter what.

6. **What does the Setup Wizard do?**

   A. It uses spells and incantations.

   B. The Setup Wizard is great for setting up your friends for practical jokes that you can play on them by using Visual Basic.

   C. The Setup Wizard finds all the files that your Visual Basic program needs and packages them in a special installation program that others can use to install your program on their computers.

   D. The Setup Wizard tries to convert you to pagan religious beliefs.

   E. The Setup Wizard searches your hard disk for any games and wrecks them.

Unit 18 Exercise

on the CD

In this unit, you got a chance to compile a real program (Shoot.VBP) and turn it into a real executable (EXE) file. Now follow the instructions below and start practicing with compiling other Visual Basic programs.

1. Load any of the Visual Basic VBP Projects that you worked with in this book.

2. Choose an icon to represent this VBP Project.

3. Compile the program.

4. Exit Visual Basic.

5. Run the program that you compiled in step 3.

Part IV Review

Unit 16 Summary

▶ **Syntax errors:** When you mistype a command or variable name.

▶ **Logic errors:** When you type the wrong command or variable name.

▶ **Math errors:** When your program calculates the wrong answer.

▶ **Boss's errors:** Things you should diplomatically overlook.

▶ **Intermediate window:** A window that lets you peek into the guts of your program while it's running.

▶ **Pause:** To temporarily stop a program from running so you can use the Intermediate window.

▶ **Instant watch:** To display the contents of a variable every time it changes.

▶ **Debug Toolbar:** A special toolbar that contains debugging related icons.

Unit 17 Summary

▶ **Bookmark:** A way of marking your current position in the code so that you can return to it later for editing purposes.

▶ **Edit Toolbar:** A special toolbar that contains all of the editor-related icons.

▶ **Breakpoint:** A highlighted BASIC line that tells Visual Basic where to temporarily stop running a program.

▶ **Watch:** A variable that appears in the Intermediate window so you can see when the variable changes its value.

▶ **Value change watch:** A variable that notifies you the moment the value of the variable changes.

▶ **Value true watch:** A variable that notifies you the moment the value of the variable becomes true.

Unit 18 Summary

▶ **EXE file:** Abbreviation for an EXEcutable file, which is a special file format that your computer understands how to use.

▶ **Compiling:** To convert your program into an EXE file that people can run on their own computers.

▶ **Icon:** A tiny picture used to represent your Visual Basic program.

▶ **P-Code EXE:** An executable that relies on tokens that are translated by an interpreter into machine code. The main advantage of using P-Code is faster compiles.

▶ **Native Code EXE:** An executable that contains only machine code instructions. The main advantages of using native code are faster execution speed and smaller EXE file size.

▶ **Setup Wizard:** A program that guides you through the process of compiling your Visual Basic program.

Part IV Test

The questions on this test cover material presented in Part IV, Units 16, 17 and 18. The answers are in Appendix A.

True False

T F 1. Debugging a program is a luxury that is safely ignored.

T F 2. The Debug.Assert command allows you to test the value of a variable or expression and then stop the program if it's not what you expected.

T F 3. The only reason to pause a program is to take a coffee break.

T F 4. You use the Step Out command if you want to leave the office during a debugging session.

T F 5. To run a Visual Basic program on another computer, you have to compile your program into an EXE file.

T F 6. A bookmark marks your place in the code without interrupting program execution in any way.

T F 7. Visual Basic programs only work if a copy of the VB40032.DLL or VB40016.DLL file is on the computer.

T F 8. The "P" in P-Code stands for personal, which means you shouldn't sell P-Code EXEs.

T F 9. The Intermediate window can help you see why your program is not working correctly.

T F 10. You can set a breakpoint by right-clicking the line of code and then choosing Toggle⇨Breakpoint from the context menu.

Part IV Test

Multiple Choice

For each of the following questions, circle the correct answer or answers. Some questions may have more than one right answer, so read all the answers carefully.

11. Why should you compile a program?

A. So you can run your program on a computer that doesn't have Visual Basic on it.

B. Because compiling is considered socially acceptable even though it's damaging to your health, much like cigarettes or alcohol.

C. To hide your BASIC code so nobody can see how you wrote your program.

D. If you don't compile a program, it'll fall apart at the seams.

E. Compiling erases a program thoroughly so nobody can find it again.

12. Why should you use the Watches window and an Instant watch?

A. To peek inside your program and see how variables are changing.

B. The Watches window gives you a glimpse of the outside world when you're trapped inside writing a program under a deadline.

C. An Instant watch is a wristwatch that only works when you pour hot water on it in the morning. Use the watch to keep track of time.

D. The Watches window helps you locate cockroaches in your house. An Instant watch helps you kill the roaches instantly.

E. The Watches window and the Instant watch work together to make sure that your program refuses to work whenever someone else uses it.

13. Why should you use the Setup Wizard?

A. Why not?

B. Because the Setup Wizard is there.

C. The Setup Wizard makes sure that all necessary files are included with your Visual Basic program when you compile the program.

D. If you don't use the Setup Wizard regularly, it may throw a spell on you.

E. The Setup Wizard is a program that helps you fantasize how a medieval existence would actually improve your life.

14. Why would you want to pause a program?

A. Because you're tired.

B. Because pausing is easier than turning the computer off.

C. So you can go to sleep.

D. To open the Watches window and set an instant watch.

E. Because pausing takes less effort than putting your fist through your screen.

Part IV Test

15. **How can you identify a math error?**

    A. Math errors occur whenever your computer uses a faulty Pentium chip that can't multiply correctly.

    B. If you set an instant watch and notice that a variable is storing incorrect data, such as adding 4 + 5 and coming up with 45, then you have a math error.

    C. A math error occurs only when you're in a hurry and need an accurate result instantly.

    D. If you give the store clerk a $100 bill to buy gum but get three $100 bills back as change, that's a math error.

    E. Math errors require complicated calculations to determine their existence; therefore, identifying math errors without using math is impossible.

16. **What happens if your program doesn't work right?**

    A. You can sell it for thousands of dollars to unsuspecting customers.

    B. You can call it version 1.0.

    C. You can weep without restraint.

    D. Vow to try something less complicated than programming, such as playing Solitaire on your computer.

    E. Use the Intermediate window to find the problem and wipe it out.

Matching

17. **Match the following errors with their official name.**

    A. Syntax error   1. When you type the wrong commands

    B. Logic error   2. When your program calculates a wrong answer

    C. Math error   3. When you realize you're with the wrong person

    D. Baseball error 4. When you misspell a command

    E. Relationship error   5. When you throw a wild pitch

18. **Match the following items with their purpose in life.**

    A. Intermediate window   1. To help you keep track of the value of your variables

    B. Icon   2. To study how a variable in your program may be getting the wrong data

    C. Instant watch   3. To graphically represent your program

    D. Watches window 4. To compile your program and make sure it has all the needed files

    E. Setup Wizard   5. To peek inside the guts of your program

Part IV Test

19. **Match the following items with their purpose in life.**

   A. Edit Toolbar   1. Holds all the debugging specific icons like Toggle Breakpoint

   B. Break icon   2. Holds all the editing specific icons like Toggle Bookmark

   C. Pressing Ctrl+G   3. No purpose whatsoever

   D. Debug Toolbar   4. To temporarily stop a program

   E. The Electoral College   5. To open the Intermediate window

20. **Match the following sports with the real reason fans watch them.**

   A. Auto racing   1. Fist fights

   B. Ice hockey   2. Car crashes

   C. Baseball   3. Fist fights

   D. Basketball   4. Fist fights

   E. Soccer   5. Fist fights

Part IV Lab Assignment

For this lab assignment, you get to compile any of the programs you created in lab assignments I, II, or III.

Step 1: Load a program that you created in a previous lab assignment

If you didn't save any of the programs you created in the previous lab assignments, go back and create a new program now. (And shame on you for not saving your work, which is something every programmer should have drilled into his or her head.)

Step 2: Set a breakpoint in your BASIC code

Where you set your breakpoint doesn't matter.

Step 3: Run your program

Your program should run and stop at the breakpoint you set in step 2.

Part IV Lab Assignment

Step 4: Use the Step Into command

The Step Into command lets you see how Visual Basic runs your program line by line.

Step 5: Exit your program and define an icon to represent your program

Visual Basic provides loads of icons that you can use to represent your program. Some icons you may want to avoid using for your program are the toilet and the toxic waste icons.

Step 6: Compile your program

Try using both the P-Code and Native Code EXE options. See which option takes the least time to generate an EXE file and which option produces the smallest EXE file. Try the various native code compilation options to see which works best with your sample program.

Step 7: Create a setup file using the Setup Wizard

Let the Setup Wizard application create a setup file on a floppy disk for you.

Step 8: Load your program on another computer

After the Application Setup Wizard has created a setup file for your program, test that setup file by running it on another computer, preferably one that doesn't have a copy of Visual Basic loaded.

Step 9: Run your program on the other computer

After the setup file finishes installing your program, run your program to make sure that it works.

Then congratulate yourself for finishing this book. (You may want to erase your program off the computer you used in step 8. Then again, if you used your boss's computer, feel free to leave it on his or her hard drive to show the progress you've made.)

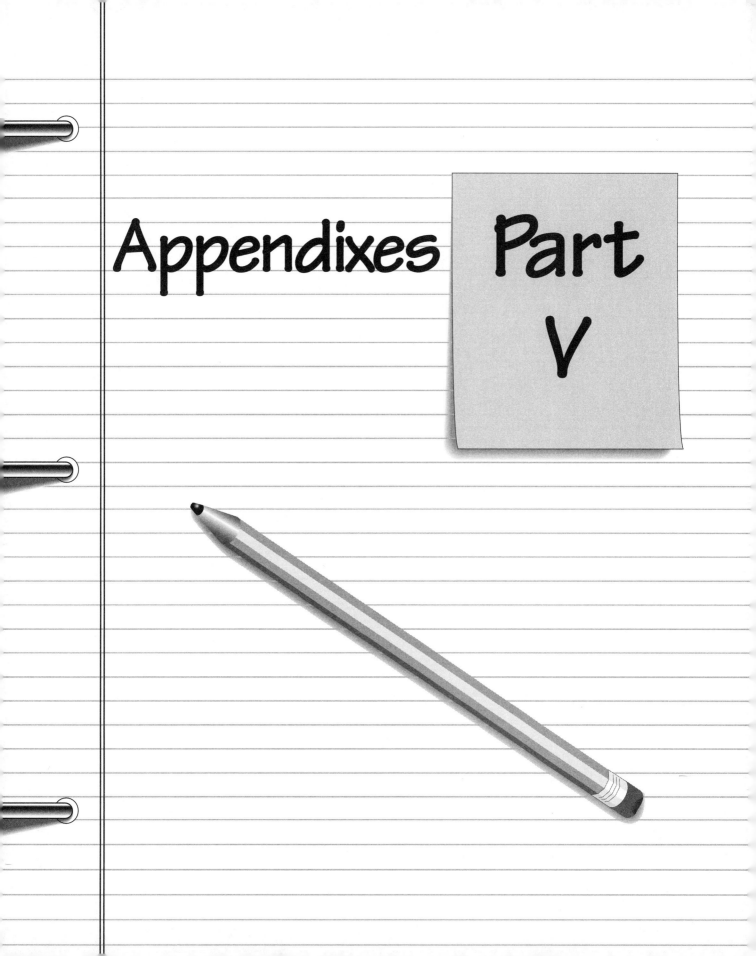

Appendixes

Part V

In this part . . .

Not many people know this, but *appendix* in the book publishing industry means "a miscellaneous category containing useful information that the publisher couldn't fit anywhere else in the book." (See? You learn something new every day.)

So this book contains two appendixes. The first appendix contains all the test answers from the tests that appeared at the end of each part of this book. While you can cheat and look at the answers first, you'll probably learn more if you honestly try answering the questions first and then check this first appendix to see if you got the right answer.

The second appendix contains information about the CD included with the book. Please read this appendix before you work with the CD.

Answers

Part I Test Answers

Question	Answer	If You Missed It, Try This
1.	True	Lesson 2-1
2.	False	Lesson 2-2
3.	True	Lesson 4-1
4.	False	Lesson 1-2
5.	False	Lesson 1-3
6.	True	Lesson 2-2
7.	True	Lesson 2-2
8.	False	Lesson 3-3
9.	True	Lesson 4-2
10.	False	Lesson 4-6
11.	A	Lesson 4-3
12.	D	Unit 3
13.	B, D	Unit 3
14.	C, E	Lesson 4-4
15.	C	Lesson 2-1
16.	D, E	Lesson 4-1
17.	A-3, B-1, C-2, D-5, E-4	Unit 2
18.	A-2, B-4, C-5, D-3, E-1	Table 4-1
19.	A-5, B-3, C-4, D-2, E-1	Lesson 1-2
20.	A-1, B-2, C-3, D-4, E-5	Review your life

Part II Test Answers

Question	Answer	If You Missed It, Try This
1.	True	Lesson 5-1
2.	True	Lesson 5-1
3.	False	Unit 5
4.	True	Unit 6 Using pictures instead of text sidebar
5.	True	Unit 10 introduction
6.	False	Lesson 6-2
7.	True	Unit 6
8.	False	Lesson 9-1
9.	True	Lesson 5-3
10.	True	Lesson 7-2
11.	B	Lesson 8-1
12.	D, E	Lesson 6-2
13.	C	Lesson 7-1
14.	B, D	Lesson 9-1
15.	A, B	Lesson 8-2
16.	A	Unit 6
17.	A-3, B-4, C-1, D-5, E-2	Units 6 and 7
18.	A-5, B-3, C-4, D-1, E-2	Lesson 8-2
19.	A-2, B-3, C-4, D-5, E-1	Units 6 and 7
20.	A-3, B-4, C-1, D-5, E-2	Review your local restaurants

Part III Test Answers

Question	Answer	If You Missed It, Try This
1.	True	Lesson 11-1
2.	True	Lesson 11-3
3.	False	Lesson 11-2
4.	True	Unit 12 introduction
5.	False	Unit 15 ActiveX controls and your machine sidebar
6.	True	Unit 13 Using the IIf() Function sidebar
7.	False	Lesson 11-2
8.	False	Lesson 14-3
9.	False	Unit 12
10.	True	Lesson 12-1
11.	C	Lesson 14-3
12.	A, C	Lesson 15-3
13.	B, D, E	Lesson 15-1
14.	D	Lesson 14-2
15.	C	Unit 15 introduction
16.	A, C, E	Unit 12 introduction
17.	A-3, B-1, C-5, D-2, E-4	Unit 15
18.	A-4, B-2, C-5, D-3, E-1	Lesson 12-3
19.	A-5, B-2, C-1, D-3, E-4	Units 13 and 14
20.	A-5, B-3, C-1, D-2, E-4	Visit your local Humane Society

Part IV Test Answers

Question	Answer	If You Missed It, Try This
1.	False	Review Unit 16
2.	True	Review Unit 16
3.	False	Review Unit 16
4.	False	Review Unit 16
5.	True	Review Unit 18
6.	True	Unit 17 Using bookmarks sidebar
7.	True	Unit 17 introduction
8.	False	Lesson 18-3
9.	True	Lesson 16-1
10.	True	Lesson 17-1
11.	A, C	Unit 18
12.	A	Lessons 16-1 and 16-3
13.	C	Lesson 18-4
14.	D	Unit 16 introduction
15.	B	Lesson 16-1
16.	E	Unit 16
17.	A-4, B-1, C-2, D-5, E-3	Unit 16
18.	A-5, B-3, C-2, D-1, E-4	Units 16 and 18
19.	A-2, B-4, C-5, D-1, E-3	Unit 16 and 17
20.	A-2, B-1, C-3, D-4, E-5	Your local sports page

Appendix B

About the CD

The *Dummies 101: Visual Basic 5 Programming* companion CD-ROM contains five entire bonus units, in addition to the exercise files that you use while you're following along with the lessons in the book.

Before you can use any of the CD files, you need to install them on your computer. Don't worry: The installation process is easy and fairly quick.

After you install the Dummies 101 exercise files, please don't open them and look around just yet. One wrong click and you can mess up a file, which would prevent you from following along with the lesson that uses the file (you'd have to go through the installation process again to get a fresh copy). Your best bet is to follow the installation instructions given in this appendix, jump right into Unit 1, and wait until we tell you to use a particular file before opening it up. Besides, the exercise files don't mean much except in the context of the lessons.

In fact, we suggest not playing around with any of the CD files and programs until you've been through the book. You open and use most of the files and programs in the course of the book, and the ones that you don't probably won't be of much use to you until you're more comfortable with Visual Basic anyway.

System Requirements

Before installing the CD files, check out the following system requirements. If your computer doesn't meet the minimum requirements, you may have trouble using the CD.

- Microsoft Windows 95 installed on your computer

- A 486 or faster processor with at least 16MB of RAM

- At least 2.29MB of free hard-disk space available to install all the software from this CD. (You'll need less space if you don't install every program.)

- A CD-ROM drive — double speed (2x) or faster

- A sound card with speakers

- A display adapter capable of displaying at least 256 colors or grayscale. (A 1,024 x 768 minimum resolution is highly recommended.)

- A modem with a speed of at least 14,400 bps

If you need more information on PC or Windows basics, check out *PCs For Dummies,* 4th Edition, by Dan Gookin, or *Dummies 101: Windows 95,* by Andy Rathbone (both published by IDG Books Worldwide, Inc.).

What's on the CD

Notes:

All Visual Basic programs include a project file, identifiable by the VBP extension at the end of the filename. These are the key files for you to look for when working with the lessons in the book. The exception: the Mydata.MDB files used in the unit on databases. Here's a list of the project files installed from the CD, along with the lesson in which the file or program is first used (if applicable) — see the lesson for more information:

Exercise Files

Marquee.VBP	Lesson 1-1
Flattax.VBP	Lesson 2-1
Message.VBP	Lesson 5-1
Vote.VBP	Lesson 6-3
Gossip.VBP	Lesson 7-2
Wordfake.VBP	Unit 8 Exercise
Dialog.VBP	Lesson 9-2
Common.VBP	Unit 9 Exercise
Refund.VBP	Lesson 10-1
Obvious.VBP	Lesson 11-1
String.VBP	Lesson 12-2
Number.VBP	Lesson 12-3
Date.VBP	Lesson 12-4
Decision.VBP	Lesson 13-1
Doloop.VBP	Lesson 14-1
Mydata.MDB	Lesson 15-1
Debug.VBP	Lesson 16-1
Buggy.VBP	Unit 16 Exercise
Break.VBP	Lesson 17-1

Shoot.VBP	Lesson 18-1
Multplay.VBP	Lesson CD2-3
Playcd.VBP	Unit CD2 Exercise
Stat_ani.VBP	Lesson CD3-1
Clock.VBP	Lesson CD3-2
Aviplay.VBP	Lesson CD3-3
2d_pie.VBP	Lesson CD4-2
3d_line.VBP	Lesson CD4-3
Barchart.VBP	Lesson CD4-4
Linchart.VBP	Lesson CD4-5

Bonus Units

Unit CD1: Pictures, Rectangles and Lines

Unit CD2: Making Noise

Unit CD3: Playing Animation and Video

Unit CD4: Drawing Business Charts

Unit CD5: Printing a Visual Basic Program

Putting the CD Files and Software on Your Hard Drive

The exercise files are sample code and documents that you use while following along with the lessons in the book. You need to put these files on your hard drive. After you're done with the book, you can remove the files with a simple uninstall process.

The CD also contains bonus units and the Adobe Acrobat Reader, a program you need to read the bonus units.

Installing the files and software

Follow these steps:

1 **Insert the Dummies 101 CD-ROM (label side up) into your computer's CD-ROM drive.**

Be careful to touch only the edges of the CD-ROM. The CD-ROM drive is the one that pops out with a circular drawer.

Notes:

Wait about a minute before you do anything else; the installation program should begin automatically if your computer has the AutoPlay feature. If the program does not start after a minute, go to step 2. If it does, go to step 4.

2 **Double-click on the My Computer icon on the Windows 95 desktop.**

3 **Double-click on the CD-ROM icon on the desktop.**

4 **Click on OK.**

The installation program will ask if you want to use the CD now.

5 **Click on Yes.**

You'll see an End User License Agreement dialog box.

6 **Click on Accept.**

You'll see the main installation dialog box.

7 **Choose whether you want to install the exercise files or software by clicking on either Install Exercise Files or Choose Software. . . .**

8 **Follow the remaining prompts to install your exercise files or software.**

If you have problems with the installation process, you can call the IDG Books Worldwide, Inc., Customer Support number: 800-762-2974 (outside the U.S.: 317-596-5261).

After installing the files . . .

The installation process puts the files in the following locations:

- Exercise files: C:\101VBP
- Extra Units: C:\101VBP\PDFS

You don't have to do anything with the files yet — the book tells you when you need to open the first file (in Unit 1).

Note: The files are meant to accompany the book's lessons. If you open a file prematurely, you may accidentally make changes to the file, which may prevent you from following along with the steps in the lessons. So please don't try to open or view a file until you've reached the point in the lessons where we explain how to open the file.

Store the CD where it will be free from harm so that you can reinstall a file in case the one that's installed on your computer gets messed up.

Accessing the CD files

You'll find detailed instructions on how to access the Dummies 101 files in Unit 1, where you first need to open a file. You can also refer to the Cheat Sheet (the yellow, perforated quick-reference card at the front of the book) for these instructions.

Removing the CD files

After you have been through the book and no longer need the exercise files, you can uninstall them. To uninstall, click on the Start button on the taskbar, click on Programs, click on Dummies 101, and click on Uninstall Dummies 101–Visual Basic Files. To remove all files, click on the Automatic button in the Uninstall window. If you feel comfortable doing a custom uninstall, click on the Custom button.

Caution: As soon as you click on the Automatic button, your files are as good as gone, and the only way to get them back is to go through the original installation process again. If you want to keep any of the files that were installed, move them to a different folder before beginning the uninstall process. You should be absolutely certain that you want to delete all the files before you click on Automatic.

Bonus Stuff

In addition to the exercise files, the CD contains five bonus units that wouldn't fit in the book. The units don't contain any essential information that you must know in order to learn Visual Basic, just some cool stuff that you may want to know how to do after you have the rest of this book down pat.

To access these units, you'll need to install Adobe Acrobat Reader, included on the CD, to your computer. To do this, follow steps 1 through 8 in "Putting the CD Files and Software on Your Hard Drive" in this appendix.

From there, follow the instructions in the Setup program to install Adobe Acrobat Reader.

To open the bonus units, follow these steps:

1 **Click on the Start button in the Toolbar.**

2 **Choose Programs➪Adobe Acrobat➪Acrobat Reader 3.0.**

3 **After the Reader software is running, choose File➪Open.**

4 **In the Open dialog box that appears, go to C:\101VBP\PDFS.**

5 **Open the PDFS folder and open the bonus unit that you want to read.**

The units have a PDF extension, so Unit CD1 will be listed as CD1.PDF, Unit CD2 will be CD2.PDF, and so on.

Unit CD1, "Pictures, Rectangles, and Lines," lets you in on the sometimes colorful stuff that you can do with your Visual Basic program, including integrating pictures and graphics. Unit CD2, "Making Noise," reveals how to use sound to enhance your program. Unit CD3, "Playing Animation and Video," shows you how to integrate multimedia into your program. Unit CD4,

"Drawing Business Charts," gives you the details on using two-dimensional, three-dimensional, line, and bar charts for business environment use. And Unit CD5, "Printing a Visual Basic Program," reveals how to print the parts of your program so you can see how your user interface looks or look over your code.

If You've Got Problems (of the CD Kind)

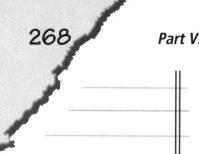

Notes:

We've tried our best to compile demo programs which will work on most computers that meet the minimum system requirements. Alas, all computers are not identical and programs may not work properly for some reason.

The likeliest problem is that you have only 16MB of real RAM but don't have certain settings turned on. If you get strange error messages, try these tips.

- Turn off any anti-virus software. Installers sometimes mimic virus activity and may make your computer incorrectly believe that it is being infected by a virus.

- Close all running programs. The more programs you have running, the less memory is left available for other programs to use. Installers typically update files and programs. If you keep other programs running, installation may not finish properly.

- Try running the software with any interfaces switched off. The interface is a program itself and uses more of your computer's precious memory.

If you have a problem in running the programs from the CD that we don't resolve here, please call the IDG Books Worldwide Customer Service phone number: 1-800-762-2974.

Index

Notes

Notes

Notes

Notes

Notes

Notes

Dummies 101 CD-ROM
Installation Instructions

The CD-ROM at the back of this book contains the practice files that you will use throughout the lessons in this book. It also contains a handy installation program that copies the files to your hard drive in a very simple process.

Note: The CD-ROM does not contain Microsoft Visual Basic 5.0 software. You must already have Visual Basic installed on your computer.

1 Insert the Dummies 101 CD-ROM (label side up) into your computer's CD-ROM drive.

Be careful to touch only the edges of the CD-ROM. The CD-ROM drive is the one that pops out with a circular drawer.

Wait about a minute before you do anything else; the installation program should begin automatically if your computer has the AutoPlay feature. If the program does not start after a minute, go to step 2. If it does, go to step 4.

2 Double-click on the My Computer icon on the Windows 95 desktop.

3 Double-click on the CD-ROM icon on the desktop.

4 Click on OK.

The installation program will ask if you want to use the CD now.

5 Click on Yes.

You'll see an End User License Agreement dialog box.

6 Click on Accept.

You'll see the main installation dialog box.

7 Choose whether you want to install all the exercise files or software.

8 Follow the remaining prompts to install either the exercise files or software.

If you have problems with the installation process, you can call the IDG Books Worldwide, Inc., Customer Support number: 800-762-2974 (outside the U.S.: 317-596-5261).

The installation process puts the exercise files in the following locations:

- Exercise files: C:\101VBP
- Extra Units: C:\101VBP\PDFS

Note: The files are meant to accompany the book's lessons. If you open a file before we tell you to in Unit 1, you may accidentally make changes to the file, which may prevent you from following along with the steps in the lessons.

❑ YES!

Please keep me informed about IDG's World of Computer Knowledge.
Send me the latest IDG Books catalog.